World Hunger

World Hunger
Twelve Myths

by

Frances Moore Lappé and Joseph Collins

A Food First Book

Grove Press
New York

A Food First Book/Published by Grove Press, a division of Wheatland Corporation 841 Broadway, New York, N.Y. 10003

First Evergreen Edition 1986
ISBN: 0-8021-5041-1 (pbk.)
First Grove Press Edition 1986
ISBN: 0-394-55626-7

Book design by Jana Janus and Norma Novy—typesetting by Diana Davis, H. S. Dakin Company, San Francisco

Printed in the United States of America

This book is printed on acid-free paper.

5   4

To the memory of our friend Harry Chapin, who believed that ordinary people could overcome hunger once we free ourselves from the myths that entrap us.

Contents

Acknowledgments

Our thanks first to Jeremy Sherman, Rachel Schurman, and Sarah Stewart. This book benefited immeasurably from your research and the tireless enthusiasm with which you left no stone unturned.

Both the research and writing of this book also benefited in innumerable ways, big and small, from expert criticisms and suggestions from colleagues around the world. To all, especially the most critical, we are indebted:

Keith Abercrombie, Will Alexander, Miguel Altieri, Marcos Arruda, David Barkin, Solon Barraclough, Medea Benjamin, Florida Botts, James Boyce, Chris Brazier, Fred Buttel, J. Baird Callicott, Robert Chambers, Barbara Chasin, Frederick Clairmonte, Stephen Commins, Belinda Coote, Phillips Cutright, Kenneth Dahlberg, Kevin Danaher, Alain de Janvry, Rene Dumont, Melanie DuPuis, Charles Elliott, Jonathan Fox, Andre Gunder Frank, Richard Franke, Mark Freudenberger, Dan Gallin, Susan George, Helena Gezelius, Terry Gips, Michael Glantz, Guy Gran, Edward Goldsmith, Kathleen Gough, Keith Griffin, Betsy Hartmann, Paul Hebinck, Steve Hellinger, Donald Hernandez, Anne-Marie Holenstein, Gerrit Huizer, Tony Jackson, George Johnson, Donald Innis, Edmond Keller, George Kent, David Kinley, Michael Klare, Uwe Kracht, Mark Lapping, Luigi Laurenti, Richard Levins, Michael Lipton, John Moore, John Mellor, David Millwood,

James Morrell, William Murdoch, David Myhre, Jay O'Brien, Ingrid Palmer, David Pimentel, Pierre Pradervand, John Ratcliffe, Bill Rau, Peter Rosset, Vernon Ruttan, Wolfgang Sachs, John Scheuring, Claudio Schuftan, T. Paul Schultz, Amartya Sen, John Sewell, S.A. Shah, Douglas Shane, Peter Smith, Pierre Spitz, Robert Stauffer, Vasant Sukhatme, John Sutter, Philip Thompforde, Lloyd Timberlake, Dexter Tiranti, Nigel Twose, Robert Wasserstrom, Michael Watts, Ponna Wignaraja, Calvin Wilvert, Ben Wisner, William Wood, S.J.

Interns at Food First backed up our research assistants. Our thanks to: Susan Beaudry, Erin Bucklen, Judy Goddess, Elizabeth Linde, Horacio Maiorana, Irene Rice, Mark Taylor, Marianna Tubman, Jennifer Watson, Shauna Whidden, and Damon Wing.

Needless to say, we remain solely responsible for any remaining errors.

Our editor William Rodarmor and copyeditor Gaen Murphree deserve our special thanks for their expert and careful work.

To all our colleagues at Food First, we appreciate your support during the period of intense concentration necessary to complete this project. Extra thanks to Publications Director Ann Kelly for your support and advice at every stage, to Donna Kelley for finding research interns for the project, to Audee Kochiyama-Holman for editing the many footnotes, and to Keith Wood for your ever-ready help with the computers.

None of Food First's work, including this book, would be possible without the support of our members. We thank each of you. While a number of foundations and churches have contributed to our work over the years, three stand out for your loyal and vital assistance: the CS Fund, the Rubin Foundation, and the Presbyterian Hunger Program. Thank you.

Frances Moore Lappé and Joseph Collins
San Francisco
June 10, 1986

World Hunger

Beyond Guilt
And Fear

For over 15 years we have sought to understand why there is hunger in a world of plenty. For us, learning had to begin with unlearning. Cutting through the simplistic and scary cliches about hunger, we arrived at some surprising findings:

- No country in the world is a hopeless basket case. Even countries many people think of as impossibly overcrowded have the resources necessary for people to free themselves from hunger.
- Increasing a nation's food production may not help the hungry. Food production per person can increase while at the same time more people go hungry.
- Our government's foreign aid often hurts rather than helps the hungry. But in a multitude of other ways we can help.
- The poor in the third world are neither a burden on us nor a threat to our interests. Unlikely as it may seem, the interests of the vast majority of Americans have much in common with those of the hungry in the third world.

Our book explains these surprising findings and many more that have freed us from a response to hunger motivated by guilt and fear. But first we must ask the seemingly grade-school question, just what is hunger? Many people assume they know—they've felt it, they've read about it, they've been touched by images of hungry people on television. But the greatest obstacle to grasping the causes and solutions to world hunger is that few of us stop to ponder this elemental question.

World Bank photo

Women grow at least half of the world's food.

What Is Hunger?

Television images haunt us. Stunted, bony bodies. Long lines waiting for a meager bowl of gruel. This is famine—hunger in its acute form, the kind no one could miss.

But hunger comes in another form. It is the day-in-day-out hunger that over 700 million people suffer.[1] While chronic hunger doesn't make the evening news, it takes more lives than famine. Every year this largely invisible hunger kills as many as 18 to 20 million people—more than twice the number who died each year during World War II.[2] This death toll is equivalent to the number killed instantly by a Hiroshima bomb every two days.[3]

Statistics like this are staggering. They shock and alarm. Several years ago, however, we began to doubt the usefulness of such numbers. Numbers can numb. They can distance us from what is actually very close to us.

So we asked ourselves, what really is hunger?

Is it the gnawing pain in the stomach when we miss a meal? The physical depletion of those suffering chronic undernutrition? The listless stare of a dying child in the television hunger appeal?

Yes, but it is more. And we became convinced that as long as we conceive of hunger only in physical measures, we will never truly understand it, certainly not its roots.

What, we asked ourselves, would it mean to think of hunger in terms of universal human emotions, feelings that all of us have experienced at some time in our lives?

We'll mention only four such emotions, to give you an idea of what we mean.

A friend of ours, Dr. Charles Clements, is a former Air Force pilot and Vietnam veteran who spent a year treating peasants in El Salvador. In *Witness to War*, he writes of a family he tried to help whose son and daughter had died of fever and diarrhea. "Both had been lost," he writes, "in the years when Camila and her husband had chosen to pay their mortgage, a sum equal to half the value of their crop, rather than keep the money to feed their children. Each year, the choice was always the same. If they paid, their children's lives were endangered. If they didn't, their land could be repossessed."[4]

Being hungry thus means anguish. The anguish of impossible choices. But it is more.

In Nicaragua four years ago, we met Amanda Espinoza, a poor campesina, who until then had never had enough to feed her family. She told us that she had endured six stillbirths and watched five of her children die before the age of one.

To Amanda, being hungry means watching people you love die. It is grief.

Throughout the world, the poor are made to blame themselves for their poverty. Walking into a home in the rural Philippines, the first words we heard were an apology for the poverty of the dwelling. Being hungry also means living in humiliation.

Anguish, grief, and humiliation are a part of what hunger means. But increasingly throughout the world, hunger has a fourth dimension.

In Guatemala in 1978, we met two poor highland peasants. With the help of World Neighbors, an Oklahoma City–based voluntary aid group, they were teaching their neighbors how to reduce erosion on the steep slopes onto which they had been pushed by wealthy landowners monopolizing the flat valley land. Two years later, the friend who had introduced us to the peasants visited our Institute for Food and Development Policy in San Francisco. We learned that one had been forced into hiding, the other had been killed. In the eyes of the wealthy their crime was teaching their neighbors better farming techniques. Guatemala's oligarchy feels threatened by any change that makes the poor less dependent on low-payi ng jobs on their plantations.

Increasingly, then, a fourth dimension of hunger is fear.

Anguish, grief, humiliation, and fear. What if we were to simply refuse to count the hungry and instead try to understand hunger in terms of such universal emotions? We discover that how we understand hunger determines what we think are its solutions.

If we think of hunger only as numbers—numbers of people with too few calories—the solution also appears to us in numbers—numbers of tons of food aid, or numbers of dollars in economic assistance. But once we begin to understand hunger as real people coping with the most painful of human emotions, we can perceive its roots. We need only ask, when have we experienced any of these emotions ourselves? Hasn't it been when we have felt out of control of our lives—powerless to protect ourselves and those we love?

Hunger has thus become for us the ultimate symbol of powerlessness.

The Causes of Powerlessness

Understanding that hunger tells us that a person has been robbed of the most basic power—the power to protect ourselves and those we love—is a first step. Peeling back the layers of misunderstanding, we must then ask, if powerlessness lies at the very root of hunger, what are its causes?

Certainly it is not scarcity. The world is awash with food, as chapter 1 will show. Neither are natural disasters to blame. Put most simply, the root cause of hunger isn't a scarcity of food or land; *it's a scarcity of democracy.*

Wait a minute! What does democracy have to do with hunger?

In our view—everything. To us, democracy is precisely the right concept because it carries within it the principle of accountability. Democratic structures are those in which people have a say in decisions that most affect their well-being. Leadership can be kept accountable to the needs of the majority. Antidemocratic structures are those in which power is so tightly concentrated that the majority of people are left with no say at all. Leaders are accountable only to the powerful minority.

In the United States, we think of democracy as a strictly political concept, so it may seem contrived to apply it to the economic questions of land, food, jobs, and income. Political democracy helps us as citizens to protect certain rights—to reside where we will, to vote, to have our civil liberties upheld, and so on. Unlike in many societies, here such universal political citizenship is taken for granted.

But along with many other societies, we lack a concept of economic citizenship. To parallel our universal political rights, we have not yet established universal economic rights, such as the right to life-sustaining resources or the right to participate in economic decision making.

What we hope to show in this book is that as long as this fundamental concept of democracy—accountability to those most affected by decisions—is absent from economic life, people will continue to be made powerless. From the family, to the village, through the national level, to the level of international commerce and finance, we will witness the continued concentration of decision making over all aspects of economic life, including what it takes to grow and distribute that on which all life depends—food. Poverty and hunger will go on destroying the lives of millions each year and scarring the lives of hundreds of millions more.

Let us look briefly at how on each of the levels antidemocratic decision making robs people of power over their lives.

First, within the family, who controls food resources? Women are responsible for growing at least half the world's food. In most African societies, the primary farmers have long been women. The resources they have to grow staple foods largely determine their family's nutritional well-being. But many African women are losing authority over land use—the result of the privatization of land ownership and a focus on export crops that began under colonialism. Credit for growing cash crops has gone overwhelmingly to men, and "women's crops" have stagnated. Especially in Africa, this shift of power within the family helps explain growing hunger.[5]

Second, at the village level, who controls the land—and how many families have none at all?

In most countries, a consistent pattern emerges—fewer and fewer people control more and more farm and pasture land. With fewer families controlling an ever greater share of the land, more and more people have none at all. Since 1960, the number of landless in Central America has multiplied fourfold.[6] By the mid-1970s, in at least 20 third world countries, 50 percent or more of the rural people were effectively landless, deprived of the most basic resource needed to feed their families.[7]

Third, at the national level, how are public resources allocated? Wherever people have been made hungry, power is in the hands of those unaccountable to their people. These antidemocratic governments answer only to elites, lavishing them with credit, subsidies, and other assistance. To protect the privileges of the wealthy minority, they increasingly funnel public resources toward the military. On average, third world governments devote less than 10 percent of their budgets to agriculture; in some poor countries the share is decreasing.[8] But during the 1970s, expenditures on arms by third world governments leapt fourfold—in Africa, 13-fold.[9] With increasing brutality, such governments fight any reform that would make control over food-producing resources more equitable.

There is yet a fourth level on which democracy is scarce—the international arena of commerce and finance.

A handful of corporations dominate world trade in those commodities that are the lifeblood of third world economies. Efforts by third world governments to bargain for higher commodity prices have repeatedly failed in the face of the preeminent power of the giant trading corporations and the government trade policies of the industrial countries.

Consumers in the industrial countries spend $200 billion a year for agricultural products from the third world, but traders, processors, and marketers reap most of the profit. Of the 15 percent of the consumer's dollar retained by third world countries, only a fraction returns to the producers themselves.[10] And the value of this 15 percent is shrinking: in 1986, the prices paid for third world raw commodities hit their lowest levels in history, relative to the prices of manufactured goods and services.[11]

Heavily indebted to international aid agencies and private banks, third world nations are also at the mercy of policies decided upon in the capitals of the industrial nations, policies leading only to further impoverishment.

In attempting to capsulize the antidemocratic roots of hunger, we have traveled a great distance—from the level of the family to that of international commerce and finance. Let us complete the circle by returning to the family.

As economic decisions are made by those unaccountable to the majority, insecurity deepens for millions of people. Economic pressures tear family bonds asunder as men are forced to leave home in search of work and joblessness leads to family violence and dissolution. More and more women shoulder family responsibilities alone; worldwide, perhaps as many as one-third of all households are now headed by women. On top of the weight of poverty, they confront barriers of discrimination against women. The breakdown of the traditional family structure does not bring liberation for them; it simply means greater hardship. Most of the hungry in the world are women and the children they care for. Most of those who die from hunger every year are children.[12]

We have still peeled off only one layer in our effort to grasp the roots of hunger. We have identified the problem: the ever greater scarcity not of food or land but of democracy, democracy understood to include the life-and-death matter of economics. But we must dig deeper. We must ask why. Why have we allowed this process to happen at the cost of millions of needless deaths each year?

How We Think About Hunger

Especially in troubled times, people seek ways to make sense of the world. We grasp for organizing principles to help us interpret the endlessly confusing rush of world events. It's a natural, human process—perhaps as human as eating itself. But living effectively depends on how well our organizing principles reflect reality.

Unfortunately, the principles around which many of us have come to organize our thinking about world hunger block our grasp of real solutions. This entire book is structured around such organizing principles. We call them myths, not to suggest that the views embodied are totally false. Many have some validity. It is as organizing principles that they fail. Not only do they prevent us from seeing how we can help the hungry, they obfuscate our own legitimate interests as well. Some fail us because they describe but don't explain, some are so partial that they lead us down blind alleys, and some simply aren't true.

What we want to do is to probe the underlying assumptions people have about world hunger's causes and cures. For we've come to believe that *the very way people think about hunger is the greatest obstacle to ending it*.

After reading our book, we hope you will find that you no longer have to block out bad news, but can face hunger squarely because a more realistic framework of understanding—to be repeatedly tested against your own experience—enables you to make real choices, choices that can contribute to ending this spreading but needless human suffering.

Our book may shake your most dearly held beliefs or it may confirm your deepest intuitions and experiences. Most of all, we hope that it convinces you that until humanity has solved the most basic human problem—how to ensure that every one of us has food for life—we cannot consider ourselves fully human.

M Y T H · 1

There's Simply Not Enough Food

MYTH: With food-producing resources in so much of the world stretched to the limit, there's simply not enough food to go around. Unfortunately, some people have to go hungry.

OUR RESPONSE: The world today produces enough grain alone to provide every human being on the planet with 3,600 calories a day.[1] That's enough to make most people fat! And this estimate does not even count the many other commonly eaten foods—vegetables, beans, nuts, root crops, fruits, grass-fed meats, and fish.[2]

Abundance, not scarcity, best describes the supply of food in the world today. Rarely has the world seen such a glut of food looking for buyers.[3] Increases in food production during the past 25 years have outstripped the world's unprecedented population growth by about 16 percent.[4] Indeed, mountains of unsold grain on world markets have pushed prices downward over the past three decades.[5]

All well and good for the global picture, you might be thinking, but doesn't such a broad stroke tell us little? Aren't people starving because of food shortages where most hungry people live—in Africa, Asia, and Latin America?

Hunger in the face of ample food is all the more shocking in the third world. In every region except Africa, gains in food production since 1950 have kept ahead of population growth.[6]

Abundance best describes the world's food supply.

During the 1970s, only 12 percent of the world's population lived in countries where food production per person was falling.[7]

One hypothetical question best highlights how misleading it is to think of food shortages in the third world as the root cause of hunger: how much of the food now available within third world countries would it take to make up for the total food lacking in the diets of each country's chronically hungry people?

According to the World Bank, the answer is but a tiny percentage.[8] In India, home of over a third of the world's hungry people,[9] the reallocation of a mere 5.6 percent of current food production would wipe out hunger, making an active life possible for everyone.[10] For Indonesia, with the second greatest number of undernourished people in the world,[11] only 2 percent of the country's food supply would make the difference.[12] And in Africa, 7.8 percent of the food supply of Tanzania and 2.5 percent of that of both Senegal and Sudan could meet the needs of the hungry.[13]

This is, we underline, a hypothetical exercise. As the World Bank itself cautions, even though enough food exists, the poor are not able to purchase it.

Thus, even most "hungry countries" have enough food for all their people right now. This finding turns out to be true using official statistics even though experts warn us that newly modernizing societies invariably underestimate farm production—just as a century ago at least a third of the U.S. wheat crop went uncounted.[14] Moreover, many nations can't realize their full food production potential because of the gross inefficiencies caused by inequitable ownership of resources. We will discuss this in chapters 4 and 6.

Finally, many of the countries in which hunger is rampant export much more in agricultural goods than they import. It is the industrial countries, not the third world countries, that import more than two-thirds of all food and farm commodities in world trade.[15] Imports by the 30 lowest-income countries, on the other hand, account for only 6 percent of all international commerce in food and farm commodities.[16]

Looking more closely at some of the world's hunger-ravaged countries and regions confirms that scarcity is clearly not the cause of hunger.

India. India ranks near the top among third world agricultural exporters. While as many as 300 million Indians go hungry, the country exports everything from wheat to beef and government officials agonize over how to get rid of mounting "surpluses" of wheat and rice—24 million tons in 1985, more than double the entire world's annual food aid shipments in a typical year.[17]

Bangladesh. Beginning with its famine of the early 1970s, Bangladesh came to symbolize the frightening consequences of people overrunning food resources. Yet Bangladesh's official yearly rice output alone—which some experts say is seriously underreported[18]—could provide each person with more than a pound of grain per day, or 2,064 calories.[19] Adding to that small amounts of vegetables, fruits, and legumes could prevent hunger for everyone. Yet the poorest third of the people in Bangladesh eat at most only 1,500 calories a day, dangerously below what is needed for a healthy life.[20]

With about 100 million people living in an area the size of Wisconsin, Bangladesh may be judged overcrowded by any number of standards, but its population density is not a viable excuse for its widespread hunger. Bangladesh is blessed with exceptional agricultural endowments, yet its current rice yields fall significantly below the all-Asia average. The extraordinary potential of Bangladesh's rich alluvial soils and plentiful water has hardly been fully used. If the country's irrigation potential were realized, experts predict its rice yields could double or even triple.[21]

Brazil. While Brazil has become the world's second-largest food exporter (after only the United States), 86 million Brazilians do not have enough to eat.[22]

Africa. Bombarded by images of barren landscapes in Sub-Saharan Africa, many of us are surprised to learn that the region is a net exporter of agricultural commodities.[23]

Despite widening hunger, food exports from the Horn of Africa—Ethiopia, Kenya, Somalia, the Sudan, Tanzania, and Uganda—were worth nearly $1 billion more in 1983 than the food imported. When all agricultural commodities are counted in, the difference rises to $1.5 billion.[24]

The Sahelian countries of West Africa are known for recurrent famines, but in most years they export more agricultural products than they import.[25] Even during the drought years 1970 to 1974, the value of the region's agricultural exports—$1.25 billion—was three times greater than the value of grain imported,[26] and such figures don't take into account unreported exports. Reports from two of the Sahelian countries, Niger and Burkina Faso (formerly Upper Volta), estimate that traders smuggle out as much as half the grain produced to sell elsewhere to customers able to pay more.[27]

While television coverage has awakened the world to hunger in the Horn of Africa and the Sahel, some of Africa's worst hunger is rarely covered. In South Africa, some 50,000 black children starve to death every year; 136 die every day.[28] Yet South Africa is a net exporter of agricultural products, even exporting corn, the basic staple of black families.[29]

Despite the productive capacity suggested by Africa's agricultural exports, by the mid-1980s food production per person had been declining for more than a decade[30] and as much as a quarter of the continent's grain consumption was reportedly coming from imports.[31] With so much of Africa's food production undercounted—especially the food poor women grow for their own families—a truly accurate assessment of the problem is impossible.[32] But repeated reports about Africa's failing agriculture and growing dependence on imports have led many to assume that simply too many people are pressing against too meager resources. Africa's

World Hunger: Twelve Myths

food crisis is real—but how true is this assumption?

Many longtime observers of Africa's agricultural development tell us that the real reasons for Africa's food problems are no mystery.[33] Africa's food potential has been distorted and thwarted.

Colonizers and, subsequently, national and international agencies, have discredited peasant producers' often sophisticated knowledge of ecologically appropriate farming systems. Promoting "modern," often imported, and ecologically destructive technologies,[34] they have cut Africa's food producers out from economic decisions most affecting their very survival.

Public resources, including research and agricultural credit, have been channeled to export crops to the virtual exclusion of peasant-produced food crops such as millet, sorghum, and root crops. In the 1980s, pressure to export to pay interest on foreign debt only reinforced this imbalance.[35]

While Africa's principal food producers are women, decisions over land use and credit have been made the domain of men.[36]

Governments beholden to urban classes demanding cheap food have paid peasants so poorly for their crops that they have often had little incentive to produce for the market.[37]

Aid policies unaccountable to African peasant producers and pastoralists have generally bypassed their needs in favor of expensive, large-scale projects. Africa receives less aid for agriculture than any other continent, and of the $14 billion pouring into the eight Sahelian nations in the decade ending 1984, less than 5 percent went to rainfed agriculture, although it accounts for 95 percent of grain production. What funds did go to farming went overwhelmingly to the irrigated systems of the richer farmers.[38]

African governments—like most in the third world—allocate, on average, less than 10 percent of their budgets to agriculture, in contrast to a much larger share going to the military and police.[39]

Many governments have also overvalued their currencies, making imported food artificially cheap and undercutting local producers of millet, sorghum, and cassava. Urban tastes then increasingly shift to imported grain, particularly wheat, which few countries in Africa can grow economically. Twenty years ago, only a small minority of urban dwellers in Sub-Saharan Africa ate wheat. Today bread is a staple for many urbanites, and wheat products account for over a third of all the region's grain imports.[40] U.S. food aid and advertising by multinational corporations ("He'll be smart. He'll go far. He'll eat bread."[41]) have played their part in molding African tastes to what the industrial countries have to sell.

Thus beneath the "scarcity diagnosis" of Africa's food situation lie many human-made and therefore reversible causes. Even Africa's high birth rates are not independent variables but are determined by social realities that shape people's reproductive choices.

A Future of Scarcity?

In contrast to the mid-1970s when we wrote *World Hunger: Ten Myths* and *Food First*, today the reality of current abundance is rarely questioned by scholars in resource economics and development. But an old debate has heated up: just how close are we to the earth's limits?

Major studies have arrived at widely varying conclusions as to the earth's potential to support future populations.[42] Most pessimistic is *Land, Food and People*.[43] This study by the Food and Agriculture Organization of the United Nations estimates that by the year 2000, many third world nations will have reached their capacity to feed their populations using current technologies. The study does note the strong potential for regional self-sufficiency (the 22 most food-deficient African countries could theoretically meet their food needs with just 11 percent of the surplus of 10 of their neighbors).[44]

In view of today's abundant food supplies as well as the potential suggested in this chapter and in chapter 6, we question the more pessimistic predictions. Only 40 years ago, China pundits predicted that that famine-ridden nation could never feed its population. Today twice as many people eat—and fairly adequately[45]—on only one-eighth the cropland per person used in the United States.[46]

Not that anyone should take the more pessimistic predictions lightly; they underscore the reality of the inevitably finite resource base entrusted to us. They should therefore reinforce our sense of urgency to address the root causes of resource misuse, resource degradation, and rapid population growth.

Lessons from Home

Finally, in probing the connection between hunger and scarcity we should never overlook the lessons here at home. Up to 20 million Americans cannot afford a healthy diet[47] and 12 percent of America's poor children are stunted by malnutrition.[48] But who would argue that not enough food is produced? Surely not U.S. farmers; overproduction is their most persistent headache. Nor the U.S. government, which has to store enough surplus cheese, milk, and butter to provide every American with almost 50 pounds[49] and enough surplus wheat to bake nearly seven loaves of bread for every human being on earth.[50]

Here at home, just as in the third world, hunger is an outrage precisely because it is profoundly needless. Behind the headlines, the television images, the superficial clichés, we can learn to see that hunger is real; scarcity is not.

Only when we free ourselves from the myth of scarcity can we begin to look for hunger's real causes. That search is what our book is about.

M Y T H · 2

Nature's To Blame

MYTH: Droughts and other events beyond human control cause famine.

OUR RESPONSE: On February 16, 1986, the *Chicago Tribune* ran the following story at the bottom of the front page: "Elderly Man Dies as a Result of Cold Weather." Surely the editor who wrote that headline didn't really believe that the weather caused the man's death. The man was probably poor, quite possibly sick and without adequate clothing; maybe he was forced to live on the street. In 1985, 400 homeless died on the streets of Chicago.[1] Who in America could blame the weather?

But many of us assume that things are somehow different in

the third world. Those who die in famines there are victims of this or that natural event—most often a drought or a flood.

A major study of droughts, floods, and other natural disasters carried out in the early 1980s by the Swedish Red Cross and the international public interest organization Earthscan came to a very different conclusion. The researchers found that the annual number of victims of natural disasters jumped sixfold between the 1960s and the 1970s—much greater than the increase in disasters or population growth.[2]

Clearly, human-made forces are making people increasingly vulnerable to nature's vagaries. Pushed onto marginal lands or deprived of land altogether, in debt to usurers who claim most of their harvests, so poorly paid that

Human not natural forces leave people vulnerable to nature's vagaries.

nothing is left to fall back on, and weakened by chronic hunger, millions die. Natural events are not the cause. They are the final blow.

Lessons from the Bangladesh Famine

In the autumn of 1974, international attention turned to one of the worst famines of modern times. The mass media readily accepted the Bangladesh government's claim that the famine taking over 100,000 lives was caused by harvest-destroying floods.

But many workers on the scene as well as later researchers argue that despite the floods at no point was Bangladesh short of food. One peasant described what happened in her village: "A lot of people died of starvation here. The rich farmers were hoarding rice and not letting any of the poor peasants see it." Asked whether there was enough food in the village, she replied, "There may not have been a lot of food, but if it had been shared, no one would have died."[3]

The 1974 Bangladesh famine was not exceptional. Widely recognized for his studies of modern famines, Oxford University's Amartya Sen has found that famines have occurred not because of a shortage of food but because people's claim to food is disrupted.[4] Where people are denied the resources to grow enough or retain enough of their own harvests to meet family needs, and where only buying power—money—gives people claim to additional food, many will go hungry and even starve if their income falls or if food prices dramatically rise.

People's income may fall precipitously because they lose their means to produce. Poor people might have to sell their land or animals because of a death in the family, for example, or a crop failure that leaves them unable to pay debts. Many such distress sales lay behind the famine deaths in Bangladesh.[5] Perhaps the price of what the poor produce suddenly drops, leaving them unable to buy enough food. Or if the income of better-off groups suddenly increases, food prices may soar beyond the reach of the poor, even with no major harvest failure.

Rumors of a future shortfall, whether true or false, can prompt well-to-do farmers and merchants to hoard food, guaranteeing a shortage for others while reaping windfall profits for themselves. As two longtime observers of rural Bangladesh commented on the 1974 famine, "while to most people scarcity means suffering, to others it means profit."[6]

One large farmer in Uganda explained candidly how she had amassed over 500 acres. "The 1980 famine helped," she said. "People were in need. For the first time, they were willing to sell land, cows—things they wouldn't dream of selling in normal times."[7]

Recurring Famine in Africa's Sahel

In the early 1970s, the much-publicized famine in the Sahelian nations of West Africa helped move us to found the Institute for Food and Development Policy.

The common assumption, reinforced by media coverage, was that the famine resulted from prolonged drought. But we learned that even during the famine years, surveys by the Food and Agriculture Organization of the United Nations—squelched by displeased aid-seeking governments—documented that each Sahelian country in West Africa produced enough grain to feed its total population.[8] Moreover, water was adequate to grow vast amounts of cotton, vegetables, peanuts (for cooking oil and livestock feed), and other agricultural goods for export. In fact, during the drought many agricultural exports from the Sahel—largely to well-fed consumers in Europe—actually increased.[9]

A decade later, drought and famine once again struck the Sahel. Poor farmers were among those who suffered most. In debt to rich farmers and merchants, they were forced to sell their crops at harvest time at rock-bottom prices and were left without enough food to survive the "hunger season." Nor did they have enough money to buy food, since merchants eagerly hiked their prices to take advantage of crop shortfalls.[10]

Because bad harvests leave ordinary farmers so much deeper in debt, they have little cause to rejoice even when good rains fall. Debt, not the weather, is the real killer of Sahelian peasants.[11]

Even in what are considered drought years in West Africa, people starve even though enough food may be near at hand. In any given year crop failure may devastate one area, while not far away farmers reap a bumper harvest, observes John Scheuring, an American agricultural scientist with years of experience in the region.[12]

And West Africa's food merchants ensure that no one with reasonable financial resources goes hungry. Due to drought in 1984, Mali's grain harvest was 400,000 tons below what had been expected, but the four major private merchants had no trouble bringing almost that much into the country from neighboring Ivory Coast for anyone who could pay for it.[13] "There's always food in the market, but we have no money," one West African peasant told University of California geographer Michael Watts.[14]

Too sophisticated to simply blame nature, many Western observers point to what they believe are deeper causes of hunger in West Africa: increased numbers of people and their livestock have simply overrun the capacity of the land. You can't blame nature for that, they tell us.

But this effort to probe deeper begs as many questions as it answers. In chapter 4, we explore the many human-made forces generating this imbalance with nature. We point, for example, to the herder's dilemma, how the declining value of each animal requires bigger herds to maintain survival income. None of these human-made forces—already evident in the Sahelian famine of the 1970s—were adequately addressed in intervening years. So by the time the next drought struck, livestock numbers had climbed once again to near the levels that contributed to the earlier crisis. Little wonder that famine—striking the poor herders most heavily—recurred with a vengeance in the 1980s.[15]

Foreign aid programs also help to explain the recurrence of famine. In the previous chapter, we noted that only a small fraction of the billions of aid dollars flowing into the region since the early 1970s has gone to rainfed peasant agriculture, though it provides the bulk of the local food supply as well as the basis of the economic well-being of most of the people.

Agriculture and forestry only got a quarter of the total aid to begin with, and most of that went to expensive (and often technically dubious), large-scale irrigation schemes, mostly to grow rice for the better off in the towns, and cotton, peanuts, and other commodities for export.[16] Less than 2 percent of the aid went to environmental restoration projects such as tree planting and soil and water conservation.[17]

So it is not surprising that during the 1982 to 1985 drought a number of Sahelian countries increased farm exports even while their food production fell.[18] Even during the drought year 1984, a record amount of cotton was exported.[19]

Ethiopia's Human-made Tragedy

We visited Ethiopia's highland villages in January and February of 1985, seeking out the causes of the widespread human suffering we had seen on television.

First, we learned how wrong we were to assume that the Ethiopian drought prevailed over the entire country or even most of it. As our jeep wound over mountain roads, we saw one valley in which the rains had brought a good harvest, followed by a valley where obviously very little rain had fallen. The very next valley had only enough rainfall to grow drought-tolerant sorghum. Ethiopia's sheer size (twice the area of Texas) and its varied geography (a splintered highland massif surrounded by lowland areas) make it highly unlikely that a drought or any other climatic condition would be nationwide.

Several agriculturalists confirmed our impression, estimating that the 1982 to 1985 drought affected at most 30 percent of Ethiopia's farmland.[20]

And while the world's attention focused on drought, an agricultural specialist within Ethiopia told us that with drainage, rich but waterlogged valley bottomlands could be planted, perhaps even doubling the cultivated land area.[21] Traveling through the relatively well-watered Awash River valley, we saw vast acreages of prime land in government-run farms producing cotton for export and sugarcane.

We also learned that for eight years prior to the drought, food production in many villages had already deteriorated—perhaps as much as 20 percent per person as a nationwide average.

If much of the country was unaffected by drought, and if food production had already dropped before it began, clearly drought cannot explain shortages that contributed to 300,000 deaths by 1985.[22] How can we understand such a tragedy?

When a military uprising overthrew Emperor Haile Selassie in 1974, the young officers charged that feudalistic landlordism, hoarding, and governmental indifference—not the years of drought—had caused the famine of the early 1970s. Peasant hopes soared soon thereafter when the new government decreed a sweeping land reform ending landlord-tenant relationships. But peasant-controlled rural development has not turned out to be the military government's priority. Instead, the central government, traditionally controlled by the Amharic ethnic group, has sought to consolidate forcibly its rule over diverse ethnic and religious groups within the "empire." Several of these groups have taken up arms in their fight for self-determination.[23]

The allocation of public resources makes the military government's priorities unmistakable. By 1984, the military slice of the annual operating budget had swollen to almost half of the entire budget.[24] Though 22 percent of the Ethiopian budget goes to agriculture,[25] little is channeled toward the roughly 7 million small farmers who grow virtually all the country's staple foods. A trifling 8 percent of the agricultural budget goes to provide them with technical assistance, credit, oxen, seeds, and chemical fertilizers.[26] Almost all of the agricultural budget is poured into the heavily subsidized government-run farms.

Worse than simple neglect, government policies actively drain peasant farmers of their resources. Since 1977, farmers have been required to sell their goods to the government at low, fixed prices.[27] Without any increase in what farmers get for their crops, in 1982 the government doubled the prices farmers had to pay for commercial fertilizers.[28] The government has also raised farmers' taxes and collects "voluntary" contributions from them to support the war effort.

With the advice of Soviet and East German planners, in 1979 the military government proclaimed collective farming as its goal for small farmers.[29] In what many see as a step in this direction, less than a year after our visit the government decreed a sweeping program to move thousands of peasant families into villages. Justified by the military government as a means to facilitate delivery of services, the program is highly unpopular with the supposed beneficiaries, relief and development workers have told us.

Lacking farm supplies and facing the prospect that the land they work today might be part of a collective tomorrow, Ethiopia's farmers find themselves with little incentive to produce beyond their families' needs, even with good rainfall. Add any natural adversity, and you have a formula for famine.

While we have focused on the military government's policies toward small farmers, we cannot overlook the more directly military dimension of Ethiopia's famine.

Between 1976 and 1980, the government imported more than $2 billion worth of weaponry from the Soviet Union.[30] The heavy interest payments on the weapons-generated foreign debt further pressured the government to concentrate on export rather than food crops. At the same time, in the East-West race for influence in the Horn of Africa, the United States has greatly stepped up its arming of neighboring Somalia, with which Ethiopia for all practical purposes has been at war since 1978. U.S. policy provides the Ethiopian military the perfect rationale for funneling resources into weapons rather than rural development.

The government's vastly disproportionate investment in government-run farms, also has a military explanation. They are considered a secure source of food for the armed forces.[31]

The mainly conscripted army—over 300,000 strong[32] and by far the largest in Sub-Saharan Africa—drains the countryside of the able-bodied young men needed for plowing and other heavy agricultural work. Villagers complained to us that their "workhorses" had been taken from them.

War itself also takes many of the country's food producers from their fields and harvests. In what many charge is a tactic of war, in 1985 the government forcibly relocated between 700,000 and 800,000 peasants from areas sympathetic to rebel forces.[33]

Suspecting rebel sympathies, the armed forces have reportedly burned fields and bombed villages in some areas of Tigray and Eritrea. The worst famine has been in war-torn Tigray, according to those who have visited the area.

Without a peaceful resolution of the conflicts and an end to the military buildup encouraged by both East and West, there is little hope for an end to famine in Ethiopia, no matter how favorable the weather.

We have focused on Ethiopia because media coverage of starvation there so reinforced the notion that drought is to blame for famine. But just as war, not drought, is at the root of the suffering in Ethiopia, so is it also in other famine-stricken countries in Africa. Of the 31 drought-affected countries in Sub-Saharan Africa in the early 1980s, only five have experienced famine. Each has occurred in the context of war: Mozambique, Angola, Sudan, Chad, and Ethiopia.[34]

Throughout history, human societies have worked to protect themselves against the vagaries of nature. Especially in large areas of Africa, periodic droughts have always challenged human survival. Precautions against their consequences have invariably been part of human culture. In the Old Testament, we read of the seven abundant years followed by seven lean years. So in much of Africa, farmers traditionally assumed that they should build up reserves to prevent famine.

Also for centuries in the semiarid areas of Africa, farmers and herders fashioned methods to cope with times of drought and other natural hardships. In chapters 4 and 5, we sketch some of these methods. Life was never easy. Hunger was probably common, but not mass starvation, except—tellingly—in feudalistic Ethiopia.

But, as noted in the previous chapter, such precautions and sound agricultural practices were overturned in the short-term interests of European colonial powers.

Reflections on Famine

Famines, it turns out, are not natural disasters but social disasters, the result of human arrangements, not acts of God. Blaming nature, we fail to see that *human* institutions determine:

- Who will have claim to food. As long as people's only claim to food is through the market—and incomes and prices remain volatile—people will die in famines no matter how much food is produced.
- Who will be chronically vulnerable. Famines are generally a disaster for the poor but an opportunity for the rich. When good rains finally return or when the flood waters recede, in most societies people's access to food-producing resources doesn't return to what it was before. Poor farmers and poor herders who were vulnerable before are likely to have been made more insecure.
- The vulnerability of the agricultural system itself—soil, drainage, seeds—to drought and other natural adversities. As long as people are forced by economic pressures to abuse the soil and to forego time-tested conservation practices, poor harvests will become more common.

If we believe that famines are caused by nature's vagaries, we will feel helpless and therefore excused from action. Learning that famines result from human-made forces, we discover hope. No one can change the weather, but we can take responsibility for establishing more stable farming systems and altering the economic rules so that people's claim to food may never be denied.

Only in this direction can we further humanity's age old quest for food security.

M Y T H · 3

Too Many Mouths To Feed

MYTH: Hunger is caused by too many people pressing against finite resources. We must slow population growth before we can hope to alleviate hunger.

OUR RESPONSE: In all of our educational efforts during the last 15 years, no question has been more challenging than, do too many people cause hunger? We've answered no, but in the eyes of some this is tantamount to irresponsibly dismissing population growth as a problem.

We do not take lightly, however, the prospect of human numbers so dominating the planet that other forms of life are squeezed out, that all wilderness is subdued for human use, and that the mere struggle to feed and warm ourselves keeps us from more satisfying pursuits.

Indeed, to us the question of population is so vital that we can't afford to be the least bit fuzzy in our thinking. So here we will focus on the two most critical questions this myth poses. Are population density and population growth the cause of hunger? And, what is the link between slowing population growth and ending hunger?

If too many people caused hunger, then reducing population density could indeed alleviate it. But for one factor to cause another, the two must consistently occur together. Population density and hunger do not.

China has only half the cropland per person as India, yet Indians suffer widespread and severe hunger while the Chinese do not.

Rapid population growth and hunger share a common cause.

Taiwan and South Korea each have only half the farmland per person found in Bangladesh, yet no one speaks of overcrowding causing hunger in Taiwan and South Korea. Costa Rica, with less than half of Honduras' cropped acres per person, boasts a life expectancy—one indicator of nutrition—14 years longer than that of Honduras and close to that of the Western industrial countries.[1]

Surveying the globe, we in fact can find no correlation between population density and hunger. For every Bangladesh, a densely populated and hungry country, we find a Brazil or a Senegal, where significant food resources per capita coexist with intense hunger. Or we find a country like the Netherlands where very little land per person has not prevented it from eliminating hunger and becoming a large net exporter of food.[2]

But what about population growth? Is there not an obvious correlation between rapid population growth and hunger? Without doubt, most hungry people live in Asia, Africa, and Latin America, where populations are growing fastest.

This association of hunger and rapid population growth certainly suggests a relationship between the two. But what we want to probe is the nature of that link. Does rapid population growth cause hunger, or do they occur together because they are both consequences of similar social realities?

Since there doesn't seem to be a correlation between population density and hunger, we propose the following thesis as most probable: hunger, the most dramatic symptom of pervasive poverty, and rapid population growth occur together because they have a common cause.

Lessons from Our Own Past

Let's begin by looking at our own demographic history. As recently as two generations ago, mortality rates in the United States were as high as they are now in most third world countries. Opportunities for our grandmothers to work outside the home were limited. And ours was largely an agrarian society in which every family member was needed to work on the farm. Coauthor Frances Lappé's own grandmother, for example, gave birth to nine children, raised them alone on a small farm, and saw only six survive to adulthood. Her story would not be unusual in a typical fast-growing third world country today.

In the United States, the move to two-child families took place only after a societywide transition that lowered infant death rates, opened opportunities to women outside the home, and transformed ours into an industrial rather than agrarian economy so that families no longer relied on their children's labor. Birth rates fell in response to these changes well before the advent of sophisticated birth control technologies, even while government remained actively hostile to birth control. (As late as 1965, selling contraceptives was still illegal in some states.)[3]

Using our own country's experience to understand rapid population growth in the third world, where poverty is more extreme and widespread, we can now extend our hypothesis concerning the link between hunger and rapid growth: both result where societies deny security and opportunity to the majority of their citizens—where adequate land, jobs, education, health care, and old-age security are beyond the reach of most people.

Without resources to secure their future, people can rely only on their own families. Thus, when many poor parents have lots of children, they are making a rational calculus for survival. High birth rates reflect people's defensive reaction against enforced poverty. For those living at the margin of survival, children provide labor to augment meager family income. In Bangladesh, one study showed that even by the age of six a boy provides labor and/or income for the family. By the age of twelve, at the latest, he contributes more than he consumes.[4]

Population investigators tell us that the benefit children provide to their parents in most third world countries cannot be measured just by hours of labor or extra income. The intangibles are just as important. Bigger families carry more weight in community affairs. Moreover, the "lottery mentality" is associated with poverty everywhere. In the third world, with no reliable channels for advancement in sight, third world parents can always hope that the next child will be the one clever and bright enough to get an education and land a city job despite the odds.

In many countries, income from one such job in the city can support a whole family in the countryside.

And impoverished parents know that without children to care for them in old age, they will have nothing.[5]

They also realize that none of these possible benefits will be theirs unless they have many children, since hunger and lack of health care kill many of their offspring before they reach adulthood. The World Health Organization has shown that both the actual death and the fear of death of a child will increase the fertility of a couple, regardless of income or family size.[6]

Finally, high birth rates reflect not only the survival calculus of the poor, but the disproportionate powerlessness of women. In highly patriarchal societies, a woman's status is largely determined by the number of children she bears—especially the number of sons. And in many societies where women would prefer fewer children, they don't have control over their own fertility. As one doctor in a Mexican clinic explained:

> When a wife wants to . . . limit the number of mouths to feed in the family, the husband will become angry and even beat her. He thinks it is unacceptable that she is making a decision of her own. She is challenging his authority, his power over her—and thus the very nature of his virility.[7]

Even where women are less dependent on men, or where family decisions are shared more equally, restricted access to health services, including birth control, limits women's ability to control reproduction. This is especially true for poor women, for whom access to health services is most limited of all.

Testing the Thesis

If our thesis that rapid population growth results largely from the powerlessness of the poor is true, then population growth will only slow when far-reaching economic and political changes convince the majority of people that social arrangements *beyond the family* —jobs, health care, old-age security, and education (especially for women)— offer both security and opportunity.

Substantial empirical evidence lends weight to this thesis. Consider the implications of the following World Bank population statistics covering three-fourths of the world's people who live in 72 countries that the bank designates low and lower-middle income.[8]

While average annual population growth rates in all industrial countries have been below 2 percent a year for decades, in these 72 countries only six had reduced their growth below 2 percent by 1982.[9] Of these, only four have experienced a dramatic drop in their growth rate since the 1960s: China, Sri Lanka, Cuba, and Colombia. Although not a country, and therefore not listed in the World Bank statistics, the

Indian state of Kerala also reduced its population growth rate below 2 percent.[10] (The remaining two slow-growing poor countries are Haiti and Jamaica, but their growth rates have not fallen since the 1960s.[11])

Population growth in these four exceptional countries and in Kerala has slowed at twice the rate of the current industrialized countries during their transition from high to low growth.[12] What do these exceptions tell us? What could societies as different as those of China, Sri Lanka, Cuba, Colombia, and Kerala have in common?

Except Colombia, they have all assured their citizens access to a basic diet through more extensive food guarantee systems than exist in other third world societies.

China. Since the 1950s, a basic ration of grain has been one of the "five guarantees" to which needy Chinese citizens are entitled.[13]

Cuba. Rationing and setting price ceilings on staples has kept basic food affordable and available to the Cuban people for nearly 25 years.[14] Under Cuba's rationing system, all citizens are guaranteed enough rice, pulses, oil, sugar, meat, and other food to provide them with 1,900 calories a day.[15]

Sri Lanka. From the postwar period to 1978, the Sri Lankan government supported the consumption of basic foods, notably rice, through a combination of free food, rationed food, and subsidized prices.[16]. Since the late 1970s, however, this elaborate food security system has begun to be dismantled.[17] Interestingly, the World Bank does not predict Sri Lanka's growth rate to continue to fall, but rather to rise slightly by the year 2000.

Kerala, India. Eleven thousand government-run fair-price shops keep the cost of rice and other essentials like kerosene within the reach of the poor. This subsidy accounts for as much as one-half of the total income of Kerala's poorer families.[18]

In most of these societies, income distribution is also less skewed than in most other countries. The distribution of household income in Sri Lanka, for example, is more equitable than in Indonesia, India, or even the United States.[19]

This positive link between fertility decline and increased income equity is confirmed by empirical investigations. While one might question the possibility of such neat precision, one World Bank study of 64 different countries indicated that when the poorest group's income goes up by one percentage point, the general fertility rate drops by almost three percentage points.[20] When literacy and life expectancy are added to the income analysis, the three factors explain 80 percent of the variation in fertility among countries.[21]

Several other critical features stand out as we try to understand why, of all low and lower-middle-income societies, these five have experienced such a rapid decline in population growth. Colombia, not known for its government interventions on behalf of the poor, appears to defy the above preconditions of security and opportunity, but not entirely.

Colombia's infant mortality is well below most lower-middle-income countries. Its health service sends medical interns to the countryside for one year's free service, unlike many third world countries, where medical services barely reach outside the capital city. Colombia has also achieved high literacy rates, and almost all children attend primary school.

Colombia's record also demonstrates that shifting resources toward women, expanding their opportunities, has a much bigger impact on lowering birth rates than an overall rise in income—a general pattern, according to Yale University's T. Paul Schultz.[22] Colombia's women appear to be achieving greater economic independence from men and therefore are becoming better able to determine their own fertility. An unusually high percentage of girls attend secondary school.[23] Colombian women are entering the work force at a rapid pace,[24] and new income from the coffee boom of the 1970s contributed to many rural women's new economic independence.[25]

Perhaps the most intriguing demographic case study—highlighting the several intertwined questions raised in this chapter—is that of Kerala. Its population density is three times the average for all India,[26] yet commonly used indicators of hunger and poverty—infant mortality, life expectancy, and death rate—are all considerably more positive in Kerala than in most low-income countries as well as in India as a whole. Its infant mortality is half the all-India average.[27]

Other measures of welfare also reveal the relatively better position of the poor in Kerala. Besides the grain distribution system mentioned above, social security payments, pensions, and unemployment benefits also transfer resources to the poorest groups. While land reform left significant inequality in land ownership, it did abolish tenancy, providing greater security to many who before were only renters. Thanks to effective farmworker organizing, agricultural wages are relatively high. Literacy and education levels are far superior to other states, particularly for women: the female literacy rate in Kerala is two and a half times the all-India average.

Like Kerala, China fascinates us because it demonstrates that even with scarce resources both hunger and rapid population growth can be addressed by shifting resources to the poorest citizens—especially to poor women.

Valuable lessons are also to be found in the experience of those countries still growing at well over 2 percent yearly, but in which crude birth rates have dropped markedly since the 1960s: Thailand, the Philippines, and Costa Rica.[28] Despite their poverty, critical health and other social indicators distinguish these countries from most third world countries, providing clues to their fertility decline. Infant death rates are relatively low, especially in Costa Rica, and life expectancy is high—for women, ranging between 65 to 76 years. Perhaps most important, in the Philippines and Costa Rica an unusually high proportion of women are educated, and in both the Philippines and Thailand, proportionately more women work outside the home than in most third world countries.[29]

But We Don't Have Time

In presenting the essence of this thesis—high birth rates result from economic insecurity—to concerned audiences over the years, at least one questioner will invariably respond, "All well and good, but we don't have time! We can't wait for societywide change benefiting the poor. That takes too long. The population bomb is exploding now."

The implication is that we should do the only thing we can do now: fund and promote family planning programs among fast-growing populations. The rest is pie in the sky.

Our response is twofold. First, demographers will tell you that even if average family size in a fast-growing society were cut by half tomorrow, its population would not stop growing until well into the next century. So every solution, including family planning programs, is a long-term one; there are no quick fixes. The second part of our answer is more surprising: simply providing birth control technology through family planning programs doesn't affect population growth all that much.

D. J. Hernandez, chief of the Marriage and Family Statistics Branch of the U.S. Bureau of the Census, has reviewed all available research to determine the contribution of family planning programs to fertility decline. Examining the research on demographic change in 83 countries, he concluded that the best studies have found little net effect from family planning programs. Hernandez observed that "perhaps as much as 10 percent but possibly as little as 3 percent of the cross-national variation in fertility change in the third world during the late 1960s and early 1970s was an independent effect of family planning programs."[30]

Naturally, Hernandez has been roundly attacked by family planning proponents. But even the study most cited by Hernandez's critics, a 1978 overview of 94 third world countries, concluded that birth control programs alone accounted for only 15 to 20 percent of overall fertility decline, with largely social and economic factors accounting for the rest.[31]

Our highlighting these findings—which reveal a relatively small impact of family planning programs on population—does not mean, of course, that we belittle their potential value. Making contraceptives widely available and helping to reduce inhibitions against their use are critical to the extension of human freedom, especially the freedom of women to control their reproduction. But these findings do confirm that what is truly pie in the sky is the notion that population growth rates can be brought down to replacement levels through a narrow focus on the delivery of contraceptive technology.

Although the experience of Kerala and Colombia suggests that birth rates can fall drastically while great economic inequalities remain, an overwhelmingly clear pattern emerges from worldwide demographic change. At the very least, critical advances in health, social security, and education must change the lives of the poor—especially the lives of poor women—before they can choose to have fewer children. Once people are motivated to have smaller families, family planning programs can quicken a decline in fertility, but that is all; they cannot initiate the decision to have smaller families.[32]

Upping the Ante

Refusing to admit the implications of these findings, many third world governments and international agencies have responded to the marginal impact of family planning programs by upping the ante: designing ever-tougher programs involving long-term injectable contraceptives, sterilization, and financial incentives and penalties.

One example is the injectable contraceptive Depo-Provera. Although considered too hazardous for general use in the United States, 1 million injections lasting three to six months have been given in Thailand alone. Known short-term side effects include menstrual disorders, headaches, weight gain, depression, abdominal discomfort, and delayed return to fertility.[33] And while long-term side effects will not be known for some time, preliminary studies suggest that Depo-Provera is probably linked to an increased risk of cervical cancer.[34]

Family planning programs that are more aimed at controlling population than enhancing the self-determination and well-being of women often fail to offer ongoing, village-level medical care to assist women in choosing appropriate methods and to monitor side effects. So the programs end up being partly self-defeating, because many women just stop using the contraceptives. In one survey in the Philippines, two-thirds of the women who had stopped using the pill and 43 percent who had had the IUD removed blamed medical side effects.[35]

In at least a dozen countries, a variety of material incentives are increasingly used to induce people to undergo sterilization or to use contraception.[36] Defenders of incentive programs stress that they are voluntary. But when you're hungry, how many choices are voluntary? Most telling is that in Bangladesh, where the majority are desperately poor, sterilizations rose dramatically when incentives were increased in 1983. Moreover, they tend to fluctuate with the availability of food. According to the *Bangladesh Observer*, during the flood months of July to October 1984, sterilizations rose to an unprecedented quarter million, accounting for almost one-fourth of all sterilizations performed between 1972 and 1982.[37]

According to author Betsy Hartmann, who has lived and worked in Bangladesh, the system invites abuse. As in many other countries, doctors and clinic staff are paid for each sterilization they perform and anyone, even outside the health system, can get a special fee for "referring" or "motivating" someone to undergo sterilization.

An extreme example suggests the abuses that can result. Donations of wheat to the poor in the aftermath of severe flooding in 1984 were made conditional on women agreeing to sterilization, Hartmann reports. After the operation, each woman received a certificate signed by a family planning officer vouching for her sterility and entitling her to a sari, money, and wheat.[38]

China's Solution?

Those who cling to family planning programs as the answer to population growth might do well to heed the current experience of China.

Through a far-reaching redistribution of land and food, assurance of old-age security, and making health care and birth control devices available to all, China achieved an unprecedented birth rate decline. But since 1979, China has taken a different tack. Believing that population growth was still hindering modernization, the Deng Xiaoping government instituted the world's most restrictive family planning program. Material incentives and penalties are now offered to encourage all parents to bear only one child. According to John Ratcliffe of UC Berkeley's School of Public Health:

> Enormous pressure—social and official—is brought to bear on those who become "unofficially" pregnant; few are able to resist such constant, heavy pressure, and most accede to having an abortion. While coercion is not officially sanctioned, this approach results in essentially the same outcome.[39]

At the same time, Ratcliffe points out, China's post-1979 approach to economic development has undercut both guaranteed employment and old-age security. This has thrown rural families back on their own labor resources, so that large families—especially boys—have once again become a family economic asset.

And what have been the consequences? Despite the world's most stringent population control program, China's birth rates have not continued to fall. If anything, they have risen slightly![40] The message should be unmistakable: people will have children when their security and economic opportunity depend on it, no matter what the state says.

Advocates of more authoritarian measures seem to forget altogether the experience of the other poor societies that along with China have reduced their growth rates to below 2 percent. Recall they are Cuba, Kerala, Colombia, and Sri Lanka. None relied significantly on social coercion or financial incentives. As health care was made available to all, Cuba's birth rates fell, for example, without even so much as a public education campaign, much less financial incentives.

No one should discount the consequences of high population density and rapid population growth, including the difficulties they can add to the already great challenge of development. While in some African countries low population density has been an obstacle to agricultural development, in most countries high population density would make more difficult the tasks of social and economic restructuring necessary to eliminate hunger. Where land resources per person are scarce, social conflict during land reform will be more intense than where resources are plentiful. In Nicaragua's agrarian reform, the luxury of ample farmland—including much unused land—allowed the government to leave many large estates untouched, while still distributing land to the landless. By contrast, El Salvador's much greater population density leaves little land idle; thus, any significant shift of land to the landless will undoubtedly involve more conflict.

No Time to Lose

In this brief chapter, we've outlined what we believe are the critical distinctions too often muddied in discussions of population:

- Unchecked population growth is a crisis for our planet not only because it threatens the future well-being of humanity but because of our moral obligation to share the earth responsibly with other forms of life.
- Population density nowhere explains today's widespread hunger.
- Rapid population growth is not the root cause of hunger, but is—like hunger—a consequence of social inequities that deprive the poor majority—especially poor women—of the security and economic opportunity necessary for them to choose fewer children.
- To bring the human population into balance with the natural environment, societies have no choice but to address the extreme maldistribution of access to survival resources—land, jobs, food, education, and health care.
- Family planning cannot by itself reduce population growth, though it can speed a decline. It best contributes to this transition when integrated into village and neighborhood-based health systems that offer birth control to expand human freedom rather than to control behavior.

We believe that precisely because population growth is such a critical problem, we cannot waste time with approaches that do not work. We must unflinchingly face the evidence telling us that the fate of the world hinges on the fate of today's poor majorities. Only as their well-being improves can population growth slow.

To attack high birth rates without attacking the causes of poverty and the disproportionate powerlessness of women is fruitless. It is a tragic diversion our beleaguered planet can ill afford.

M Y T H · 4

Food vs. Our Environment

MYTH: Pressure to feed the world's hungry is destroying the very resources needed to grow food. To feed the hungry, we are pushing crop and livestock production onto marginal, erosion-prone lands, clearing age old rain forests, and poisoning the environment with pesticides. Clearly, we cannot both feed the hungry and protect our environment.

OUR RESPONSE: We should be alarmed—a many-pronged assault on the environment is destroying the resources on which food production depends. Environmental scientists alert us to these threats:

- More than half of the world's arid and semiarid lands—one-fifth of the earth's land surface and home to 80 million people—is at risk of being turned into deserts.[1]
- At current rates, half of the world's surviving rain forests will be leveled by the end of this century.[2]
- With global pesticide use increasing from virtually nothing only 40 years ago to over 5 billion pounds a year,[3] at least three persons are poisoned by pesticides somewhere in the world every minute and an estimated 10,000 die annually.[4]

That an environmental crisis is undercutting our food-producing resources and threatening our health is no myth; but myths and half-truths confound our grasp of the root causes of the crisis and, therefore, our ability to move toward solutions.

Clearing forests, but not to feed the world's hungry.

In many parts of the world, once-productive lands now resemble desolate moonscapes. But claiming that population pressure and overgrazing cause spreading deserts is no more useful than saying that a person whose throat had been slit died from a lack of blood! That may describe what happened, but it hardly helps us understand why.

Similar descriptive but not explanatory approaches confuse us as to the necessity of pesticides in feeding the hungry and to the reasons behind the felling of rain forests. They block us from seeing that a tradeoff between our environment and the world's need for food is not inevitable. Alternatives do exist and no doubt many more are possible. Indeed, environmentally sound alternatives can even be more productive than environmentally destructive ones. In our next chapter, we explore these possibilities.

World Hunger: Twelve Myths

How to Make a Desert

Over hundreds of years, many of the farmers and pastoralists in West Africa's Sahelian region and much of the continent's other semiarid areas fashioned an interactive mix of food crops, trees, and livestock. For the most part, the system maintained soil fertility and protected the land from wind and water erosion. Its diversity helped ensure some harvests even in years of poor rainfall, which were common.

In the late nineteenth century, by contrast, occupying colonial powers viewed the land as a mine from which to extract wealth. In West Africa, colonial administrations imposed on local farmers monocultures of annual crops for export, notably peanuts, for cooking oil and livestock feed, and cotton, for French and British textile mills.[5] But growing the same crops year after year on the same land, without any mixing of crops, trees, and livestock, rapidly ruined the soils. Just two successive years of peanuts can rob the soil in Senegal of almost a third of its organic matter.[6]

Rapidly depleting soils drove farmers to push export crops onto even more vulnerable lands. Geologically old sediments, well-suited for grazing grasses or tree crops but too delicate to withstand hoeing, were torn up for continuous planting. Ever less land was left fallow.

Especially in East and southern Africa, Europeans seized the fertile and well-watered lands for themselves—even the legendary Livingstone's trek through Africa was in part a search for the best land for cotton. Relocating and confining Africans to areas least suitable for farming, the Europeans made localized overpopulation inevitable.[7] Thus even when the population living off the land was but a fraction of today's, food-producing resources in Sub-Saharan Africa were rapidly being destroyed.

With formal independence (for most European colonies in the early 1960s) the pattern only intensified. To generate foreign exchange to finance Western lifestyles for a new urban elite and launch industrial investments, postcolonial African governments have pressured that more, not less, be produced.[8] Falling export prices in the late 1970s and early 1980s put pressure on governments to make up in volume what they were losing in value. And farmers themselves, receiving meager and falling prices for what they grew, had to produce even more just to meet their food and cash needs.

By crowding livestock herders into ever smaller areas, the spread of export crops has contributed to overgrazing. Government restrictions on herders' traditional practice of migrating in response to rainfall patterns has compounded the problem further.

Adding still greater pressure, livestock numbers have swelled dramatically during the last two decades,[9] in part because pastoralists have sought to offset the uncertain and generally sinking barter value of their animals.[10] A pastoralist trading a milk cow for grain in Niger in the 1970s got only half as much millet as he would have 30 years earlier.[11] For poor herders, more animals have become a survival strategy. For wealthy herders and merchant farmers, they are a source of wealth and prestige.[12]

Governments have promoted bigger herds to expand the supply of meat for export, largely to pay for imports of goods for urban elites. Aid projects have also exacerbated the problem, placing drinking wells for livestock where grass cover has been too poor to sustain the animals.[13]

Little wonder that in more and more areas, the numbers of animals have grown beyond the rangeland's endurance. With so many assaults on soil fertility and protective cover, it is no surprise that drought, wind, and rain create deserts. The underlying explanation, however, hardly has to do with feeding increasing numbers of hungry people.

Soil Destruction at Home

Bringing our focus back to the United States should be enough to dispel the notion that population pressure is the root cause of soil erosion.

Even by official estimates, about one-quarter of U.S. farmland is losing topsoil faster than nature can rebuild it, with the worst erosion occurring on some of our best land.[14] As of the late 1970s, the Department of Agriculture reported that the United States was losing 3 billion tons of topsoil every year—enough to fill New York's Yankee Stadium 21,000 times![15]

Just as in the third world, the dramatic expansion in the early 1970s of row crops for export—primarily corn and soybeans—has greatly accelerated soil losses. In the first three years of the export boom, soil erosion in the Corn Belt leapt 39 percent.[16] Lest we imagine that this irreplaceable loss was at least feeding the world's hungry, keep in mind that close to two-thirds of the edible agricultural exports from the United States go to feed livestock to produce foods the hungry can never afford.[17]

With erosion continuing unabated into the 1980s, national alarm mounted—and conservation measures were incorporated into the 1985 farm legislation. This is a positive turn, without question. But even if these measures can help to counterbalance market pressures to overuse soil, repairing the damage already done to our land would take generations: nature needs at least a hundred—and can take thousands of—years to build a single inch of topsoil.

Wholesale Destruction of Rain Forests

Perhaps even more grievous than soil erosion and desertification is the wholesale destruction of tropical rain forests: deserts can be reclaimed, but age old rain forests may well be irreplaceable.[18]

Just within this century, forests in the tropical third world have declined by nearly half.[19] Each year more than 27 million acres of tropical forests are being destroyed worldwide:[20]

- At the current rate of destruction, the Brazilian rain forests will be gone in 35 years.[21]
- For every 10 acres of Central American rain forest in 1961, only six were left by the late 1970s.[22]
- Two-thirds of the forests of the Ivory Coast have been lost since 1960.[23]
- The rich lowland rain forests of Kalimantan (Indonesian Borneo) may be exhausted by the 1990s.[24]

Such leveling of rain forests destroys the world's richest and least studied plant gene pool that could help improve many important food, fiber, and drug crops as well as develop new ones. Two anticancer compounds, for example, derive from the periwinkle plant found only in Madagascar.[25] Harvard University's Edward O. Wilson has argued that the mass extinction of genetic material underway today is unprecedented in our planet's lifetime.[26]

Deforestation destroys the homes of and poses a genocidal threat to millions of indigenous forest peoples.[27] It also leads to massive soil erosion, exacerbating floods and silting rivers. Moreover, many scientists worry that the wholesale destruction of tropical forests is profoundly altering climates worldwide.[28]

Women and children suffer the most from deforestation. After all, women are typically responsible for collecting firewood, and as it becomes more scarce, they must spend even longer hours gathering it.[29]

What lies behind such ominous devastation? Is it growing numbers of people in search of land to grow food? Evidence from around the world strongly suggests otherwise.

Brazilian Amazonia. Every day as many as 30 buses and flatbed trucks carrying poor Brazilian families arrive in the Rondonia region of the Amazon River basin. Like hundreds of thousands before them, these desperately impoverished farmworkers come in search of land. They cut down and burn areas of forest, plant crops, and then move on after a few years when the soil is exhausted, only to start the cycle again.

Some commentators have been quick to point at Brazil's large and rapidly growing population as the explanation for the influx of settlers. They fail to ask why settlers have been forced into an area where eking a living from the land is so difficult. Certainly Brazil should have enough land for all, since its ratio of cropland to people is more generous than even that of most Latin American countries.[30]

Landless Brazilians are not forced to clear new areas because of insufficient land elsewhere in Brazil, but because a relatively few families own most of that rich resource. Two percent of Brazil's landowners have taken control of 60 percent of the nation's arable land, at least half of which lies completely idle.[31] A mere 340 of the country's largest landowners own more land than 2.5 million poor peasant farmers.[32] For decades, wealthy land moguls have resisted pressures for more equitable distribution of land. A reform decreed in 1964 by the military government had by 1969 distributed land to only 329 peasant families.[33] In 1985 alone, wealthy landlords and their hired killers murdered over 200 peasants whose demands for land they feared.[34]

Such astounding concentration of land ownership has left 12 million rural day workers completely landless, not to mention millions of impoverished families who abandoned the countryside for the infamous urban *favelas* out of economic desperation. Moreover, to rid themselves of the rural disenfranchised whose demands they fear, landowners have been rapidly mechanizing their large farms (with generous government subsidies) and pushing hundreds of thousands of tenants and sharecroppers off the land.[35] So ever more landless farmworkers must compete for ever fewer jobs.

In this light, we can understand why the landed elites and their government tout the new frontier of the Amazon as the solution for the landless: in the eyes of the privileged, it is a handy escape valve against mounting pressure for justice.

But this escape valve is no more than a cruel hoax. Throughout the 1970s, government radio and television ads proclaimed:

> For the man without land in the northeast [a region known for its large estates and millions of landless, hungry people], the land without owner is the Amazon.

But most of the landless who make the considerable sacrifices to get themselves to Amazonia only get to add their names to the government's long waiting lists.[36] They wind up with few options but to clear and "squat" on the forest lands of indigenous peoples and on national parks, always at risk of being driven off or killed. Having done the work of clearing the land, many squatters are then dispossessed by the much more powerful ranchers.[37]

Even if the squatters could remain, cleared tropical forests cannot support farming anyway. For all their Tarzan-movie lushness, tropical rain forests lack deep, fertile soils: they are lush because nutrients are stored in living vegetation. In the heat and humidity, dead leaves and other organic matter decay and are assimilated into new plant life so rapidly that soil is only an inch or so deep and nutrient poor. Not surprisingly, once the protective tree canopy is removed, torrential downpours soon wash away what soil there is. So while Brazil has ample lands suitable for farming, Amazonia has very little.[38]

Colombia. About a million acres of forest are felled every year, and peasant squatters have axed and burned several hundred thousand acres of woodlands in Colombia's Macarena National Park. According to *Latinamerica Press*, they've even had the backing of local congressional representatives. "For those politicians," writes Miguel Varon, "invasion of national parks is a preferable alternative to land reform, which would result in the dismemberment of the largest estates owned by the nation's oligarchy."[39]

Ranchers of the Tropics

Brazil. Further refuting the view that simple people-pressure is destroying the Amazonian rain forest is the fact that most[40] of the destruction has been done by a handful of big-time ranchers, steeply subsidized by the Brazilian government.[41]

From the mid-1960s onward, the Brazilian government has granted kingdom-sized concessions, ranging up to several million acres each, to wealthy individuals and corporations including Volkswagen, Nestlé, Mitsubishi, Liquigas, King Ranch, and Swift-Armour. With the government covering more than three-quarters of the financial outlay, they have bulldozed millions of acres to replace rain forests, home to probably 2 million or more species of plant and animal life, with largely a single crop—pasture grass for cattle. The beef produced is not for hungry Brazilians; it goes mainly to Western Europe, the Middle East, and North America.[42]

Apparently many of these ranches have failed because the soils are so quickly depleted that they won't sustain even pasture grasses. Toxic weeds have also vexed the operations. Even the most well-managed ranches may not stay afloat without continued massive government subsidies.[43]

At enormous public expense, the Brazilian government—with millions in World Bank loans—is constructing highways through Amazonia to serve the ranches and other large-scale schemes. The new highways also reflect the national security obsession of the military.[44] In the process, a wide swath—6 to 10 miles on each side of the highway—has been cleared.[45]

Central America. Often following the roads cut by logging operators, the region's biggest landowners have converted vast acreages of rain forests to pasture over the past 25 years.[46] And international lending agencies—especially the World Bank and the

Inter-American Development Bank—have helped spur Latin America's fledgling livestock industry with billions of dollars in loans.[47]

What is the result of all this effort? Less food, not more! While an acre of land devoted to corn and sorghum can produce over 1,200 pounds of grain a year, that same land devoted to cattle ranching barely yields 50 pounds of meat.[48] Does the beef at least ease Central America's hunger problem? No, most countries export more than half of their beef production—and some 90 percent of that goes to the United States.[49] While beef exports in the 1970s soared 448 percent, beef consumption per person in the region declined by 14 percent.[50] Poor Central Americans rarely, if ever, eat meat. Indeed, a North American pet typically eats more meat than most Central Americans.

Logging the Tropics

Commercial logging is also bringing down rain forests in the Amazonia, the Philippines, Malaysia, the Ivory Coast, Honduras, and elsewhere.[51] In Indonesia for instance, lumber multinationals Weyerhaeuser and Georgia-Pacific have leveled an estimated 2 million acres a year—at least four times more than the area affected by peasant slash-and-burn farming.[52] Commercial logging is notoriously wasteful: to get at a very few marketable species of trees like mahogany, logging companies destroy virtually whole forests. Lumber exploitation also leads to even more widespread destruction by agriculture since roads cut by logging companies open up forests to farmers and ranchers.

And with wholesale felling of trees and insufficient replanting, these operations offer only a brief windfall. Of the 33 third world countries that are now net exporters of forest products, only 10 are expected to remain so by the turn of the century. Already Ghana's timber exports have dropped to less then a tenth of what they were in the early 1970s.[53]

Growing more food for increased numbers of people in the tropics does not generate this demand for lumber. The demand comes from the industrial countries, where consumption of lumber has increased tenfold since 1950 and far exceeds that by all tropical countries. The United States alone consumes more than 70 percent of all tropical plywood and veneer in world trade.[54] Pressed to make interest payments on foreign debt, many governments will no doubt encourage stepped-up logging for export to earn foreign exchange.

Such logging and ranching in the tropics represent the kind of development that redistributes wealth upwards. The benefits provided by the forests—biological diversity, water catchments, soils, rivers, fertile land for gardening under forest-fallow systems, as well as energy sources for labor-intensive local industries—are available to all local people, including even the poorest with no

World Hunger: Twelve Myths

market power. But commercial logging and ranching liquidate such benefits in favor of those accruing mainly to existing elites and to affluent groups, largely foreign interests in the West. Permanent, broadly distributed benefits are exchanged for temporary, highly concentrated ones. The whole process reflects the grossly unequal distribution of power, nationally and internationally.[55]

Rapid population growth in the tropics does contribute to pressure on rain forests, just as more people and bigger herds contribute to desertification in Africa. But "to blame colonizing peasants for uprooting tribal people and burning the rain forest," write two rain forest ecologists, "is tantamount to blaming soldiers for causing wars."[56] We agree. And we hope our book helps focus attention on the cause of the "war" itself.

Pesticides and Our Food Security

Now let's turn to the third area of concern raised in this chapter—the threat to health and the environment from pesticides.

We too found ourselves wondering whether people's legitimate food needs will not require using ever more pesticides. Already over 5 billion pounds of pesticides are used annually throughout the world.[57] In the United States alone, more than a billion pounds of pesticides are injected each year into our environment—that's over four pounds for every American and nearly double the amount as recently as 1964.[58]

Worldwide, pesticides now add $14 billion to farmers' costs,[59] but the human health toll is even more staggering. Pesticide poisonings may be as high as 1.5 million each year.[60] In California alone, 14,901 farmworkers were officially recorded as suffering from pesticide-related illnesses between 1962 and 1983. And the number of poisonings of farmworkers in the state doubled between the 1960s and the 1970s.[61] At least 15 herbicides have recently been detected in surface and groundwater across the country.[62]

In the third world, the health threat is magnified. At least a quarter of the pesticides that U.S. corporations export are banned, heavily restricted, or have never been registered for use here.[63] Most end up in fields where workers are not provided protective clothing and where safety precautions are the last concern of the farms' owners. On cotton and banana plantations in the Philippines, the Ivory Coast, and in Central America, we found pesticides being indiscriminately sprayed from airplanes and from cannisters strapped to the backs of unprotected workers.

A schoolteacher in Trinidad told us that each time the sugarcane plantations have been aerially sprayed, most of the children in her classes stay home sick the next day. They have fainting spells, vomit, and suffer bad skin rashes.

Following the deaths of two teenage girls in Malaysia from field exposure to paraquat in 1985, the Health Ministry divulged that 1,200 workers had been killed since 1980 by exposure to just this one pesticide.[64]

Increasingly, pesticides are manufactured in the third world where plant safety regulations are less stringent. The combination of lethal ingredients and deficient safety precautions was dramatically demonstrated by the 1984 leak at the Union Carbide pesticide plant in Bhopal, India, that killed more than 2,000 people and injured 200,000.[65]

While pesticides most endanger exposed factory workers and farmworkers, today everyone is at risk. "The weight of evidence is clear," says Charles Benbrook, executive director of the National Academy of Sciences' agricultural board, "exposure to pesticides is a cause of cancer."[66]

The U.S. Environmental Protection Agency (EPA) now formally considers pesticides the nation's number one environmental problem, yet it tests pesticide ingredients at a glacial pace. To date, the EPA has been able to provide assurances of safety for only 37 of the more than 600 active ingredients used in 45,000 pesticides on the market.[67] Even after accelerating its pace of review, the agency can study only 25 such ingredients a year.[68] As a result, the EPA often relies on test results furnished by the manufacturers. It probably shouldn't. A U.S. court recently found that manufacturer-contracted tests upon which hundreds of pesticides were approved by the government were fraudulent.[69]

Becoming aware of the mounting use of pesticides, involving both immediate harm and untold future hazards, we had to ask ourselves if pesticide use is really essential to our food security. In assessing this complex question, we had to struggle to fix the following facts in our minds—they run so counter to what is widely assumed about the necessity of and benefits from pesticides:

- Between 20 and 30 percent of the pesticides in the United States are used not in agriculture at all but on golf courses, parks, and lawns.[70]

- Despite great increases in amounts and toxicity since the commercial introduction of pesticides in the late 1940s, crop losses to insects, disease, and weed pests have actually increased from 32 to 37 percent.[71]

- Often, less than 0.1 percent of the pesticides applied to crops actually reaches target pests. The rest moves into ecosystems contaminating the land, water, and air.[72]

- U.S. farmers could cut insecticide use by as much as 50 to 75 percent with no effect on crop production, simply by using better pest management techniques.[73]

42   *World Hunger: Twelve Myths*

- For corn and wheat, together accounting for 30 percent of all pesticides used on U.S. cropland,[74] researchers estimate that crop losses from pests would increase only 1 or 2 percent even if no pesticides were employed.[75]

What these five facts brought home to us is that much of the threat from pesticides is not related to food production at all and that therefore a large portion of pesticides currently used on food crops could be eliminated without a significant drop-off in production.

And what about the third world? Do pesticides there help produce food for hungry people?

In the third world, the bulk of pesticides are not used to grow the staple crops of the poor but are applied to export crops.[76] In West Africa, the figure is over 90 percent.[77]

Because pesticides are so expensive and because they are used largely by politically influential owners of large commercial farms, third world governments spend hundreds of millions of dollars annually subsidizing pesticide use.[78] Spared the full cost, producers are much more likely to use pesticides extravagantly, compounding the hazards.[79]

The Pesticide Treadmill

The striking increase in pesticide use worldwide, with sales climbing at 12.5 percent each year, results in part because pesticides lock farmers onto an accelerating treadmill. In Central America, in little more than 10 years, pesticide applications per growing season leapt from 5 to 28, while the number of insect species requiring control went from two to eight. Soon pesticide costs came to account for half of all production costs.[80]

Ever more pesticides are needed simply to combat resistant organisms *resulting from the pesticides themselves*! Insects have now developed resistance to all major classes of pesticides.[81]

Malaria's recent resurgence is one of the most alarming consequences of pesticide overuse and insects' capacity to develop resistance and adapt behaviorally to even the most deadly human concoctions. Pesticides DDT and later dieldrin were used widely from the 1950s on to wipe out the mosquitoes that carry the disease, and by the 1960s world health officials were rejoicing at their victory. During that decade in Sri Lanka, for example, malaria cases dropped from 3 million to fewer than 25. But even by the early 1970s, DDT-resistant mosquitoes were pushing infection levels to previously unknown levels.[82]

This environmental and health castastrophe wasn't just the result of an ill-conceived public health strategy. Authorities now partly blame the overuse of pesticides in agriculture—especially on cotton in Central America and on Green Revolution rice in India—

for spreading resistance and speeding the deadly return of malaria. With DDT used in cotton production in El Salvador, two public health experts estimate that each kilo of the insecticide added to the environment will lead to 105 new cases of malaria.[83]

A Mounting Response to Environmental Destruction

Since we began our work in the early 1970s, we have witnessed the rise worldwide of increasingly vocal and effective responses to the environmental destruction we have discussed in this chapter.

Citizen organizations are contesting the right of governments and corporations to tear down irreplaceable rain forests to benefit a few.

The United States. In the United States, the Natural Resources Defense Council, working with other organizations, has successfully pressured the World Bank to halt lending to Brazil for development schemes that destroy Amazonian rain forests.[84]

Malaysia. The logging of a proposed national park was halted by a Malaysia-wide campaign led by the Consumers' Association of Penang.[85]

Central America. The Environmental Project on Central America is supporting ecologically sound alternatives in the region. Each year it sends brigades to help plant trees.[86]

India. In the Uttarakhand region of the Indian Himalayas, thousands of poor women villagers united in a Tree Huggers movement that sucessfully pressured the government to ban the felling of trees in the region by commerical contractors and launched reforestation efforts responsible for planting a million trees.[87]

Worldwide. With the growing awareness worldwide of the hazards of pesticides, the international Pesticide Action Network has launched the Dirty Dozen campaign targeting the 12 most hazardous pesticides.[88] The network also disseminates information about viable alternatives to ever-increasing dependence on chemical pesticides.

To promote the often ingenious methods developed by millions of farmers over hundreds of years, the International Alliance for Sustainable Agriculture was formed in 1983. Its goal is the spread of tried-and-true farming methods enhanced by the latest scientific knowledge that can produce food economically and without harming the environment or public health.[89]

Hard Questions

Surely there are areas where population density exacerbates environmental destruction. But a superficial diagnosis that blames the growing number of people (who often are victims themselves) leads us nowhere. Even where environmental destruction is severe, would cutting the population in half solve the problem?

We must dig for root causes, asking, why are peasants denied productive agricultural land and forced onto lands that should not be farmed or resettled in rain forests? Why are big operators allowed—and even publicly subsidized—to tear down tropical forests? If desertified areas are helped to regenerate, who will control the process, who will benefit, and who will lose? Why do most of the farmers who use chemical fertilizers and pesticides think they cannot afford the risk of shifting to less chemical-intensive methods? Why are environmentally sound alternatives for food production little known and even suppressed rather than fostered? And finally, can humanity afford to treat food and the resources to produce it just like any other commodity?

Hard questions like these must be confronted if we are serious about protecting and even enhancing for future generations our planet's finite food-producing resources as well as an environment safe for all life. While we have a long way to go in developing our answers—and no one answer will fit every place and people—we hope this book helps clear our vision so that the right questions can be raised.

M Y T H · 5

The Green Revolution Is the Answer

MYTH: The miracle seeds of the Green Revolution increase grain yields and therefore are a key to ending world hunger. Now biotechnology—actually manipulating the genes of plants—offers an even more dramatic production revolution just down the road. More food means less hunger. In Asia, the Green Revolution is working—in Africa, it's long overdue.

OUR RESPONSE: Improving seeds through experimentation is what people have been up to since the beginning of agriculture,[1] but the term Green Revolution was coined in the 1960s to highlight a particularly significant breakthrough. In test plots in northwest Mexico, improved varieties of wheat dramatically increased yields. The "miracle" seeds quickly spread to Asia, and soon new strains of rice were developed in the Philippines.

By the 1970s, the term revolution was well deserved, for the new seeds—accompanied by petrochemical fertilizers, pesticides, and, for the most part, irrigation—had displaced the traditional farming practices of millions of third world farmers. By the mid-1980s, Green Revolution seeds were being sown on roughly half the rice and wheat acreage in the third world.

Clearly, the production advances of the Green Revolution are no myth. Thanks to the new seeds, 50 million extra tons of grain a year are being har-

New technology has increased food production, yet more people are hungry.

vested, Green Revolution promoters tell us. And it's also true that we're on the brink of a second Green Revolution based on further advances in biotechnology. Although it may not arrive as quickly as press accounts suggest, its impact may be even more pervasive.[2]

But has the Green Revolution actually proven itself a successful strategy for ending hunger? Here the debate heats up! Let us capsulize two dominant sides in this debate.

Proponents claim that by increasing grain production, the Green Revolution has alleviated hunger, or at least it has prevented it from becoming even worse as populations keep growing. Traditional agriculture just couldn't meet the demands of today's burgeoning populations. Moreover, they assert, dealing with the root causes of poverty that contribute to hunger takes a very long time and people are starving now. So we must do what we can—increase production. The Green Revolution buys the time desperately needed by third world countries to deal with the underlying social causes of poverty and to cut birth rates. In any case, outsiders—like the scientists and policy advisors behind the Green

Revolution—can't tell a poor country to reform its economic and political system, but they can contribute invaluable expertise in food production.

The above view was rarely questioned when we began our work over 15 years ago. It was the official wisdom. But in response to many independent analyses, including the work of our institute[3] and the experience of the Green Revolution itself, today this "wisdom" is being increasingly challenged.

Those of us challenging the Green Revolution strategy know that production will have to increase if populations continue to grow. But we've also seen that focusing narrowly on increasing production—as the Green Revolution does—cannot alleviate hunger because it fails to alter the tightly concentrated distribution of economic power, especially access to land and purchasing power. If you don't have land on which to grow food or the money to buy food, you go hungry no matter how dramatically technology pushes up food production.

Introducing any new agricultural technology into a social system stacked in favor of the rich and against the poor—without addressing the social questions of access to the technology's benefits—will over time lead to an even greater concentration of the rewards from agriculture, as is happening in the United States.

Because the Green Revolution approach does nothing to address the insecurity at the root of high birth rates—and can even heighten that insecurity—it cannot buy time while population growth slows. Finally, a narrow focus on production ultimately defeats itself as it destroys the very resource base on which agriculture depends.

We've come to see that without a strategy for change that addresses the powerlessness of the poor, the tragic result will be more food and yet more hunger.

This debate is no esoteric squabble among development experts—it cuts to the core of our understanding of development and therefore deserves careful probing. So first we will explore why a narrow production strategy like the Green Revolution is bound to fail to end hunger, drawing on the experience of the past quarter century. Then, recognizing that this debate itself overlooks critical considerations, we will step outside its confines to ask, what approach could offer genuine food security?

More Food and Yet More Hunger?

In 1985, the head of the international body overseeing Green Revolution research, S. Shahid Husain, declared that the poor are the beneficiaries of the new seeds' output. He even went so far as to claim that "added emphasis on poverty alleviation is not necessary" because increasing production itself has a major impact on the poor.[4]

Husain's statement must have embarrassed many promoters of the Green Revolution because by the 1980s few of even its avid defenders would make such a sweeping claim.

In fact, some within the World Bank—which finances the research network Husain chairs—concluded in a major 1986 study of world hunger that a rapid increase in food production does not necessarily result in food security, that is, less hunger. Current hunger can only be alleviated by "redistributing purchasing power and resources toward those who are undernourished," the study said.[5] In a nutshell—if the poor don't have the money to buy food, increased production is not going to help them. At last! was our response—for this fundamental insight was a starting point of our institute's analysis of hunger more than a decade ago.

The bank's study goes on to tell us that the number of hungry people increased throughout the world during the 1970s, reaching 730 million by the end of the decade.[6]

And where are these 730 million hungry people?

Beginning in 1984, Africa's acute famine awakened Westerners to hunger there, but Africa represents about a fifth of the hunger in the world today. We are made blind to the day-in-day-out hunger suffered by hundreds of millions more.

By the mid-1980s, newspaper headlines were applauding the Asian success stories—India and Indonesia, we were told, had become "self-sufficient in food" or even "food exporters."[7] But it is in South Asia, precisely where Green Revolution seeds have contributed to the greatest production success,[8] that live roughly two-thirds of the undernourished in the entire world![9] There both the absolute number and the proportion of people who are hungry have risen since 1970.[10]

India. In spite of the nation's 24 million ton grain surplus,[11] per person consumption of grain hasn't increased in 20 years, and nearly half the population lacks the income necessary to buy a nutritious diet.[12] (This we learn from a U.S. Department of Agriculture article with the unlikely title "India's Agricultural Success Story.") In recent years per person availability of grain in India has even declined.[13]

Thailand. The Green Revolution helped push rice production up over 30 percent in the 1970s, but with exports of rice increasing nine times faster, per person availability of rice has fallen.[14]

The Philippines. This country is home to the world-famous rice research center from which improved varieties spread throughout Asia, yet two-thirds of the children are malnourished even in Luzon, the "rice granary" of the Philippines.[15]

Mexico. Here in the birthplace of the "miracle" wheat seeds, we find hunger worse today than it was when those seeds were first sown.[16]

Zimbabwe. Now we're told that better seeds can end hunger in Africa. In Zimbabwe, improved seeds have increased yields, yet nearly 30 percent of all children are stunted by malnutrition.[17]

How can there be more food and yet more hunger?

The volume of output alone tells us little about hunger. Whether the Green Revolution or any other strategy to boost food production will alleviate hunger depends on the economic, political, and cultural rules that people make. These rules determine who benefits as a *supplier* of the increased production—whose land and crops prosper and for whose profit—and who benefits as a *consumer* of the increased production—who gets the food and at what price.

The Green Revolution:
A View from the Farm

In theory, the Green Revolution was to alleviate hunger by helping poor farmers produce more food for themselves and generate more income from their land.

But the new seeds' potential to relieve poverty and hunger by making farmers more prosperous depends—to start with—on *what portion of the poor are farmers*. This seems pretty elementary, but it is often overlooked—despite the fact that nearly 1 billion people in the third world are either landless or have too little land to feed their households. Half of them are in India and Bangladesh alone.[18]

The Green Revolution and the Landless

Those with little or no land gain if jobs and wages increase, but investigators dispute whether either has in fact happened. Some early studies reported improvements in both yields and wages,[19] but a 1985 International Labour Office study of rural Asia concluded that "contrary to expectations, the [Green Revolution] . . . has not led to increased labour absorption in agriculture."[20] In five of the eight Asian cases examined in the study, agricultural wages also failed to rise.[21]

Whether the landless benefit hinges in large part on how those profiting from the new seeds use their new wealth. Do they replace workers with machines, thereby reducing the number of jobs? Rice threshers—developed by the same research center responsible for the new strains of rice—are already displacing women's labor in the Philippines and Thailand.[22] Just since 1973, the number of tractors has doubled throughout the third world.[23]

Much also depends on the political organization of the landless. In the Indian state of Kerala where agricultural workers are well organized, real wages of farmworkers have risen, in contrast with most of India.[24]

The Green Revolution and Poor Farmers

The initial thrust of the Green Revolution excluded the majority of poor farmers in many countries. In Mexico, poor farmers' primary crops are corn and beans, but the focus of Mexico's Green Revolution has been wheat. Wheat output leapt three times between 1960 and the early 1980s, while corn production limped far behind; corn increased about two-thirds by the early 1970s and afterward experienced no sustained growth.[25] Even the poor farmers who grew wheat were displaced by the big growers in Mexico's northwest, backed by generous government credit and an expensive government-built irrigation network.[26]

Similarly, in India until the mid-1970s, the Green Revolution was almost exclusively a wheat revolution. Yet when the new seeds were first introduced in the 1960s, wheat covered only 9 percent of Indian farmland. The new seeds needed careful irrigation, yet only 17 percent of Indian farmland was irrigated.[27] And both wheat and irrigation were to be found in India's *already* most prosperous areas.

More recently, plant scientists have put more emphasis on rainfed agriculture and on a wider variety of crops—maize, cassava, potatoes, cowpeas, millet, sorghum, and so on—grown and eaten by the poor.[28] But the question still remains. Can improving seeds—even those used by the poor farmers—alleviate their hunger and poverty?

By the mid-1980s, we were told that Green Revolution critics (like us) were dead wrong in claiming that only the big farmers benefit. "Neither size nor tenure has been a serious constraint on the MV [modern variety of seeds] adoption," wrote two respected agricultural economists in 1984.[29] Many smaller, poorer farmers are adopting the new seeds. But in societies where ownership of farm assets is tightly concentrated, what happens?

Consider India. In most of the subcontinent, it "is generally true" that "the poor benefit from the Green Revolution but not equally or proportionately because of the several advantages enjoyed by the rich and the handicaps suffered by the poor," concluded one of the architects of India's Green Revolution, D. P. Singh, in 1980. The gulf between the two, he says, widens "in absolute as well as relative terms."[30]

What are those handicaps suffered by the poor?

Most of all, the poor lack clout. They can't command the subsidies and other government favors accruing to the rich. Neither can the poor count on police or legal protection when wealthier landowners abuse their rights to resources.

The poor also pay more and get less. Poor farmers can't afford to buy fertilizer and other inputs in volume; big growers can get discounts for large purchases. Poor farmers can't hold out for the best price for their crops, as can larger farmers whose circumstances are far less desperate.[31]

World Hunger: Twelve Myths

In much of the world, water is the limiting factor in farming success, and irrigation is often out of the reach of the poor. Canal irrigation favors those near the top of the flow. Tubewells, now promoted by development agencies, favor the bigger operators, who can better afford the initial investment and have lower costs per unit.[32]

Credit is also critical. It's not uncommon for small farmers to pay interest rates several times as high as big farmers—reaching over 100 percent annually.[33] Government subsidized credit overwhelmingly benefits the big farmers.[34]

So what, some will say. If the poor are using the improved seeds, haven't they gained, even if not as much as the better off?

But poor and rich participate in a single social dynamic—their fates are inevitably intertwined. A study of two rice-growing villages in the Philippines dramatizes this reality. In both villages, large and small farmers alike adopted the new seeds. In the village where landholdings were relatively equal and a tradition of community solidarity existed, the new technology did not polarize the community by disproportionately benefiting the better off. But in the village dominated by a few large landowners, their greater returns from the Green Revolution allowed them to advance at the expense of the small farmers. After 10 years, the large farms in the village had grown in size by over 50 percent.[35] Land absorbed by the rich meant less for the poor.

Where a critic might want to blame the Green Revolution for the greater misery of poor farmers, the real fault lies in a social order permitting a tight grip on resources by only a few families.

Who Survives the Farm Squeeze?

With the Green Revolution, farming becomes petrodependent. Some of the more recently developed seeds may produce higher yields even without manufactured inputs,[36] but the best results require the right amounts of chemical fertilizer, pesticides, and water.

So as the new seeds spread, petrochemicals become part of farming. In India, adoption of the new seeds was accompanied by a threefold rise in fertilizer use per acre in the 1970s alone.[37] Because farming methods that depend heavily on chemical fertilizers do not maintain the soil's natural fertility and because pesticides generate resistant pests, farmers need ever more fertilizers and pesticides just to achieve the same results.[38] At the same time, machines—though not *required* by the new seeds—enter the fields as those profiting use their new wealth to buy tractors and other machines.

This incremental shift we call the industrialization of farming. What are its consequences?

Once on the path of industrial agriculture, farming costs more. It can be more profitable, of course, but only if the prices farmers get for their crops stay ahead of the costs of petrochemicals and machinery. Some Green Revolution proponents claim striking increases in net incomes from farms of all sizes once farmers adopt the more responsive seeds.[39] But recent studies also show another trend: outlays for fertilizers and pesticides may be going up faster than yields, suggesting that Green Revolution farmers are now facing what U.S. farmers have experienced for decades—a cost-price squeeze.[40]

A village study in the prime rice-growing area of the Philippines showed that as farmers' costs—the money spent on fertilizers, pesticides, and fuel—rose between 1970 and 1978, their return measured as a share of the value of their crop fell from one-third to only one-tenth. If yields had increased enough, farmers could still have profited. But they didn't, and returns to farmers decreased not just proportionately but absolutely.[41]

Village studies in Tamil Nadu, India, tell a similar story. Farm income fell between the early 1970s and early 1980s for both large and small farmers, despite greater output.[42] Elsewhere in Tamil Nadu during the same period, rice yields doubled and large and medium farmers gained, but poor farmers, even though they too reaped higher yields, ended up even worse off than before.[43]

Given the heavy costs of agricultural inputs and farmers' lack of bargaining power over the prices of their crops, farmers in many Asian countries are plagued by mounting debts. In Thailand, 5 million rural families are now carrying a total debt of over $1 billion on a per family basis equal to more than each family's entire yearly income.[44]

To anyone following farm news here at home, these reports have a painfully familiar ring—and why wouldn't they? After all, the United States—not Mexico—is the true birthplace of the Green Revolution. Improved seeds combined with chemical fertilizers and pesticides have pushed corn yields up threefold since 1950. As larger harvests have pushed down the prices farmers get for their crops while the costs of farming have shot up, farmers' profit margins have been drastically narrowed since World War II. By the early 1980s, profit per acre had fallen to a third of pre–Green Revolution years.[45]

So who survives today? Two very different groups: those few farmers who chose not to buy into industrialized agriculture and those able to keep expanding their acreage to make up for their lower per acre profit.

Among this second select group are the top 1 percent of farms by income, those the U.S. Department of Agriculture has dubbed superfarms. In 1969, the superfarms earned 16 percent of net farm income; by 1982, as the cost-price squeeze tightened, they had captured 60 percent![46] By 1984, the average income of half of all farm families—even counting income from jobs off the farm—was less than $14,000. But for the top 1 percent the average net income from farming *alone* was well over $400,000.[47]

Superfarms triumph, not because they are more efficient food producers[48] or because the Green Revolution technology itself favored them, but because of advantages that accrue to wealth and size.[49] They have the capital to invest and the volume necessary to stay afloat even if profits per unit shrink. They have the political clout to shape tax policies in their favor. Over time, why should we expect the result of the cost-price squeeze to be any different in the third world?

In the United States, we've seen the number of farms drop by more than half since World War II and average farm size double in 30 years. The gutting of rural communities, the swelling of inner-city slums, and more recently the exacerbation of unemployment—all have followed in the wake of this vast migration from the land. Think what the equivalent rural exodus would mean in the third world, where the proportion of jobless people is already double or triple our own.

Big Winners Off the Farm

So far we've tried to clarify which farmers "win" in the Green Revolution. But the biggest winners may not be farmers at all. "Neither the farmer nor the landlord reaped the benefits of the Green Revolution," writes researcher Hiromitsu Umehara about the Philippines. "The real beneficiaries were the suppliers of farm inputs, farm work contractors, private moneylenders and banks." In his village study in central Luzon, their share of the value of the rice harvest rose from one-fifth to more than one-half in only nine years.[50]

In the United States, the same pattern holds. Not only has the share of the consumer food dollar going to the farmer dropped from 42 to 27 percent since 1950, but of that 27 percent the farmer must pay out an ever bigger share to banks and corporate suppliers.[51]

The pressure toward the industrialization of agriculture—leading to ever bigger and fewer farms—may be no more inherent in the new seeds themselves than in any farm technology that costs money. But any strategy to increase production that does not directly address this underlying dynamic will ultimately contribute to the displacement of rural people, and thus, especially in the third world, to greater poverty and hunger.

The Green Revolution: The Price of Dependency

The more dire consequences of displacing people from the land is one obvious difference between the industrialization process now under way in the third world and that well advanced in U.S. agriculture. But there's a less visible difference. Here the manufacturers of farm inputs are largely based in this economy. So as corporations selling inputs to farmers capture a bigger share of the national food dollar, at least it ends up in part creating jobs and returning profits here.

But what about countries in the third world that must import most of their fertilizers, pesticides, irrigation equipment, and machines? Benefits leave the country altogether. In India, the cost of importing fertilizer rose 600 percent between the late 1960s and 1980.[52] And India has exceptional industrial capacity and is unusually well endowed with its own fertilizer-making resources. Even where multinational firms establish plants in third world countries to produce, for example, fertilizers and pesticides, profits are controlled by the parent company.

The next breakthroughs of the Green Revolution promise to make farmers and entire nations even more dependent on a handful of corporate suppliers. The first stage relied on improving seeds by breeding for desired qualities. These seeds were for the most part developed within the public domain in research institutes funded by governments and international lending agencies.[53]

The new stage—including cloning plants in tissue culture from single cells and gene splicing (recombinant DNA techniques)—enables much more rapid and specific selection. Its techniques can be applied to virtually any crop and even to livestock. Unlike the earlier stage, these new biotechnology techniques are largely being pursued within the private sector. Their products will be patented by major chemical, pharmaceutical, and energy companies that already have acquired a major share of the seed industry.[54]

Some concerned analysts, such as Jack Doyle of the Washington, D.C.–based Environmental Policy Institute and author of *Altered Harvest*, fear that among the consequences will be even greater dependency of third world farmers on imported inputs. If a new seed is genetically engineered to work only with a certain herbicide or a particular chemical growth regulator, for example, a farmer must purchase the whole package. What will farmers' cost savings be if they buy the genetically engineered seed—and then have to buy still another product? asks Doyle.[55] Moreover, if the corporate research strategy is to produce hybrids that are reproductively unstable—that don't reproduce themselves in the farmers' fields—farmers will be compelled to buy new seeds each year, adding still further to production costs and therefore to risk.[56]

Even those who see great potential benefit for third world agriculture in biotechnology breakthroughs, such as Cornell's Frederick Buttel and Ohio State's Martin Kenney, are concerned about what one might call research dependency. The widespread patenting of biotechnology processes and products will make it more difficult for third world scientists to adapt biotechnologies to the needs of their countries. Moreover, poor farmers just don't make an attractive market. Take, for instance, the development of salt-tolerant rice seeds. This one breakthrough would enable rice cultivation on almost 150 million acres in Southeast Asia now affected by high salinity. But given the meager buying power of most farmers on that less favorable land, why would a private company pursue such a costly project?[57]

The Green Revolution: A View from the Dinner Bowl

So far we've asked only how the potential of growing more food to help end hunger is shaped by the economic ground rules governing production—that is, who has the power to determine the distribution of rewards from the greater yields. The same question applies as we turn to consumption.

Almost half of India's rural people are net food buyers,[58] yet important food crops most eaten by the poor have not been primary targets of the Green Revolution. While consumption of Green Revolution wheat increased in India, per capita consumption of legumes—peas, beans, and lentils, which are important protein sources for the poor—dropped by one-half.[59]

And has the Green Revolution lowered prices so that the poor without land could buy more food?[60] The Green Revolution has restrained prices, and in Colombia it appears to have helped lower them.[61] But while the price of grain in world markets has fallen since 1970, prices *within* key Green Revolution countries have not.[62]

Food prices don't fall just because production goes up; greater food output doesn't necessarily mean greater availability. Some governments, such as those in India and the Philippines, have simply used the Green Revolution to displace imports, not augment supply. This helps explain why, despite India's Green Revolution in wheat and rice, grain available per person today is no greater than 20 years ago.

Food prices will not fall if merchants hike their own profits instead of passing on savings to consumers. Much also depends on whose voices are heard by policymakers. The Indian government, more responsive to lobbying by affluent grain producers than to the needs of the hungry, has not allowed grain prices to fall, despite record grain surpluses.[63] Moreover, the industrial model of agriculture imparts its own pressure to keep prices up. Once dependent on costly industrial inputs, farmers just can't go on producing if prices fall too much.

The Hidden Food Revolution

Journalists eagerly report on the globe-spanning network of Green Revolution research laboratories where breakthroughs in plant genetics are being achieved. With so much attention focused on the Green Revolution, we fail to perceive a much more sweeping food revolution underway in the third world, one far more dramatic than the increased consumption of new strains of wheat or rice.

The consequence of this revolution is to shrink, not expand, the food supply.

Mexico is but one example of this hidden revolution. While two-thirds of Mexico's people are chronically undernourished[64] and its population is growing fast, no greater area is planted today in the foods most consumed by the poor—corn and beans—than 20 years ago.[65] Even the acreage in wheat[66]—the crop targeted by Green Revolution research and investment—doesn't hold a candle to Mexico's real postwar boom crop.

The real winner is sorghum, a feed grain used mostly to produce poultry, eggs, and milk for urban classes. Sorghum was virtually unknown in Mexico in 1958, but by 1980 it covered twice the acreage in wheat![67]

Sorghum spread at such spectacular speed largely in response to the demand for livestock products by the top 15 percent of Mexicans whose purchasing power enables them to consume half of Mexico's food.[68] Sorghum also spread because it requires less labor, is drought resistant, and farmers don't have to worry about midnight harvests by hungry peasants because this variety is *not* for human consumption.[69]

Twenty-five years ago, livestock consumed only 6 percent of Mexico's grain. Today livestock consume from one-third to one-half of Mexico's grain,[70] including as much as one-fifth of Mexico's Green Revolution wheat.[71] Only a fraction of the nutrients fed to livestock returns to humans. At least 25 million Mexicans are too poor ever to eat meat, and even poultry and dairy foods are largely beyond their reach.[72]

Worldwide over 40 percent of all grain goes to livestock.[73] And in the third world, *the demand for feed is growing 75 percent faster than the demand for food*.[74] Increasingly soybeans and cassava, both basic foods for many third world peoples, are grown as livestock feed for export from the third world, as we describe in chapter 8.

In the late 1970s, we traveled to northwest Mexico to see with our own eyes where the breakthrough wheat research was carried out over 20 years ago. We wound through mile after mile of cropland, all well watered by costly government-built irrigation. Mostly we saw cotton, grapes, and vegetables—asparagus, cucumbers, tomatoes, and peppers—largely destined for export.

World Hunger: Twelve Myths

Stopping at a government agricultural research station, we asked why this prime land was planted in export crops when we had seen so many hungry people. Scribbling a few figures on a scrap of paper, the young agronomist explained, "It's quite simple. An entrepreneur in this area can make 20 times more by growing tomatoes for export than food for Mexicans."

The story of northwest Mexico is not unique. Overall, food exports, often luxury items, are growing twice as fast as total food production in the third world.[75] Thus, perhaps more decisive for the hungry than the much-heralded Green Revolution is this almost invisible one. In this revolution, production shifts out of basic foods and toward the tastes of those who can pay. They are not the hungry.

The Green Revolution: Some Lessons

Having seen food production advance while hunger widens, we are now prepared to ask, under what conditions are greater harvests doomed to failure in eliminating hunger?[76]

First, where farmland is bought and sold like any other commodity and society allows the unlimited accumulation of farmland by a few, superfarms replace family farms and all society suffers.

Second, where food is bought and sold like any other commodity and society tolerates vast inequalities in income and wealth, farmland shifts to produce sorghum for livestock or tomatoes for export, while people starve for lack of beans and corn.

Third, where the main producers of food—small farmers and farmworkers—lack bargaining power relative to suppliers of farm inputs and food marketers, producers get a shrinking share of the rewards from farming.

Under these economic ground rules, mountains of additional food could not eliminate hunger, as hunger in America should never let us forget.

Fortunately, many societies are experimenting with different economic ground rules. China is but one such society, along with others we highlight in other chapters. We do not propose China as a model—no society is—but its experience is instructive. Almost half of all land in the world now planted with Green Revolution rice is in China, but the results of greater production in that country contrasts dramatically with India's experience.

China's relatively low infant death rate and impressive life-expectancy statistics suggest much less widespread hunger than in India. "Probably less than 3 percent of China's population suffers from undernutrition," estimates Oxford University scholar Keith Griffin.[77] In India, almost half the population is too poor to buy the food they need.[78] In China, farmland cannot be bought and sold, helping to ensure that the vast majority of rural Chinese people have a direct claim on food-producing resources. Moreover, a basic diet is guaranteed to those who cannot work.[79]

There is another lesson to be learned from China. While China's record in overcoming chronic hunger is outstanding, Amartya Sen, an authority on the etiology of famines, points out that China's lack of an independent press and vehicles for political opposition allows the government to fail to respond adequately to acute food shortages, such as the 1959 to 1961 famine.[80] Civil liberties are critical, we underline in chapter 12, in keeping a government accountable to its people's food needs.

In chapter 7 and in our concluding essay, we include examples of other societies experimenting with new rules. Many are not tossing out private ownership of farmland or market distribution of food but attempting to make effective everyone's right to food.

Towards an Agriculture We Can Live With

The post–World War II Green Revolution represents not just the breeding of more responsive seeds and a (flawed) strategy for ending hunger; it is a way of viewing agriculture. In the Green Revolution–cum–industrial agriculture framework, farming means extracting maximum output from the land in the shortest possible time. It is a "mining" operation. In this process, humanity seeks to defeat its competition—nonfood plants, insects, and disease. So agriculture becomes a battlefield, in a war we believe we're winning as long as growth in food production stays ahead of population.

In this war, weapons are chosen through a cost-calculus derived from the marketplace, from the apparently extrahuman economic laws of supply and demand. If the market tells farmers that more pesticides and chemical fertilizers will produce enough to cover their costs, then, of course, they use them.

But there's one big problem: intent on winning the war, we fail to perceive how the food-producing resources on which our very security rests are being diminished and destroyed. In this chapter, we have noted how the potential of food resources is diminished as prime land gets channeled into feed and luxury export production. In the previous chapter, we touched upon some of the modes of destruction—desertification, soil erosion, and pesticide contamination. But the list goes on:

• Groundwater is being rapidly depleted.

- Overuse and poor drainage are causing the salinization of water used in agriculture.
- Prime farmland is being gobbled up by urban sprawl.
- The world's plant genetic resources, essential for developing new seed varieties, are shrinking. In India, which had 30,000 wild varieties[81] of rice only half a century ago, no more than 50 will likely remain in 15 years. (The industrial countries are heavily dependent on the third world's genetic diversity. Every current Canadian wheat variety, for example, contains genes that have recently come from up to 14 third world countries.)[82]
- Fossil fuels, on which the industrial model of agriculture rests, are being depleted. Marcia Pimentel of Cornell University estimated that to feed the world's population with a diet produced and consumed on a U.S. Green Revolution model would deplete the world's proven oil reserves in just 10 years![83]

And this is only a partial list! Yet none of these threats is addressed within the Green Revolution framework. We therefore have to ask if there are alternative approaches up to the challenge of feeding today's growing populations.

Over thousands of years, in many areas of the world, agricultural systems have evolved along principles that are fundamentally different from industrial agriculture. Productivity is an important goal, but not above stability and sustainability. Today the emerging field of agroecology—built on the ecological principles of diversity, interdependence, and synergy—is applying modern science to improve rather than displace traditional farming wisdom.

Industrial agriculture is simple; its tools are powerful. Agroecology is complex; its tools are subtle. Industrial agriculture is costly both in money and energy. Agroecology is cheap in dollars and fossil fuel energy, but in knowledge, labor, and diversity of plant and animal life it is rich.

Traditional rice farming in Asia, for example, produced 10 times more energy in food than was expended to grow it, but today's Green Revolution rice production cuts that net output in half, according to Cambridge University geographer Tim Bayliss-Smith. The gain drops to *zero*, he reports, in a fully industrialized system, such as that of the United States.[84]

Why such a difference? Instead of continuous production of one crop, agroecology relies on intercropping, crop rotations, and the mixing of plant and animal production—all time-honored practices of farmers throughout the world. With intercropping, several crops grow simultaneously in the same field. Rotating cereals with legumes (fixing nitrogen in the soil for use by other plants) and interplanting low-growing legumes with a cereal or in stubble help to maintain soil fertility without costly purchased fertilizers. Mixing annual and perennial crops better uses the soil's lower strata and helps prevent the downward leaching of nutrients.

Geographer Donald Innis of the State University of New York at Geneseo explains the scientific basis of intercropping. Because different plants have different needs and different timings of those needs, intercropping takes better advantage of available light, water, and nutrients so more total growth takes place. Instead of depleting the soil as does monocropping of row crops (with soil between the rows exposed to rain and wind erosion), intercropping increases the organic matter content of soils, thereby promoting better tillage and higher yields. It also insures against disaster, since the more plant varieties, the less chance of all failing simultaneously.[85]

Integrating crops and animals on the same farm allows the return of organic matter to the fields. Using some animals—geese in rice farming, for example—can reduce weeds without herbicides. Animals also provide emergency income and food, adding overall stability to the farmstead. Limiting pest damage by crop rotation and intentional diversity, along with careful timing of planting and harvesting, can maximize yields without the heavy doses of pesticides that threaten farm families' and consumers' health.

Miguel Altieri and M. Kat Anderson of the University of California at Berkeley highlight three types of traditional agriculture from which much can be learned:

- Paddy rice culture, which can produce edible aquatic weeds and fish as well as rice
- Shifting cultivation involving complex combinations of annual crops, perennial tree crops, and natural forest regrowth
- Raised bed agriculture, the ancient Aztec method of constructing islands of rich soil scraped from swamps and shallow lakes

Striking plant and genetic diversity typifies each of these farming systems. Throughout the tropics, farming systems involving both crops and trees commonly contain over 100 plant species used as construction materials, firewood, tools, medicinal plants, livestock feed, as well as human food.[86]

Poor farmers throughout the world are eager to build on this inherited land-use wisdom, according to Altieri. He describes, for example, the development of a model farm in Chile that is not much bigger than one acre but combines forage and row crops, vegetables, forest and fruit trees, as well as animals. The farm can supply most of the food requirements of a family even with scarce capital resources. Poor farmers visit the project, learn the system, and then take it to their communities to be adapted to local conditions.[87] In Chile, the Pinochet government has cut off assistance to farmers, but, says Altieri, "the most rapid rates of agricultural progress will occur where government and other institutional resources back such changes that small farmers are already keen to make."[88]

Agroecology does not mean going backward—it means applying modern biological science to improve rather than displace traditional agriculture. But why, then, has traditional agriculture been perceived simply as an obstacle to development?

If It Could Have Worked, It Would Have

In a heated response to our criticisms of the Green Revolution, one of its most distinguished defenders recently told us that the notion of an alternative, drawing on lessons from traditional agriculture, is hopelessly naive. Obviously, if traditional agriculture could have fed the third world's growing populations, it would have; today's terrible hunger is proof of its failure.

Did traditional agriculture really fail, or was it destroyed by the forces we touch upon in chapter 4? Such disdain for traditional farming practices clearly bolsters the role of corporate suppliers of manufactured inputs. Calgene is one such supplier, a U.S.–based biotechnology firm proud of its seeds with "built-in management," such as resistance to herbicides. Norman Goldfarb, Calgene's chief executive, recently suggested that such seeds would be particularly relevant in Africa. "In Africa, there are a lot of unsophisticated farmers," he said. "You can't even expect them to drive a tractor straight; you might ask them to put the seed on the field evenly."[89]

Goldfarb's arrogance reflects more than simple ignorance. It typifies a widespread blindness to traditional agriculture's potential. Because its principles profoundly contradict the rules that guide industrial agriculture—particularly allowing market values almost exclusively to dictate use of resources—traditional agriculture has been undervalued. Criteria derived from industrial agriculture are simply inadequate for assessing traditional approaches.

In measuring success, industrial agriculture asks, how much of the main commercial crop is produced this year per acre and per labor hour? But in traditional agriculture, where intercropping of several crops is more common, such a single measure grossly underestimates production. And judging productivity by how *few* people can produce a given quantity of food—the industrial yardstick—is hardly appropriate in societies where many people are out of work. Finally, traditional agriculture asks how much can be harvested not just this year, but indefinitely into the future.

To move beyond industrial agriculture thus involves rethinking how we judge performance. What happens when we evaluate an entire farming system—including its year-to-year stability, its sustainability, and the productivity of its diverse elements—instead of just this year's output of the top cash crop?

In preindustrial farming, two or more crops in the same field produce a total output that would require as much as three times more land if the crops had been cultivated separately, according to Innis.[90] As many as 22 crops in the same field is not unknown in traditional systems.

Such systems hold special importance for Africa where fragile soils have been seriously abused for many decades but considerable knowledge of alternatives still remains.[91] In West Africa's Senegal, for example, where soils have been depleted by cash crops, a recent study suggests that the traditional mix of millet, cattle raising, and a parklike cover of acacia trees could support a population almost double the present density, already considered high. Acacia trees yield nitrogen the soil so badly needs and high-protein pods for animal feed. The tree's drought-tolerant tap root goes down almost 100 feet and, conveniently, the leaves fall just before the short crop-growing season, so the trees do not compete with millet for sunlight, moisture, and nutrients.[92] Authors of the study want to persuade the World Bank and other developers of Africa's semiarid regions that such successful systems can still be reestablished.

As industrial agriculture spreads, not only the skills and land-use wisdom underlying such intricate systems but the vast multitude of plant varieties they use are rapidly being displaced. However, more than half of all the world's farmers still use traditional methods. The remainder of the twentieth century may be the most critical in the history of agriculture. Will we open our eyes to this alternative path to food security before it is too late?

A Metaphor

This chapter opened with a sketch of one of the arguments used by proponents of the Green Revolution. Outsiders, we are told, are not the ones to instigate the political and economic reforms essential to ending hunger. All that concerned foreigners can really offer is expert technical help—like the Green Revolution—to boost production.

In chapter 10, we document the many ways U.S. citizens—whether we like it or not—mightily affect the lives of people within the third world, often blocking the very changes needed to alleviate hunger. As outsiders, we *can* help reverse the nature of our influence. But from this chapter another response emerges: should not the many negative consequences of our "expert" advice render us more humble in assuming that our development model is superior to the values and knowledge that have been developed in many third world societies over hundreds, even thousands, of years?

The Green Revolution–cum-industrial model single-mindedly asks, how can we get more out of the land? And to anyone raising questions, the response is, how heartless you are—without the Green Revolution many more people would be dying of hunger!

Perhaps a metaphor will clarify our answer. Imagine for a moment our global food resources as a large house gradually burning to the ground. The fire destroying the house represents all the ways in which our present food-producing resources are being degraded and diminished. How does the Green Revolution respond to the catastrophe? It rushes into the burning dwelling to rescue as many people as possible. Its defenders then declare, look, the Green Revolution works, it saves lives.

There's only one problem. The house is still burning! The fire is consuming all who remain and making the house uninhabitable for those who will need its protection in the future. And much evidence suggests that the rescue team itself—the Green Revolution—inadvertently adds oxygen to the flames as it smashes down the doors to save as many victims as possible. The "oxygen" is its single-minded pursuit of production that contributes to the soil erosion, soil exhaustion, groundwater overuse, and so on that helped start the fire in the first place.

Clearly, congratulating the rescue team for saving lives is beside the point. We must rebuild the dwelling and make it fireproof.

As we put out the flames and begin to rebuild, we must never forget that, as we have shown in this chapter, increased production can go hand in hand with greater hunger. So even if the house were made sound, keeping its doors open for all depends on social forces, not technical ones. By social forces we mean the rules people make through custom, laws, and—too often—through brute force that govern the life-and-death question of who eats and who doesn't. The new, fireproof dwelling can offer genuine security only as people change those rules—as they make the claim to food, the right to life itself, effectively universal.

The model of industrial agriculture that the Green Revolution carries with it is constructed by the rules of the market and the unlimited accumulation of productive resources. In later chapters, we stress that ending hunger does not necessitate throwing out the market or property ownership. It will require, however, transforming such rules from dogma into mere economic devices serving the entire community, no longer a privileged few. Here are some questions that can free us from dogma and allow us to begin addressing the underlying forces generating hunger:

• How can claims to land and other food-producing resources and to income to buy food be made equitable?

- How can poor farmers—the majority of the world's food producers—augment production and maintain and improve soil fertility without increasing their dependency on costly technologies?
- How can decisions leading to the destruction of food-producing resources be brought under democratic direction so that the destruction can be reversed?

Only by facing such questions squarely can we assume our rightful responsibility—no longer abdicating our morality to supposedly automatic laws of the marketplace. Once moving in this direction, farming practices could be based on a more sophisticated calculation of cost-effectiveness. Melding traditional wisdom and growing scientific appreciation of our complex biological interdependence with plant and animal life, we could then finally achieve food security for everyone now and responsibly safeguard resources needed by future generations.

M Y T H · 6

Justice vs. Production

MYTH: No matter how much we believe in the goal of greater fairness, we face a dilemma. Since only the big growers have the know-how to make the land produce, redistributing control over resources would undercut production. Reforms that take land away from the big producers will lower food output and therefore hurt the hungry people they are supposed to help.

OUR RESPONSE: Fortunately, justice and production turn out not to be competing goals; instead they are complementary. The discouraging notion of an inevitable tradeoff between the two is still widely held, in part because so many people do not perceive the ways in which unjust food production systems—those dominated by a few—are *inefficient*. They both underuse and misuse food resources. People will understandably fear change in the direction of greater fairness until it becomes clear precisely how injustice blocks development.

Wealthy landowners hardly need to use every acre. And by all indications they don't. In Brazil, large landowners cultivate on average only 11 percent of their arable land.[1] And in Central America the same pattern holds: large farmers cultivate only 14 percent of their land.[2]

With so much land left unused by the big operators, it is no surprise that small farms are

*The small farmer is almost always more productive than the large
landowner.*

almost always more productive. A recent study of 15 countries
(primarily in Asia and Africa) found that per acre output on small
farms can be four to five times higher than on large estates.[3] Even
comparing output only on actually cultivated land, small farms are
still significantly more productive.[4]

Small farmers achieve higher output per acre in part because
they work their land more intensively than do big farmers. In
Colombia, small farms use labor five times as intensively as large
ones.[5] In Kenya, farms under 10 acres use an average of nine times
more labor per acre than do farms with 100 acres or more—resulting
in six times more output per acre than the bigger farmers achieve.[6]

Combine the superior performance of small farms with the fact
that large landholders, those least productive, control more[7]—and
better—land than small farmers. Only then is it possible to begin to
appreciate how profoundly *counter*productive are present, elite-
controlled farm economies.

In the United States, a different measure of efficiency is commonly used—not output per acre, but return per dollar invested.
Using this yardstick, government and independent studies con-

World Hunger: Twelve Myths

clude that a relatively small American family farm can operate at full efficiency.[8] One such study found, for instance, that a small wheat farm in North Dakota could be just as efficient as its seven-times-larger neighbor.[9]

While costs per unit of production generally decrease as the size of an operation increases, all such economies of scale have an upper limit. Most U.S. farms have now grown beyond that limit; they are bigger than can be justified by any efficiency criterion.[10]

If these studies are accurate, why then do so many people believe that bigger is better—that large-scale operations are most efficient?

The Illusion of Efficiency

At first glance, it is easy to confuse the very size of a large-scale operation with proof of superior know-how. The real reasons for the success of the big producers—advantages resulting from wealth and political pull—are all but invisible. They include preferential access to credit, irrigation, chemical fertilizers, pesticides, technical assistance, and marketing services. Policies of governments and aid institutions are also biased in their favor, as we document in chapters 5 and 10. With this understanding, small producers' ability to out perform the big growers becomes all the more impressive!

Motivation for Good Farming Undermined

Where a few large landowners control most of the land, rental and sharecrop arrangements are common, and wage laborers do much of the farm work. All of these arrangements undermine the best, most careful use of the land, compared to farming systems in which those who work the land have a direct stake in its long-term productivity.

Without secure rights to their land, how could one expect the millions of poor tenant farmers in the third world to invest in land improvements, judiciously rotate crops, or leave land fallow for the sake of long-term soil fertility?

In Bangladesh, where a large part of the country's farmland is worked by sharecroppers,[11] most have cultivated the same plot for three years or less. Landlords often prefer to evict tenants regularly because they fear that long-term tenants might someday assert legal rights to the land. Consider the disincentive built into the sharecropping system.[12] Suppose a poor farmer goes 200 taka into debt to buy improved seeds and fertilizer. He realizes a 400 taka increase in output, but then has to hand over half his crop and 200 taka plus interest to repay the landlord. He ends up with no gain at all! It's not hard to understand why much of Bangladesh's excellent food-producing resources are so underdeveloped—it reflects not peasants' "backwardness" but their good economic sense.

In the United States, a similar pattern exists. Tenant-operated farms, for example, have higher rates of topsoil loss than owner-operated farms. In Iowa, tenant farms lose a third more topsoil than owner-operated farms.[13] And the 1951 report of a major research group is even more relevant today. The report concluded that tenure problems in the Corn Belt were one of the major stumbling blocks to the adoption of conservation practices.[14]

Hired labor also characterizes big-scale farming. For the first time in U.S. history, most farm work is now performed by people who don't themselves live on a farm.[15] In the third world, laborers also do much of the work on big estates. They have still less stake in the operation than tenants, and they naturally worry about their wages, not the landowner's or the agribusiness corporation's yields. State farms—another form of large-scale operation in which workers often do not have a direct stake in output—have faced similar motivation problems. In Cuba, we found that on small, privately owned farms, despite less access to irrigation and nitrogen fertilizer, sugarcane yields consistently surpass those on huge state farms in the same provinces.[16]

Cooperation Thwarted

Monopoly control over food-producing resources also thwarts their full use by undermining the motivation for community cooperation needed to develop them.

Historically, cooperation has played a crucial role in agricultural development. A study by the UN Food and Agriculture Organization notes that "repair and maintenance of rural water courses, reservoirs, tanks, etc. . . . have always been the responsibility of the community."[17] In Bangladesh, for example, cooperation in digging and maintaining ponds for irrigation and fish cultivation was common before 1793, the year the British instituted individual land ownership. Today when 10 percent of rural households have come to control over half the land while almost half of the families have virtually none, village cooperation is a thing of the past. Traveling in rural Bangladesh, we were struck by the many ponds, once a village asset, now silted up and useless.[18] Why should the land-poor majority pitch in if the benefits go mainly to the village's few better-off landowners? For their part, the landowners find that thanks to aid programs they can irrigate with a pump, dispensing altogether with the need for a pond.

The Misuse of Food Resources

Thus far we have asked how antidemocratic farming systems controlled by a few thwart the fullest and most careful use of resources.

But we can go further, approaching the problem from the perspective of the big landowner or absentee investor. Seeking the greatest profits in the shortest time, big growers are willing to overuse the soil, water, and chemical inputs without thought to eroding the soil, depleting the groundwater, and poisoning the environment. Since they are likely to have other income-generating investments and can take over additional land if need be, why should they concern themselves about the long-term viability of a particular piece of land, to say nothing of the health of workers and the larger community exposed to toxic chemicals?

In Nicaragua under the Somozas, wealthy cotton growers increased output by 80 percent in only eight years[19] and at the same time succeeded in turning their country into the pesticide capital of the world. Mother's milk in Nicaragua contained 45 *times* the amount of DDT considered tolerable by health authorities. Wealthy cotton growers had vastly expanded production by escalating applications of DDT.[20]

In the United States, with more and more farmland in the agricultural heartland owned by nonfarmer investors with no attachment to the land beyond annual profit statements, we can expect abuse of the land to increase. For example, when John Hancock Mutual Life Insurance bought up the Hauck family farm in Wabasha County, Minnesota in 1984, it proceeded to undo conservation practices that the Haucks had built up over decades. The farm's annual soil loss had soon increased tenfold.[21] Absentee ownership of this type is on the rise; farm management companies are predicted to control a quarter of American farmland by the early 1990s.[22]

The Wealth Produced Leaves Town

Surely more bushels of grain is not the only goal of farm production; farm resources must also generate wealth for the overall improvement of rural life—including better housing, education, health services, transportation, local business diversification, and more recreational and cultural opportunities.

But when a few control most of the land, what happens to the wealth produced? It leaves town! We remember visiting northwest Mexico, an area with some of the country's most lucrative farm production. But stopping in neighboring towns, we saw only squalor. Wealth from the rich farmland, pocketed by a few, had gone into savings accounts in foreign banks, fancy cars, and private planes for hopping over the border on shopping sprees. Virtually none of that wealth stayed around to enrich the community. And our firsthand observations are confirmed by rural economists. A UN study mission to rural Sri Lanka in the early 1980s concluded the rural areas were in a "chronic and worsening condition of underdevelopment" because the "rural surplus is extracted by the banking process mainly for use outside the rural sector."[23]

In our own country, we find a similar misappropriation of agricultural wealth. In family farm communities, the wealth produced stays around, notes the author of a now classic study contrasting two California communities in the rich San Joaquin Valley. "In towns surrounded by family farms, the income earned in agriculture circulates among local business establishments," while in corporate-farm towns "the income is immediately drained off into larger cities to support distant, often foreign enterprises." Where family farms predominate there are more local businesses, paved streets and sidewalks, schools, parks, churches, clubs, and newspapers, better services, higher employment, and more civic participation.[24]

The Fruits of Reform

As we came to grasp the many ways in which agrarian systems controlled by narrow elites both underuse and misuse resources, we found ourselves asking if virtually any alternative could be worse. Wouldn't greater production—certainly more sustainable production—have to follow where access to land, credit, and knowledge is more fairly shared?

A World Bank–International Labour Organization study in six countries—India, Malaysia, Brazil, Colombia, Pakistan, and the Philippines—reinforced our sense that the answer to that question must be yes. The study considered the likely productivity impact of a more equitable distribution of land and concluded that land reform could bring significant production gains not only in land-abundant countries in Latin America but even in the land-scarce, intensively farmed countries of Asia.[25] Other factors remaining the same, transforming the countryside into uniformly small, family-owned and worked farms would boost agricultural output by amounts ranging from 10 percent in West Pakistan to 28 percent in Malaysia and Colombia.[26] In northeast Brazil, the study argued that redistribution of farmland into small holdings could raise output an astounding 80 percent.[27]

Unfortunately, testing such predictions as to the benefits of fairer access to land isn't easy. Big landowners use all of their considerable power to resist. In the mid-1980s, large landowners in Brazil were so frightened of land reform that they invested $5 million to buy arms and hire gunmen to protect their land against peasant occupations.[28] In El Salvador, death squad activity—representing the landed oligarchy—has concentrated with particular fury on those peasants demanding their rights under the land reform.[29]

Modern history offers relatively few examples of genuine agrarian reform. Nevertheless, in this century several far-reaching re-

World Hunger: Twelve Myths

forms have been carried out. Examining their impact can tell us a great deal about the concerns raised in this chapter.

Japan. Fearing social unrest in the aftermath of World War II, a conservative government carried out a major land reform with prodding and support from U.S. occupation forces. Transforming tenant-farmers into owner-cultivators, the reform not only resulted in greater equity but may also have removed a constraint on the growth of Japanese agriculture.[30] Today Japanese cereal yields per acre are the highest in all of Asia.[31]

South Korea. Whereas more than half of South Korea's agricultural households had been landless, only 3 percent remained without land after a sweeping land reform in the early 1950s. More than a quarter of the cropland was redistributed, with all beneficiaries ending up with roughly the same amount of land. Within a decade, yields far surpassed prereform levels.[32]

Taiwan. In the years 1949 to 1953, mainland Chinese forces—driven out of China by the peasant-based Red Army demanding land reform—themselves imposed reforms on the Taiwanese landed aristocracy. They increased the proportion of farm families owning their land from 33 to 59 percent, reduced the share of farmland worked by tenants from 41 to 16 percent, and reduced rents and insecurity on the remaining tenancies.[33] As a result, agricultural productivity rose, income distribution became more even, and rural and social stability were enhanced.[34]

China. In the early 1950s, the Chinese undertook perhaps the most far-reaching land reform ever attempted. Half a billion rural people were affected. Looking back over 40 years of agrarian change in China, we can say that when authority over the use of the land was wrested from wealthy landlords and eventually passed into the hands of large administrative units, production increases were not exceptional. But when responsibility for land was further devolved to individual families and rewards were made more commensurate with effort (bringing rural incomes more in line with urban ones),[35] production advanced well ahead of population growth. Agricultural output per capita grew a phenomenal 39 percent in just six years.[36]

Nicaragua. By 1986, the post-Somoza government's agrarian reform had granted secure property titles to 60 percent of the nation's campesinos. Their holdings then amounted to 15 times more land than all of the country's campesinos farmed before the reform. Despite the U.S.–financed counterrevolutionary war, the production of several important crops has set records. Cotton yields on new peasant cooperative farms in 1985 were higher than on the estates of wealthy private growers.[37]

Zimbabwe. Almost as important as land itself, agrarian reform also involves redistributing credit. In 1985, the Zimbabwe government allocated substantially more credit to small peasant producers. It had already granted women the formal right to own property, and women then gained access to credit and training as well.[38] These changes help to explain why Zimbabwe achieved a million-ton surplus in 1985, despite seven years of the worst drought in decades. Its small farmers increased their corn output tenfold over any preindependence year.

In addition to these specific examples, we have examined the results of several overview studies of the impact of agrarian reform. While production has not always increased as a result of reform, the historical record does not support the fear that reform will undercut production. "Usually reforms cannot be shown to have hampered agricultural production and productivity, at least not after some initial difficulties were overcome," was the guarded summary in a 1970 study.[39] A more recent World Bank review of five land-reform efforts in Latin America reported that with the possible exception of Peru, the effects of reform on agricultural production were generally positive.[40]

If land reform has been able to achieve marked production success, why, we ask again, do so many people still believe that the outcome must be the opposite, the undermining of production?

In part the answer is that some reforms and attempted reforms have indeed seen a falloff in production, at least in the initial years. The reasons seem to hold true in a range of countries.

In every genuine effort to redistribute land, entrenched interests feel threatened. Fearing that land and power will be taken from them, landowning elites have been known to sabotage production. Either they liquidate what they can of their resources—slaughtering livestock, for instance—in order to take their wealth out of the country; or they try to disrupt the economy in hopes of stirring popular discontent against the government carrying out the reform. If support from foreign sources gives the privileged oligarchy hope that it can successfully resist the changes, it is all the more likely to attempt such sabotage.[41]

Giving Reform a Bad Name

People are understandably confused when governments speak of land reform but use policies that protect, not alter, the status quo. When the potential of reform is measured by the consequences of these fake land reforms, the conclusions can be pretty discouraging.

Mexico. In the 1930s, the government of Lázaro Cárdenas enacted a sweeping land reform that raised the hopes of millions of peasants. But subsequent governments never came through with the other ingredients essential to genuine redistribution of productive resources—credit, improved seeds, irrigation, and so on—which have remained the province of wealthy, politically powerful growers. After four decades, 2 percent of landowners control three-quarters of the land, and more than half of all rural adult workers remain landless.[42]

El Salvador. Designed under the direction of the U.S. government, El Salvador's land reform left untouched the backbone of the rural oligarchy, the coffee estates, and ignored the needs of the landless majority in the countryside. Haciendas turned into cooperatives by the reform were starved for credit, technical assistance, and timely provision of seeds by government agencies controlled by a political party opposed to reform. To "demonstrate" the economic costs of reform, the cooperatives were sabotaged.[43]

Examples of such fake reforms abound—in the Philippines, Honduras, Pakistan, India, and other countries. Carried out by governments beholden to the rural oligarchy, they inevitably leave the rural power balance intact. Such "reforms" can therefore contribute neither to greater production nor to the alleviation of poverty at the root of hunger.

Not Size but Structure of Decision Making

Shifting the power balance to favor the poor majority is the heart of genuine land reform. But we should not let the size question confuse us on this point. As we challenge the assumption that bigger is better, please understand that we are not talking about size itself. We are evaluating the consequences of different structures of power and accountability. Size is often a handy stand-in for these concepts. But to refer to big landowners is actually to refer to a particular authoritarian structure of power, where a few make all the decisions over the use of a vital resource, farmland. But a very big farming operation might also be governed by a nonauthoritarian structure—say, as a producer cooperative where work and reward are shared and leaders are genuinely elected.[44] Moreover, just because an agricultural system is dominated by small farms we should not assume it is necessarily equitable. If small farmers are at the mercy of those who control distribution of farm inputs and marketing of farm commodities, they are powerless even if large operators do not monopolize the land.

Production for What?

While common sense and historical experience convince us that fairer control over agricultural resources can bring greater, not lower output, a more fundamental consideration ought never to be forgotten.

Even if one could prove that an elite-dominated agricultural system were more productive, we would still ask, *so what?* Is not food production of value *only* if it fulfills human needs? If a society's agricultural system is strikingly productive but its citizens go hungry, of what use is it?

The problem of production must therefore never be posed in isolation. The question must not be what system can produce the most food, but under what system—elite controlled or democratically controlled—is hunger most likely to be alleviated.

If as a result of a redistribution of assets the poor gained more buying power, the composition of crops would likely respond to their needs and the production of luxury crops might slump. Families with more land might for the first time consume all they need, thus failing to increase marketed production. Indeed, the market value of production might fall—yet hunger could be falling too. Our point is simply a reminder that we should never focus so narrowly on production that we forget why we care in the first place, forget that our real concern is how to end needless hunger.

Many people have been made to believe that we must choose between a fairer economic system and efficient production. This tradeoff is an illusion. In fact, the most inefficient and destructive food systems are those controlled by a few in the interests of a few. Not only can greater fairness release untapped productive potential and make long-term sustainability possible, it is the *only* way that production will contribute to ending hunger.

M Y T H · 7

The Free Market Can End Hunger

MYTH: If governments just got out of the way, the free market could work to alleviate hunger.

OUR RESPONSE: Unfortunately, such a market-is-good-government-is-bad formula can never help address the causes of hunger. Such thinking misleads us into believing that a society can opt for one or the other, when in fact every economy on earth combines the market and government in allocating resources and distributing goods.

Even the division between so-called capitalist and socialist societies is hardly clear-cut. In West Germany's "capitalist" economy, government expenditures are a significantly bigger share of the gross national prod-uct than in Spain's more "socialist" one.[1] Nicaragua's economy relies as much on the market as does Mexico's.[2] South Korea and Taiwan, the favorites of free-market purists like Milton Friedman, owe much of their striking growth records to numerous government interventions, not the least of which have been government-imposed land reforms and support for key industries.[3]

Worst of all, such black-and-white thinking blocks us from identifying the truly critical questions we must ask to learn how *either* the market *or* government can alleviate hunger.

Defenders of the market have a lot of evidence on their side—certainly any society that has tried to do away with the market has faced serious

Markets can respond to human needs to the degree that income is widely dispersed.

headaches.[4] The problem comes when a useful device gets raised to the level of dogma. We lose sight of what it can and cannot do. For all the market's virtues, three of its shortcomings contribute directly to the causes of hunger.

We recently had the opportunity of publicly responding to perhaps the market's greatest advocate, Nobel laureate Milton

Friedman. Friedman insists that the most salient virtue of the free market is that it responds to individual preferences. In our response we said we thought that the preference of most individuals is to eat when they're hungry—yet more than half a billion people living in market economies are *not* eating.

The lesson is unmistakable: the first shortcoming of the market is that it does not respond to individual preferences—or even needs. It responds to money.

Let's look at the hunger consequences of this simple lesson. From the beginning of our book, we've described the increasing concentration of decision-making power over all that it takes to grow and distribute food—fewer and fewer people owning more and more land, controlling credit, water, marketing channels, and so forth. As the poor in ever greater numbers are pushed from the land, they are less and less able to make their demand for food register in the market.

In parallel urban development, a small elite often controls banking, industry, and commercial institutions. In Chile, for example, after only six years of the Pinochet military regime's free-market economics, the country's five largest financial clans had taken control of two-thirds of the country's 250 largest firms. In the Philippines, the Marcos family and their rich friends came to control a huge share of that nation's corporate assets. With such concentrated power, the wealthy are free to indulge in investments that employ relatively few workers and to resist workers' demands for a living wage.

Under these conditions, what does the market do? The only thing it can: it responds to the tastes of those who can pay, the privileged minority. They alone have the income to make what economists call effective demand. Production inevitably shifts to items desired by the better off, such as meat, fresh fruits and vegetables, imported VCRs, and Chivas Regal. In chapter 5, we spoke of an invisible food revolution in which basic foods for the majority are increasingly displaced by luxury crops for the minority. In international commerce, food flows from the hungry to the well-fed, as we document in our next chapter.

Here in the United States, we witness the same affront to logic and our sensibilities. While soup lines lengthened in the early 1980s, the food industry spawned a record number of new-fangled food items—2,000 in 1982 alone—including Pac Man cereal and a juice treat for dogs.[5]

Left to its own devices, the market simply mirrors inequalities in wealth and income and should be seen for what it is: a useful device and nothing more. We must not delude ourselves into thinking that it registers the needs and wishes of all people.

A second drawback of the market is that it is blind—blind to the social and resource costs of the production engine it is supposed to drive.

An example from the United States will make this clear. During the 1970s, U.S. agricultural exports boomed, rising sixfold in value in only a decade. At their peak in 1981, our agricultural exports brought in over $44 billion in foreign exchange. What a bonanza! the market told us. All that grain could pay for imported oil.

But the market failed to tell us that producing all that grain required an energy expenditure equivalent to at least a third of the money generated,[6] that topsoil was eroding from prime farmland at an accelerated and alarming rate, and that the push to export was pumping groundwater out of the earth much faster than nature could replenish it.

The market also failed to tell us about the social costs of farmers being made more vulnerable to the vagaries of the international market. Hundreds of thousands of livelihoods wiped out, increased rural landlessness, the decline of whole rural communities, and the shocking sight of farmers on food stamps—to all of this destruction the market is blind.[7]

Finally, left to its own devices, the market has another drawback that undermines some of our most deeply held values. It leads to the concentration of economic power. Those with greater economic power undercut and gobble up those with less. The 1980s "merger mania" involving some of the largest corporations in the United States is only the most recent manifestation of this tendency. In 1984 alone, $122 billion went into over 2,500 mergers that even *Business Week* doubts were economically justified.[8]

The resulting concentration of economic power directly contributes to hunger and seriously compromises political democracy. We will return to this theme in chapter 12. This is relatively easy to see when we look at the third world. The connection between hunger in El Salvador and the fact that six families control as much land as 300,000 peasants is obvious. Can we see such a connection between the accelerating concentration of economic power and needless human suffering here at home?

Let's take the example of U.S. agriculture again. At the mercy of international markets, U.S. farmers in the 1970s experienced an incredible concentration of reward. By the early 1980s, a mere 1 percent captured 60 percent of net farm income, as we noted in chapter 5. Market theory alone doesn't explain such a dramatic transformation. In theory, the market rewards hard work; in reality, it *requires* hard work and production, but only *rewards* those who have considerable equity in their land—those who have wealth. They have easier access to credit and can therefore better withstand the market's inevitable swings, and only the wealthy can expand to make up in volume what all are losing in profits per acre, as a production push leads inevitably to price-depressing gluts.

Once made aware of the market's drawbacks, it might be tempting to throw out the market altogether in favor of government control. But to get at the root of hunger, we must take a more thoughtful, studied approach.

How Can the Market Work to End Hunger?

For those who believe in the usefulness of the market and who also want to end world hunger, the urgent question is, under what conditions can the market respond to human needs and preferences?

Since, by definition, the market responds to economic power and not to need, the answer in our view is fairly straightforward. *The more widely dispersed is purchasing power, the more the market will respond to actual human preferences and needs and the more power the market will have to end hunger.*

In other words, what must be promoted is not the market but the customers! For where there are customers, there will be entrepreneurs—and voilà! The market booms. In China, to the extent that the greater use of the market works to serve broad-based development goals, it is because purchasing power is relatively widely distributed, the fruit of making access to work and productive resources more equitable.

For those who believe in the utility of the market, the challenge is to promote policies that counter the concentration of buying power and ensure its wider dispersion. But this prescription raises a final question. Focused on the market, we have yet to take up the equally challenging issue: under what conditions can government serve genuine development?

Ending Hunger: Is There a Role for Government?

Those who see government, by definition, as the obstacle to development fail to appreciate the role that government has played in our own society's development. Without public support for infrastructure, including not only roads, bridges, railroads, and the like but also public education and public health, where would our nation be?

Government is clearly essential to development. But having acknowledged that, the temptation is to debate *how much* government versus *how much* market will best contribute to development.

This simple tradeoff helps us little. It fails to probe the nature of government's contribution. For example:

- Is a government's public health budget spent largely on big hospitals in urban centers using expensive imported technology, as in the Philippines? Or is that same amount of money spread throughout the countryside, as in the Indian state of Kerala, to support primary health clinics serving the majority?[9]
- Is the government's agricultural budget going to costly state farms, while ignoring the needs of the majority of rural producers, as in Ethiopia?[10] Or is priority given to small farmers through cheaper credit and appropriate technical assistance?
- Is the government using its foreign exchange earnings to import late-model combines and computers for the country's wealthiest farmers, as in South Africa, or does a greater share of the earnings go to import tools and fertilizers to help small farmers who grow staple foods?

These and many similar questions are the really meaningful ones to ask about the nature of a government's role in development. They will be answered according to whom a government sees itself as accountable. A government beholden to a wealthy elite will use its resources for that group's disproportionate gain. A government that knows its survival depends on the support of the majority will work to respond to that majority's needs.

In addition to vital human and material infrastructure, many societies recognize two other critical roles for government. We feel they are just as important in determining whether it can help alleviate hunger.

Government as Protector of the Market

As we emphasized above, the market left to its own devices will concentrate wealth and purchasing power and therefore undermine its usefulness in meeting human needs. But a government responsible to majority interests can make rules and allocate resources to counteract the tendency toward concentration. These two instruments of economic life need not be in competition. Here's where the government can *help* the market!

Specifically related to hunger, such a mandate requires genuine land reform—including enforcing rules to keep ownership from becoming reconcentrated. It means tax and credit policies that benefit poor farmers. And it requires that all public policies —credit, tax, land, social welfare, or workplace reforms—actively disperse buying power. Perhaps most critical to such wide dispersion is making sure that anyone who wants a job can get one.

This isn't interference with the market. Policies that disperse purchasing power actually help the market do what it is supposed to do—respond to human needs and preferences.

Do We Have a Right to Eat?

Finally, government's role is to protect rights. Indeed, government uniquely has the power to do so, for nothing is an effective right until government protects citizens' enjoyment of it. We have a meaningful right to free speech, for example, only to the degree that the courts will stop anyone who tries to prevent us from speaking.

A few societies have decided that among basic human rights should be the right to life itself—that indeed this right should be of primary concern. For—as we ask in chapter 12—how can we enjoy any other right without it?

Not all democratic societies protect the right to life. Many protect life only when threatened by physical assault, not by physical deprivation. Some, like our own, assume that while government should organize fire departments and police forces for the physical safety of its citizens, those citizens should fend for themselves when it comes to getting a decent job, enough to eat, or affordable medical care.

Only when the concept of basic rights is enlarged to include life itself, is government obligated to ensure that each citizen has access to employment, a healthy diet, and adequate health services. *This does not mean necessarily that government itself provides these goods; it means only that government ensures no one goes without them.* A variety of approaches can be discovered in a wide spectrum of societies.

Consider the experience of the Indian state of Kerala, which we highlighted in our discussion of population in chapter 3. Within India, Kerala has considerably less hunger than the rest of the country, as suggested by an infant death rate half the all-India average and a much longer life expectancy. Kerala still tolerates extreme concentrations of landownership but has mitigated the effects by turning poor renters of farmland into owners. And it no longer treats food grain and certain other basic goods as mere market commodities to be sold to the highest bidder. Fair-price shops keep food prices low.[11]

In the industrial world, the Scandinavian countries illustrate a positive role for government in protecting family-farm agriculture. Take Sweden, for example. Although wealth is still tightly concentrated in Swedish society, Swedes some time ago decided that farming and food were too important to be left to the market alone. So in Sweden, only working farmers can own farmland, and sales of farmland are closely monitored by county boards to ensure that prices paid are not so high as to eliminate family farmers from the competition.[12] Moreover, wholesale food prices are not allowed to fluctuate with the market, wreaking havoc on the family farm. Instead they are periodically set when farm representatives, government, agribusiness, and consumer food cooperatives sit down at the negotiating table.[13]

These far-flung illustrations suggest a growing willingness to acknowledge the failure of the market alone to alleviate hunger. To the degree that hunger in urban Mexico was eased for some during the 1970s, for example, it was not the result of greater output but increased government price subsidies for consumers.[14] Even the World Bank in its previously mentioned study *Poverty and Hunger* concluded that growth alone could not alleviate chronic hunger in an acceptable period of time—direct intervention in the market is necessary to enhance the ability of the hungry to acquire food.[15]

In such a brief book, we cannot hope to provide answers to the critical controversy over the proper role of the market and government as instruments of development and promoters of human freedom. More modestly, we hope to show that hunger will never be eliminated if our vision is blocked by rigid dogma, detached from real life experience. The government-*or*-market tradeoff fails to help us grasp the truly urgent questions we must address in order to end hunger.

Under what conditions can both the market and government serve to alleviate hunger? Clearly the answer to such a question cannot be found in economic theory alone, but rests on the relationship of citizens to decision-making power. For neither the market nor government can end hunger as long as control over economic resources is in the hands of a few and political authority responds largely to the booming voice of wealth.

CHAPTER EIGHT

MYTH · 8

Free Trade Is The Answer

MYTH: Without protectionist barriers, world trade could reflect the comparative advantage of each country—each exporting what it can produce most cheaply and importing what it cannot. Third world countries could increase exports of those commodities favored by their geography, and their greater foreign exchange earnings could be used to import what they need to alleviate hunger and poverty.

OUR RESPONSE: The theory of comparative advantage sounds perfectly sensible. Growth in exports generates increased foreign exchange earnings to fuel a nation's development. Didn't all of us learn in junior high school how natural it is that Pedro's family in South America can grow coffee for us while we in turn can export industrial goods his country needs and that in a world of unhampered free trade we all win?

Such an appealing theory! It falls apart only when we apply it to the real world.

If increased exports contributed to the alleviation of poverty and hunger, how can we explain that in so many third world countries exports have boomed while hunger has continued unabated or actually even worsened?

Brazil. By the mid-1980s, Brazil's phenomenal success in boosting agricultural exports had placed that country second only to the United States among world agricultural exporters.

Export agriculture means that the poor majority in the third world often lose out to better-off consumers abroad.

Soybeans, virtually unplanted in Brazil 20 years ago, had by the end of the 1970s become that country's number one export,[1] almost all of it going to feed Japanese and European livestock. At the same time, the hunger of Brazilians has markedly worsened, spreading from one-third of the population 20 years ago to two-thirds by the early 1980s.[2]

Thailand. In the 1970s, cassava exports—to feed livestock abroad—expanded so fast that Thailand is now the world's leading exporter.[3] During the second half of the 1970s, frozen fruit and poultry exports were tripling every year![4] Yet more than half of Thai preschoolers are undernourished,[5] and some 50,000 children die each year of malnutrition.[6]

Central America. From 1950 to the mid-1970s, agricultural exports from Central America grew at an impressive 8 percent a year.[7] From 1960 to 1980, beef exports increased almost sixfold.[8] Yet by 1984 in El Salvador, with countless small farmers losing their livelihood as they were pushed off their land, 72 percent of all Salvadoran infants were found to be underfed.[9]

Africa. Export earnings from coffee—a major export for 13 African countries—increased almost fourfold over the decade of the

1970s. Among the successful coffee exporters are Ethiopia, Zaire, and Uganda—all notorious for their widespread hunger. Export revenues for Kenya quadrupled between 1970 and 1980,[10] yet malnutrition has been increasing.[11]

Chile. Farm exports, principally table grapes and fresh fruits, increased 30-fold in the decade following General Pinochet's military takeover in 1973.[12] According to official figures, the poorest 40 percent of Chileans consume only three-quarters of the calories they need daily.[13]

These far-flung examples tell a story. Where the majority of people have been made too poor to buy the food grown on their own country's soil, those who remain in control of productive resources will, not surprisingly, orient their production to more lucrative markets abroad. Fruits, vegetables, coffee, feed grain, sugar, meat, and so on are shipped out of the third world and voilà!—the global supermarket, part of the invisible food revolution we described in chapter 5.

In the global supermarket, even Fido and Felix can outbid the third world's hungry. Vast quantities of fish caught in third world waters end up feeding pets in Europe and North America.[14]

Comparative Advantage Reconsidered

Exports increase while the well-being of the majority of people deteriorates because reality does not fit the neat logic of comparative advantage.

What's the Advantage?

While it is popularly assumed that a nation's comparative advantage lies in its geographic endowment, the relative qualities of soils and climates turn out to have virtually nothing to do with who produces what. Low wages are the real advantage of most third world nations.

When the Ministry of Trade of the Philippines placed an ad in U.S. business magazines headlined "WE WANT YOU TO TAKE (COMPARATIVE) ADVANTAGE OF US," its message was right on target.[15] A Philippine banana worker can expect no more than about $1.50 a day; a Sri Lankan tea worker is lucky to bring home 72 cents.[16] Such wages reflect business and landowner power to block collective bargaining and circumvent whatever meager minimum wage law may be on the books. Mexico exports tomatoes, for example, not because its climate is better than Florida's or California's (except for a couple of weeks in late winter) but because Mexican farmworkers make less in a day than their Californian counterparts do in an hour![17]

Global corporations are also key in determining to what ends third world nations put their land and other resources. After organized field workers in Hawaii had achieved the most livable wages in farmwork and land costs skyrocketed, Del Monte and Dole shifted production of virtually all canned pineapple to the Philippines, where labor organizing was in effect prohibited under Marcos and land was obtained by taking it from poor farmers. Pineapple field workers average $3.25 to $5 an hour in Hawaii,[18] but only a fraction of that in the Philippines.[19]

Third world agricultural production can also appear low cost because public subsidies are hidden from view. Even as they tout their allegiance to the free market, governments beholden to wealthy interests selectively subsidize their production.

Brazil. Was Brazil's soybean export boom built on its natural advantage in that crop? Or did it reflect the advantage given to big landowners in the form of massive amounts of generously subsidized government credit to plant soybeans—loans at 15 percent interest even when inflation rates hovered around 120 percent?[20]

Mexico. How much of the striking growth in the export of fruits and vegetables from northwest Mexico has been a product of the area's geographic advantage and how much has been due to heavy government investment in irrigation—in some years accounting for over 90 percent of all public expenditures in agriculture?[21] The beneficiaries? Some of the nation's wealthiest farmers.

The Philippines. Part of Del Monte's "natural advantage" in the Philippines, has been the government's willingness to lease the company large tracts of good land to grow pineapples for export for what is believed to be less than $18 per acre a year.[22]

Sri Lanka. Sugar production will no doubt rise as partially foreign-owned companies develop new large-scale sugar operations. Not only has the Sri Lankan government assured the companies a 10-year tax holiday, it promises to protect them from falling world sugar prices and inflation.[23] Now that's some advantage.

So the first false assumption is that the advantages on which export success depends are positive, geographic endowments. Actually, they all too often reflect the power of a minority to suppress wages and get big subsidies from the government.

Who Benefits from the Foreign Exchange?

A second assumption underlying the comparative advantage theory is that the foreign exchange earned by exports contributes to overall development, benefiting the vast majority. This assumption is rarely spelled out—maybe the counter evidence is all too obvious!

In the late 1970s, we flew to the island of Mindanao in the southern Philippines. Looking out from the airplane window, 50,000 acres of banana trees stretched as far as the eye could see. Only a decade earlier, small farmers grew a variety of crops there.

Then in the mid-1960s, Del Monte, Dole, and other multinational firms began offering contracts to the area's biggest landowners to grow bananas for export to Japan. Bananas boomed, soon making the Philippines the world's fourth largest banana exporter.[24]

Bananas from the Philippines represent precisely the export success that free trade advocates prescribe for the third world. But have the Filipino people benefited? Those who labor to produce the fruit earn little more than a dollar a day, live in overcrowded barracks, and are regularly exposed to pesticides.[25] The foreign exchange does not return to southern Mindanao to improve *their* lives and *their* communities.

The displacement of local foods by export commodities is often defended on the ground that a more valuable export commodity can earn enough foreign exchange to finance imports of a much greater quantity of basic food. Theoretically, such advantages are enormous, but in the real world the theory means little.

Mexico. Export earnings during the 1970s shot up a spectacular 12-fold while the portion used to import food fell from 12 to 9 percent.[26] And of that already small share, four-fifths consisted of imports of luxury foods—meat, feed grains, and alcoholic beverages available only to the better off. In absolute dollars, imports of food luxuries rose 55-fold over the decade![27]

Kenya. Export earnings climbed over fourfold during the 1970s, yet by 1980 the share spent to import food remained only 14 percent.[28] Of those food imports, the portion spent on luxuries doubled to 40 percent—representing a 15-fold increase on dollars spent on imported luxury foods.[29]

Thus, while undernutrition afflicts as much as half of the rural people in these countries, export earnings did little to meet their needs.

Moreover, when a government pushes export crops, local staples are sure to lose out in competition for land, farm credit, farm inputs, and technical assistance. As Brazil's agricultural exports expanded, the production of beans, corn, plantains, and many other popular staples fell. For Brazil's urban population, food supplies per person dropped by a fifth during the 1970s.[30] With wages rising at only half the rate of food prices, the poor majority in Brazil—even those who could find work—undoubtedly found themselves increasingly hungry.[31]

Even when a substantial portion of export earnings *is* used to import food supposedly to compensate for such declines—in contrast to the examples above—what gets imported is less likely to reach the poor than locally produced foods. Furthermore, as countries import foods that cannot be economically grown locally and the population acquires a taste for the imported food, long-term dependency develops. As Peru has imported more and more wheat, the per person production of corn has fallen by one-third and that of potatoes by more than one-half since 1970.[32] Peru's president recently lamented the radical transformation of his country's diet:

> The huge consumption of foreign food products has caused . . . the people [to] lose faith in their ability to control their own geographical environment. Food imports are not just a foreign exchange problem; they also make a country lose touch with its sense of its own history and geography. The mass consumption of wheat, which comes from another geographical area . . . ended the usefulness of the Andes. Peruvians . . . without moving from their land, are exiled from their own history.[33]

A belief in exports as the wealth-generating answer to under-development also ignores how a shift to cash crop production—whether for export or the domestic market—can undercut consumption by altering decision making within families. "Cash crops may encourage men to take over women's land rights," writes Lloyd Timberlake in *Crisis in Africa*. "When cash crops are introduced, women may lose rights to both cash and food." In Africa, "wives nearly universally oppose cash crops because they reduce the amount of land available for food."[34] Timberlake notes that women spend more time cultivating their husband's cash-crop plots than their own food-crop plots. This wouldn't be so bad if they got a portion of the cash income, but they usually don't; it's considered male income. Studies suggest that where promoting cash crops shifts control over farming resources away from women, the nutrition of the entire family suffers.[35]

We want to underline that such conflict between export crops and food crops is unnecessary. In many peasant farming systems a mix of food and export crops—yams and cocoa in Ghana, bananas and coffee in Tanzania, corn and tea in Kenya, for example—provides both food and some cash income for the household. Such mixed farming can also be beneficial agronomically, as we suggested in chapter 5.

No Bargaining Power, No Advantage

A third questionable assumption lies behind the comparative-advantage advocacy of export-led growth as the answer for the third world's poor.

Let's set aside for a moment the economic and social inequities within third world countries in order to ask, *even if* foreign exchange earnings were in the hands of governments accountable to the needs of the poor majority, is exporting agricultural commodities likely to be profitable for third world countries today? Given the current structure of international trade, we would have to say no.

To begin with, very little of the value of their exports stays within third world countries. Of every dollar that consumers in the industrial countries spend on products from the third world, only 15 cents remains in the country of origin.[36] The other 85 cents goes to banks, traders, processors, and distributors based in the industrial countries. While most third world nations lack the industrial capacity to export anything but raw commodities, the real profit lies in processing and marketing.

Moreover, the prices of third world agricultural exports are falling relative to the costs of imported manufactured goods.[37] By 1985, prices of primary products had dropped to the lowest levels since estimates were first compiled in 1957.[38] The impact on third world countries begins to sink in when we consider that if the prices of raw materials had remained at 1973 or even 1979 levels, most third world countries—especially those in Latin America—would face no debt crisis today.[39]

Given falling commodity prices, it is quite possible for a country to increase its export volume yet end up with the same or even less in foreign exchange earnings.

Examples abound. In 1981, the Sudanese government, determined to boost foreign exchange revenues in order to meet payments on the world's greatest per capita debt, offered greater incentives to boost cotton production. Exports of cotton did triple in just two years.[40] But as the world price fell over the same period, total earnings improved only slightly.[41] If the costs of all the imported inputs used to produce it were taken into account, cotton is quite possibly an actual *drain* on the nation's foreign exchange, we were told by U.S. government economists and others when we visited the Sudan in 1985.[42]

Between 1981 and 1983, Malawi managed to increase its export of sugar, yet falling sugar prices shrank foreign exchange earnings by more than half.[43] The world sugar price has continued to fall—by 1985 to its lowest levels in history and certainly way below production costs, no matter how miserly the wages paid to the workers.

Why do so many third world countries appear to be on a trade treadmill falling ever farther behind? Simply put, third world exporters find themselves in a buyers' market. They lack bargaining power.

Over half of the countries in the third world obtain more than 50 percent of their export earnings from just one or two crops or minerals.[44] When prices fall, many countries have no alternative source of foreign exhange earnings; they cannot hold out for better prices. In fact, they feel even more compelled to step up exports. Timberlake finds a tragic parallel with parents' attitudes toward having babies: "If children are dying, more—not less—children are needed. And if crop prices are falling, more—not less—cash crops are needed."[45]

Of course, this response undercuts prices still further.

To compound the problem, most third world agricultural exports are produced by dozens of nations—62 countries produce coffee, for example—all competing for relatively stagnant markets. Production of many important commodities—sugar, coffee, and bananas to name only three—typically exceeds world demand.

Many of these commodities are also luxuries like cocoa and bananas, which means that consumers in the industrial world can always cut back if prices go up. And whenever prices of some raw commodities do rise, processors and marketers in the industrial nations invest heavily in substitutes. Think of the proliferation of sugar substitutes over the last 20 years. And further advances in biotechnology are likely to produce a whole new wave of even more widely used substitutes.[46]

While third world producers face many competitors, they have relatively few buyers. For each commodity, a handful of multi-national firms dominate world trade and processing. Unilever, for example, controls 80 percent of world trade in edible oils[47]—and they are fully capable of playing one source of supply against another.

To financial analyst Peter F. Drucker, these many trends (combined with changes in manufacturing processes that drastically reduce the use of third world minerals as well) suggest that the relative prices for third world exports are likely *never* to pick up on their own.[48] Given such a structure of world trade, we question whether third world nations can benefit from export promotion, no matter how successful in upping the volume.

How About Export-Led Industrialization?

Not just export agriculture, of course, but export-led industrial development is also promoted as the path of progress for poor nations. Just look at South Korea and Taiwan! Since the beginning of their export-led growth in the 1960s, the gross national product of both countries has grown by an average of 10 percent yearly. Can't other third world countries follow their example?

This book's brevity and its agricultural focus doesn't permit a full response, but we will point out that these countries' experience tells us little about the benefits of the export-led growth model now being prescribed by the International Monetary Fund and the World Bank. In both countries, export growth depended heavily on strong government protection for infant industries and later on extensive, ongoing government planning. Moreover, both Taiwan and South Korea received a massive influx of U.S. foreign aid, inconceivable for most third world countries in the 1980s. Finally, to the degree that their export earnings contributed to societywide development, the explanation lies partially in prior sweeping land reform—albeit authoritarian—that contributed to more equitable distribution of income than within most third world countries.[49]

To appreciate the risks of export-led growth along the lines now prescribed, one need only look to Sri Lanka. Over the last decade it has tried to take the recommended medicine—foregoing protection of domestic industry and trying to compete in both domestic and foreign markets with the advanced capitalist countries. But significant sustained growth has not been forthcoming. Debt is mounting as imports grow much faster than exports. Sri Lanka now brags that it has the cheapest wage in Asia. But how are the Sri Lankan people faring? Once celebrated for its near victory over hunger, Sri Lanka now finds hunger on the rise again.[50]

Reflections on the Pitfalls and Promises

Because the title of the first book we authored together was *Food First*, some mistakenly believe that we are against trade—that we advocate autarky, with all of us eating from our own backyards. But *food first* does not mean food *only* or that export crop production is in itself the enemy of the hungry. We believe trade *can* contribute to development. Our purpose in this chapter is simply to warn against the uncritical notion that trade in itself represents progress, that exports in themselves generate resources for alleviating hunger and poverty.

In most third world societies, the poor are hurt by export-oriented agriculture:

- It allows local economic elites to ignore the poverty all around them that limits the buying power of local people. By exporting to buyers in higher-paying markets abroad, they can profit anyway.
- It provides incentive to both local and foreign elites to increase their dominion over third world agriculture and fuels their determination to resist economic and social reforms that might shift production away from exports.
- It mandates subsistence wages and miserable working conditions. Third world countries compete effectively in international markets only by crushing labor organizing and exploiting workers, especially women and children.
- It throws the poor majority in third world countries into competition with foreign consumers for the products of their own land, thus making local staple foods more scarce and more costly.

But recognizing the positive *potential* of trade, we then must ask the same question we asked of the free market in the preceding chapter: under what conditions can trade contribute to development?

Where third world citizens achieve more equitable claims over the use of resources, including the use of foreign exchange; where agricultural workers are free to organize and bargain collectively and can build solidarity with their counterparts across national borders; where third world governments cooperate to limit their self-defeating competition and challenge the multinational trading corporations' control over markets—under these conditions foreign exchange generated by agricultural exports can contribute to genuine, broad-based development.

Genuinely rewarding trade also requires self-reliance in at least the basics for survival. How else can a nation avoid selling its products at rock-bottom prices, as it desperately seeks foreign exchange to stave off famine? Consider how in recent years China's greater food self-reliance has put it in a position to use the world market, instead of being used by it. For years China has exported rice and imported wheat, coming out ahead. In this case, no one's survival was dependent upon the imported wheat or threatened by the export of rice. This was true only because for three decades, despite limited resources, Chinese policy has placed a high priority on producing basic foods as well as on ensuring adequate purchasing power for most citizens.

Free traders might call our preconditions for nonharmful trade utopian and dismiss them out of hand. But what is more utopian than clinging to a textbook model of comparative advantage, stubbornly refusing to peek out at the real world? Of course, agricultural exports are not themselves the enemy of the hungry; but in this real world of extreme power differentials, export-oriented agriculture both reflects and fuels the forces generating needless hunger.

M Y T H · 9

Too Hungry To Revolt

MYTH: If initiative for change must come from the poor, then the situation truly is hopeless. Beaten down and ignorant of the real forces oppressing them, poor people are conditioned into a state of passivity. They can hardly be expected to bring about change.

OUR RESPONSE: Bombarded with images of poor people as weak and hungry, we lose sight of the obvious: for those with few resources, mere survival requires tremendous effort. The poor often travel great distances just to find work, labor long hours, and see possibilities where most of us would see none. Survival demands resourcefulness and learning the value of joint effort.

If the poor were truly passive, few of them could even survive!

But this myth centers on the question of initiative. Can those at the bottom of the social hierarchy, often treated worse than animals, come to realize their innate dignity, grasp their potential for creative action, and then work effectively for change? We know the answer is yes, but how can we be so confident? Because our work has helped us perceive the many examples all around us.

We'll never forget our first research trip together. We drove into northwest Mexico in the fall of 1976. There we talked to poor peasants who only days before had seized land promised to them for decades by the Mexican government. Standing in the middle of the barren fields, we

Nowhere do people go on watching their loved ones die needlessly of hunger.

saw no tools, no houses, nothing. We tried not to reveal our skepticism, while wondering to ourselves how they would ever make it.

But in 1985 when institute colleague Medea Benjamin visited the same area, she discovered that we had greatly underestimated the courage and ingenuity of the peasants. In nine years, not only had they achieved yields comparable to those of the neighboring big landowners, but they had developed their own credit, marketing, and insurance systems—so that today they are no longer dependent on a government that had proven itself unresponsive to their needs.[1]

A few years later visiting the Philippines, we met banana-plantation workers who labored 12 to 14 hours a day but still found energy to try to start a union. Holding clandestine meetings, they were risking their jobs and even their lives. The evident courage of the Filipinos we met on this trip, made us, perhaps, less surprised than most Americans when in 1986 millions of Filipinos stood firm against the Marcos dictatorship.

World Hunger: Twelve Myths

In Nicaragua, we met peasants who inspired our book *Now We Can Speak*. Under the Somoza dictatorship, many had worked for decades to get land of their own. One told us how he and his entire family had finally saved enough money to buy some land, but the big landowner in the area—threatened by their success—had their crop burned. Unable to repay a bank loan, his family lost their land. But he did not give up. Concluding that his family's only hope was to overthrow Somoza, he chose to fight. Not long after the victory over Somoza, his family received land under the government's reform program. They now work the land as a producer cooperative with other families. Listening to their story, we sat on sacks of newly harvested beans, tangible proof that their suffering had not been in vain.[2]

Since the overthrow of the Somoza dictatorship, tens of thousands of Nicaraguan peasants have continued to insist—albeit at notably less risk of repression—that they too get access to land. Unlike the families we just mentioned, many landless peasants found the pace of the land reform excruciatingly cautious during the first several years of the revolution. They protested vigorously, holding rallies and marches on government offices. Many refused to join progovernment rural associations and voted for parties opposed to the Sandinista party; some even aided the efforts of the *contras* trying to overthrow the government. Largely in response to such pressures, the government more than doubled the pace of the land redistribution. By 1986, Nicaragua's peasants controlled 15 times more land than they had under Somoza.[3]

In Honduras, where 26 years of so-called land reform benefited only 9 percent of the landless, peasants are now finding strength through unified action. Marcial Caballero, head of the National Peasants Union, told researchers from our institute how his own family's land had been seized by big landowners. For his family and thousands of others, he said, the promised and long-awaited land reform amounted to no more than "reclaiming what was ours to begin with."

Several years earlier, Caballero's family together with 64 other landless families moved onto land controlled by a big export company. "The company manager showed up with six armed men and started to threaten us. 'Get out of here today, you filthy peasants, or I'll use your blood as fertilizer,' he shouted. He turned around and saw all the peasants behind him holding our machetes and rifles, and he changed his tune."

Beaten and jailed in the aftermath of this confrontation, Caballero became even more determined. "I went to work with the peasant union," he told us, "so I could help other poor people fight for their rights."[4] Then in the spring of 1985, the union orchestrated a nationwide series of land recoveries, occupying 75,000 acres. Since the peasants could claim that the land was rightfully theirs under the agrarian reform law and since they obviously weren't going to wait any longer, the government was forced to investigate the claims of each of the groups involved in the land takeovers.[5]

Prices that peasants receive for their crops can be nearly as important as the land itself. In the early 1980s, in the West African country of Senegal, peasants in scores of villages organized to demand a higher price for peanuts, their principal cash crop. To demonstrate village solidarity, some communities decided to share and eat their meals together. Threatened by the united peasant action, the government of Senegal increased the price paid to farmers for peanuts by more than 50 percent.[6]

Credit is another key link in the exploitation of the poor. In India, the Working Women's Forum, an organization of over 36,000 mostly poor, illiterate women, is breaking this link through a credit organization that they themselves control. The women—mostly small food and cloth vendors—are organized into mutual guarantee loan groups connected to national banks. Each group is made up of 10 to 20 women from the same neighborhood who apply for loans together.

The group element is the key to their success. The group pressures members to repay the loans since each member's credit worthiness affects the group's repayment record. Likewise, members pressure the group's leader—who collects and deposits the payments—to carry out her responsibilities honestly and efficiently. And it works—the loan repayment rate is over 90 percent!

The success of the Working Women's Forum has led it to establish its own cooperative bank as well as to tackle other basic economic needs, including daycare centers, skills training, and health care. Thanks to the forum, women are gaining the confidence to confront civic authorities, the police, and moneylenders, all of whom contribute to their poverty.

The Spark of Change

Many Americans imagine that the conflict today in many parts of the third world—in Central America, in South Africa, in the Philippines—is being stirred up by outside ideologues taking advantage of the desperation of the poor. This view fails to appreciate the varied sources of initiatives for change and how often the poor themselves understand only too well the mechanisms of their oppression.

The poor "have an understanding of the working of the economic system and can describe in detail the processes (wage exploitation, money lending, bribery, and price discrimination) through which exploitation takes place," write four Asian development specialists with years of experience in organizational work with the rural poor.[7] And this view confirms our own experiences in many different parts of the world.

And where the poor aren't rising up against their exploiters, we shouldn't presume that their fatalistic attitudes stand in the way. More likely they have realistically assessed the forces poised against them. Lasse and Lisa Berg, writing of their experiences in India in their book *Face to Face*, observe that while middle-class Indians often explain their daily actions as based on religious beliefs the poor almost never do. "If asked why they do not revolt," note the Bergs, "they do not answer that they want to be reborn to a better position; they answer that they are afraid of the landowner or the government or the police."[8]

But the poor's perception of the possibility for change can change. It is changing, as we see in many countries where there are growing movements involving poor people.

The example of others can show that change is possible. In the village of Shivalaya in southern Bangladesh, Karima's small son died because her husband, a landless laborer, did not have enough money for medicine. Despite her poverty, her illiteracy, and women's customary dependency on men and isolation from one another, Karima was determined to prevent such a tragedy from happening again.

Over a period of weeks, she brought together other landless women from the village. Together they decided to save money—taka by taka—so that any member could borrow to buy medicine in an emergency. They also persuaded the village teacher to help them learn to read and keep basic accounts. Two years later, during which time they had often talked over their common problems and their numbers grew, they decided to pool all their money. With this sum they rented a small plot to grow potatoes and sugarcane. Their profits went to buy better tools and a calf, which they fattened and sold at a nice profit. They then planted vegetables for local markets and raised a few chickens. Part of their profits helped launch a basic nutrition education program.

As word of the accomplishments of these women from poor, landless families spread, poor women from nearby villages came to see for themselves. In less than two years, some 30 cooperatives started by over a thousand landless women had sprung up. As the movement continued to spread from village to village, a number of the women's cooperatives had initiated programs such as small schools to teach themselves and their children better farming techniques.[9]

The belief that one's sacrifice has meaning, even if the rewards are not in one's own lifetime, can be a force for change. History has shown the willingness of human beings to face indignities and suffer brutality for goals realizable only beyond their own lifetimes. Why? Each of us would probably answer that question differently. Many people will unhesitatingly do what they would never do for themselves, if they believe it has even a chance of bettering the lives of their children. In the next chapter, we include the words of a young Guatemalan woman who made such a decision.

For many, religious faith—instead of instilling a fatalistic acceptance of their misery—inspires the decision to act. Many Nicaraguans who participated in the overthrow of Somoza told us that their religious convictions ultimately left them no choice but to act. "The priest in my community helped me to understand that we all are made in God's image and so we too have rights, above all the right to live," one peasant told us. "And that means we have the right to land to feed our families."

Religious faith motivated many in the Philippines who worked for years to free their country from the Marcoses. Who will forget the televised images of nuns blocking the way of army tanks on the streets of Manila? In Haiti, in the final years of the Duvalier tyranny, the key resistance movement grew out of over two thousand grass-roots Christian communities and the Catholic radio station's broadcasts in Creole about the injustices and horrors of the regime.[10]

Experience outside the village can be a catalyst. "The essential ingredient for change is mental—it all starts with a vision," Pierre Pradervand, a development worker with years of experience in West Africa, wrote us. Often someone from the community who has gone away for a while returns with an expanded sense of what is possible.[11] In the Sahelian countries, hundreds of the tens of thousands of men who left their villages and lived and worked in France have returned. In any number of villages in Mali, Burkina Faso, and Senegal, some of these young men have taken up farming—some starting and others joining village-level self-help associations among local farmers. Invariably, the older generation of peasants receive the young returnees with skepticism, but in many cases—once everyone sees what working together can achieve—such associations are providing concrete hope for self-reliant development in the Sahel.

Even a disaster can help by shaking up old patterns and perceptions. In Kuala Juru, a tiny fishing village in Malaysia, fishermen banded together to confront the destruction of their river by chemical pollutants. While they did not stop the pollution, the experience of joining together in protest led to a common strategy to rebuild their shattered economy. They switched from individual fishing to cooperative farming of cockle, a fish more resistant to the pollutants. All members share the harvests and profits, and the collective savings of the cooperative have allowed it to set up a coffee shop and sundries store.[12]

Getting on Board

Many of us see the poor as passive victims because of the selective way news of the world comes to us. How many poor people have you seen interviewed on the evening news or in your newspaper? The newsmakers appear to be only government officials and business leaders, never poor people. We must regularly bring alternative sources of news into our lives; otherwise, the real struggles for change will remain invisible. The search for news that reveals more of the real world is a goal of Food First. That's why in the final section of this book, we suggest some of the periodicals we have found useful.

Thinking of the third world's poor as passive also confuses us about the nature of our responsibility. Visualizing hungry people as so oppressed as to be ignorant and immobilized makes us think our responsibility is to go in and set things straight. In our next chapter, we challenge this assumption.

Wherever people are suffering needlessly "the train is already moving"—that is, movements for change are already underway. Appreciating this truth, we understand our responsibility differently. It is not to start the train, but *to remove the obstacles in its path* and to get on board ourselves!

M Y T H · 10

More U.S. Aid Will Help The Hungry

MYTH: In helping to end world hunger, our primary responsibility as U.S. citizens is to increase and improve our government's foreign aid.

OUR RESPONSE: Once we learned that hunger results from antidemocratic political and economic structures that trap people in poverty, we realized that we couldn't end hunger for other people. Genuine freedom can only be won by people for themselves.

This realization doesn't lessen our responsibility, but it does profoundly redefine its nature. Our job isn't to intervene in other countries and set things right.

Our government is *already* intervening in countries where the majority of people are forced to go hungry.

Our primary responsibility as U.S. citizens is to make certain our government's policies are not making it harder for people to end hunger for themselves.

In light of the demonstrated generosity of many Americans, most of us would probably be chagrined to learn that U.S. foreign aid is only 0.2 percent of our nation's gross national product (GNP)—that's half the percentage of GNP West Germany provides, for example, and less than one-quarter of that provided by the Netherlands.[1]

For the world's hungry, however, the problem isn't the stinginess of our aid.

A first step in putting ourselves on the side of the hungry is to change our government's definition of the national interest.

In 1985, Secretary of State George Shultz stated flatly that "our foreign assistance programs are vital to the achievement of our foreign policy goals."[2] But Shultz's statement shouldn't surprise us. Every country's foreign aid is a tool of foreign policy. Whether that aid benefits the hungry is determined by the motives and goals of that policy—by how a government defines the national interest.

For many years, but especially during the Reagan administration, our national interest has been defined as protecting the status quo throughout the third world. Our government acts as if U.S. interests are threatened by any experiment that doesn't mimic the U.S. economic model—the free market and unlimited private accumulation of productive assets. Viewing the world as divided between two opposing camps, U.S. policymakers see any nation seeking to alter its economic ground rules as in the other camp and thus an enemy.

Such a definition of our national interest lines up our nation's might—with our tax dollars and our country's good name—against the interests of the hungry. As we have seen, change—profound, societywide change in control over food-producing resources—is a sine qua non for ending hunger. It is impossible to be both against change and for the hungry.

Aid Against Change

Looking at our foreign aid, we want to highlight seven of the consequences of the current definition of the national interest.

First, U.S. economic assistance is highly concentrated on a few governments. Its focus has nothing to do with poverty. Out of the 70-odd governments receiving almost $34 billion in U.S. bilateral economic assistance in the first half of the 1980s,[3] just 10 countries got over half of all assistance (see table 1). Israel and Egypt together got almost one-third. In fiscal 1985, the 31 low-income under-

---

Table 1

Top 10 Recipients Get Over Half of All U.S. Economic Assistance*
Fiscal Years 1981–1985

(In Millions of Dollars)

1.	Egypt	5,444.1
2.	Israel	5,215.0
3.	El Salvador	1,286.1
4.	Pakistan	1,153.7
5.	Turkey	1,103.5
6.	India	1,084.8
7.	Bangladesh	857.3
8.	Sudan	819.6
9.	Costa Rica	655.5
10.	Philippines	637.8

*Economic Assistance includes Development Assistance, Economic Support Fund, PL 480 Food Aid, Peace Corps, and International Narcotics Control.

Sources: U.S. Agency for International Development, *Congressional Presentation Fiscal Year 1987*, Main Volume, Parts I and II.

developed countries receiving U.S. economic assistance got about $1 per person, compared to almost $28 per person for the high-income recipient countries.[4]

The world's 10 poorest countries—most of them in Africa—received less than 5 percent of all U.S. bilateral economic assistance in fiscal year 1985.[5] Despite famine and widespread poverty in Sub-Saharan Africa, only one of the top 10 recipients, Sudan, is in this region. In Central America, three governments designated U.S. allies—Honduras, El Salvador, and Costa Rica—received over $69 per person in 1985, while the 48 nations of Sub-Saharan Africa got only about $3 per person that year.[6]

Second, the distribution of U.S. food aid is not related to need. When many Americans hear about foreign aid, they automatically think of ships loaded with food, but such aid constitutes only 14 percent of our total bilateral foreign aid.

Most food aid is used to bolster politically allied governments. During the war in Indochina in the early 1970s, for example, U.S. government allies there received nearly 20 times more food aid than the five African countries then suffering famine. In 1985, the United States shipped nearly four times more food aid per capita to the countries of Central America than it did to the entire famine-ravished region in Sub-Saharan Africa.[7]

Over half of U.S. food aid is not given away but sold on credit to recipient governments that are then free to resell the food to any of their citizens who can pay for it.[8] But if the hungry lack food precisely because they lack the money to buy it, what chance do they have of benefiting from this type of food aid? Indonesia is a rice exporter, yet the United States supplies that country with about $45 million in food aid a year; the Indonesian government resells 90 percent of it. Recipient governments keep the proceeds from sales of food aid, so these funds become another form of general support.

Under intense pressure from its own citizens and international public opinion, the U.S. government has offered significant emergency food relief, as in 1984 and 1985 to African famine victims.[9] Usually, only about 10 percent of U.S. food aid goes to emergency relief.[10]

Third, food aid can actually forestall agricultural development that could alleviate hunger. A number of studies indicate that food aid has been a direct disincentive to production, undercutting prices local producers must receive to stay in business.[11] But food aid can potentially do even more harm: it takes the recipient government off the hook! Counting on cheap food aid, a government can indefinitely postpone confronting the inequities and resulting inefficiencies in its own agricultural economy.

Bangladesh, for example, has received $1.5 billion in food aid since 1972 from the United States alone, not to mention significant quantities from other nations. Yet Bangladesh's martial-law government has refused to enforce the two land reform measures on its books that might move the country toward a more equitable distribution of land, a prerequisite to improved food production.[12] Historically, the Bangladesh government has sold most of its food aid through a ration system that, according to the U.S. Embassy there, is designed "to keep potentially active Dacca dwellers supplied with low-priced grain."[13]

And because food aid usually consists of wheat, dairy products, and other surplus commodities from temperate-zone countries, food aid can shift tastes away from foods that can be produced in tropical regions. Since the beginning of our food aid in the 1950s, over half of Titles I and III (two of the three major U.S. food aid categories) to Africa has been in the form of wheat, even though, as we noted earlier, wheat grows well in very few African countries.[14] For many countries, such a shifting of tastes is no small concern—it makes long-term food self-reliance even more difficult.

Fourth, U.S. economic aid is concentrated on governments dead-set against economic reforms on behalf of the poor. Locked into a view of the world as divided between two competing camps, the U.S. government willingly abets governments resisting structural reforms as long as they claim to be in our camp. El Salvador, Pakistan, Bangladesh, and the Philippines under Ferdinand Marcos—all have been among the top recipients of U.S. economic aid, yet are notorious for their intransigent, often brutal, resistance to reforms benefiting the majority.

After Marcos imposed martial law in the Philippines in 1972, U.S. tax dollars provided almost $1 billion in economic aid—not to speak of military aid. While touting land reform, the Marcos regime used U.S. aid to pursue economic policies that placed control of agricultural land and credit into ever fewer hands—notably those of his family and cronies.[15] At the same time, hunger deepened dramatically in the Philippines.[16]

While El Salvador ranks third among per capita recipients of U.S. economic aid, its government defends the economic structures that have made Salvadorans among the five hungriest peoples in Latin America.[17] According to Massachusetts Institute of Technology's Martin Diskin, the Salvadoran land reform, designed by the U.S. Agency for International Development (AID), has failed utterly to address the needs of more than half the rural population that lacks enough land even to feed their own families.[18]

Fifth, the U.S. government uses the cutoff of aid as a form of punishment. Americans are understandably appalled when they see countries dependent on the Soviet Union apparently forced to back it up in the United Nations as a condition for Soviet help. Does the United States use its aid similarly? In 1983, miffed by Zimbabwe's unwillingness to toe the line on two votes in the United Nations, the United States cut its aid to that country by nearly half.[19] Later that same year, the Reagan administration pushed a bill through Congress linking future aid allocations to an annual review of each country's voting record in the UN.[20]

Once identifying the national interest as threatened by any change that veers from the U.S. development model, our government can justify denying aid to the very countries making the greatest reforms. Anticipating the election of reform-oriented Salvador Allende to the Chilean presidency in 1970, then U.S. Ambassador to Chile Edward Korry declared, "Not a nut or a bolt will reach Chile under Allende. Once Allende comes to power we shall do all within our power to condemn Chile and the Chileans to utmost deprivation and poverty."[21] Korry's was not an empty threat. When Allende began implementing reforms passed by the Chilean congress to improve living conditions for his country's poor majority (including a far-reaching land reform[22] and the nationalization of the copper industry), the U.S. government quickly cut its aid to Chile to almost nothing.[23]

Nicaragua is the most recent example. Far-reaching reforms in land, education, and health services have won the Nicaraguan government no kudos from Washington. Not only did the Reagan administration cut off food and development aid, pressure other governments and multilateral agencies like the World Bank to do likewise, and impose a trade embargo, the administration has also directed and funded the attempted overthrow of that government.[24]

Sixth, military aid—now the biggest category of U.S. foreign assistance—helps to arm governments against their own hungry people. Under the Reagan administration, military aid has become the largest category of U.S. aid—swelling from 22 percent in fiscal 1980 to 37 percent of our total aid budget in fiscal 1985![25] During the first half of the 1980s, the number of countries receiving U.S. military assistance grew from 57 to 95, and the amount rose 83 percent, even after adjusting for inflation.[26]

Military aid to Latin America shot up 12-fold over this period.[27] Even more troubling, the number of African nations receiving U.S. military aid more than doubled, from 16 to 38, as U.S. military aid to Sub-Saharan Africa grew by over 40 percent.[28]

As the previous chapter reminds us, no one goes on passively watching their land stolen and their children needlessly die of hunger. People resist—at first peaceably, but when peaceful demands are met with armed violence, some decide they must risk taking up arms themselves. Rigoberta Menchú is one young Guatemalan peasant woman who ultimately had to ask herself the most wrenching question a human being may ever face: must I risk my life so that my children might live?

We don't need very much advice, or theories, or documents: life has been our teacher. For my part, the horrors I have suffered are enough for me. . . . It was this that made us decide to fight. This is what motivated me, and also motivated many others. Above all, the mothers and fathers. They remember their children. They remember the ones they would like to have with them now but who died of malnutrition, or poisoning [from pesticides] in the *fincas* [plantations], or had to be given away because they had no way of looking after them.[29]

Rigoberta took up arms against a government that killed not only several members of her family but more civilians than perhaps any other in the hemisphere.

"Governments fear an armed population and are preparing," says former Assistant Secretary of State Charles William Maynes. "The extraordinary increase in arms sales to Africa and Latin America . . . reflect elite fears of internal insecurity more than external aggression."[30] Part of the arms to which Maynes refers are subsidized sales under our military aid program.

So while Americans imagine U.S. aid as bags bursting with grain or tractors loaded on ships headed for faraway ports, a much more accurate picture would be ships loaded with machine guns, riot control equipment, armored vehicles, and military helicopters. Since World War II, U.S. aid has provided "gifts" of more than $47 billion worth of military equipment and training to the third world, a substantial portion of which goes to military-controlled governments.[31] The United States is second only to the Soviet Union as a supplier of military hardware and training to the third world, and probably has the dubious distinction of being the world's largest donor of military arms to the third world.[32]

"The military used to be confined to security affairs, [but] now you will find military men in the judicial, legislative, administrative, and executive bodies," is how one Filipina described the growing dominance of the military while the Marcos government was a major recipient of U.S. military aid.[33] Between 1972 and 1985, the number of military personnel in the Philippines *rose fivefold*. With the power of the military so deeply entrenched, the challenge for Filipinos working to overcome the Marcos legacy and fight hunger and poverty is made incalculably more difficult.

No doubt U.S. military assistance has abetted the growth of military influence in many other third world societies as well. One-third of the governments receiving U.S. aid are under some form of military rule.[34] Twenty-six of these governments—the Mobutu Sese Seko dictatorship in Zaire, for example[35]—are notorious for violence against their own people.[36]

Part of our military aid is simply invisible, and here we are not referring to covert aid. While it is difficult to know exactly how much, undoubtedly proceeds from the resale of U.S. food aid as well as the AID-administered Economic Support Fund enable recipient governments to buy more arms. The Economic Support Fund provides grants and loans to U.S. allies, the uses of which range from importing U.S. goods to paying interest on the recipient's foreign debt. Take Pakistan, for example. If the martial-law regime of General Zia were not the Economic Support Fund's fourth largest recipient—$200 million in 1985 alone—could the regime afford to spend almost half of all government revenues on the military?[37]

Finally, even most development assistance fails to help the poor and hungry. Only 16 percent of U.S. bilateral aid is even called development assistance. (Remember that two-thirds of U.S. bilateral aid goes for military buildups and overall budgetary support.)[38]

How is this development aid spent? During the 1960s and early 1970s, much of it went to install infrastructure (power plants, transportation and communication facilities and the like) benefiting mainly businessmen, landlords, and others in an economic position to take advantage of such facilities. In more recent years, the trend has been toward smaller-scale projects, including agricultural credit programs and the development of small and medium-size businesses. But even these smaller-scale aid projects fail to reach the poorest, concluded a major study by the World Bank and International Monetary Fund.[39]

This general finding is born out in AID's own program evaluations. One recent report reviewing 12 years of small-farm credit programs noted that benefits are "highly skewed against the small farmer and the landless poor."[40] The reasons for this failure are clear enough—very few of the poor had titles to farms large enough to satisfy the requirements of a credit application. Since the majority of rural poor in most third world countries are landless, even the best farm credit program could never help them.

While the poor may not be the chief beneficiaries of AID's development assistance projects, one group that does benefit handsomely includes the U.S. corporations and universities that get AID contracts. Under current law, our aid is "tied," meaning that any outside goods or services paid for with U.S. aid funds must come from the United States—even if they could be purchased more cheaply elsewhere. In fiscal 1984, 20 U.S. corporations and universities received over $159 million in AID funds,[41] equal to almost half of U.S. development assistance to Sub-Saharan Africa that year.[42]

Trying to understand the impact of official foreign aid for our book *Aid as Obstacle: Twenty Questions about Our Foreign Aid and the Hungry,*[43] we found that we first had to ask ourselves, how likely is it that resources channeled through the *powerful* will help the *powerless*?

The already better off are positioned to capture a disproportionate share of any economic gains offered by development aid. And with their new resources, they can often further tighten their grip over land and other productive resources, thereby worsening the plight of the poor. Thanks to a bribe to a technician, an irrigation pump earmarked for a cooperative of poor farmers in Bangladesh winds up belonging to the village's richest landowner; he graciously allows his neighbors water from the new well in exchange for a third of their harvests. The pump and the added revenue give the "water-lord" the incentive to take over more land by foreclosing on the small farmers in debt to him. Thanks to his heightened prosperity, the landowner can now buy an imported tractor, eliminating desperately needed jobs for the village's landless families.

This and similar scenarios, endlessly repeated, entrench the already well off and add to their incentive to fight demands for democratic control over productive resources. In Bangladesh, as in so many countries, rich landowners are known to hire thugs to intimidate and even murder villagers who dare to protest or organize self-help cooperatives.[44]

Only projects that reinforce the poor's initiatives to tackle the extreme inequalities in power within the village (such as those highlighted in chapter 9), have a chance of improving the lives of the majority. Most foreign governments are unlikely to risk such projects for fear of antagonizing a "friendly" government.

But we hesitate even to use this space to question the possibility of government-sponsored development projects helping the poor within elite-dominated societies. To do so may mislead, for it is so easy to lose sight of the big picture.

No matter how sensitively designed the aid project, prospects for the poor majority—whether they will have land, jobs, food, or economic security—hinge largely on forces *outside* their villages. To whom is their government accountable? To whom are international bankers who make loans to their government accountable? And what about the corporations dominating trade in their country's exports? Such questions point us to what we call the iceberg. Foreign aid is only the tip.

The Iceberg

Over and above its foreign aid program, through numerous other overt channels (not to mention covert ones, like the CIA), the U.S. government supports governments of its choosing, often in ways diametrically opposed to the interests of the hungry. Focusing only on official aid can blind us to these many other ways we citizens of the United States are linked to the lives—and hopes—of the hungry.

The Export-Import Bank (EXIM) and the Commodity Credit Corporation (CCC) can have a greater impact on the economy and policies of a third world country than official U.S. foreign aid, although few Americans have ever even heard of these U.S. government agencies. Both offer financing and loan guarantees—backed by U.S. taxpayers—to foreign purchasers of U.S. products. In a typical year, these two agencies alone channel about one and one-half times as much U.S. government support to the third world as the Economic Support Fund and development assistance portions of U.S. aid combined.[45]

When under pressure from human rights activists, Congress outlawed U.S. foreign aid to Chile in 1975, financing through the Export-Import Bank and the Commodity Credit Corporation more than made up for the lost aid.[46] From the 1940s until 1978 (when antiapartheid pressure forced Congress to cut off EXIM loan guarantees for South Africa) the EXIM provided Pretoria nearly $1 billion worth of credit authorizations, vastly more than was authorized for all the black-ruled states of southern African.[47]

Many of the EXIM's loans go for power generation (especially nuclear and hydroelectric), high-technology equipment (such as computers, CAT scanners, and communications satellites) and aircraft, largely benefiting industrialists and the better off in the third world, along with some of the biggest U.S. corporations.[48]

These alternative sources of government support have grown substantially in recent years. Since the 1970s, the EXIM's "exposure" (the amount of money it loans, guarantees, or insures) to Chile, for example, has grown about fivefold to reach $36 million.[49]

The International Monetary Fund (IMF) has become decisive in recent years in determining who can afford to eat in many third world countries. The United States holds the largest voting block and an effective veto in this 148-member "lender of last resort."[50] When a country's debt mounts to the point that it cannot get loans from other sources, it has virtually no choice but to turn to the IMF. But after a country has drawn down a certain amount of its loan credits, the IMF stipulates specific policy changes as conditions for its help. And being in the IMF's good standing is necessary to get more loans from other international agencies and private banks.

So far about 50 governments have had to try to meet the IMF's conditions, which typically include devaluing the currency and slashing social services and public subsidies on staple foods, energy, and transport. And to earn more foreign exchange (mainly to pay interest on loans), governments are told to step up export production at the expense of domestic needs, as we documented in chapter 8.

IMF-mandated austerity reforms have a far greater impact on the poor majority than any foreign aid projects—and they are devastating. Increased unemployment, galloping inflation, and drastically eroded purchasing power are predictable results. Between 1979 and early 1985, food prices in Brazil rose twice as fast as wages.[51] During the first half of the 1980s in Jamaica, after the currency was devalued by 250 percent, the price of basic foods like milk, flour, and rice quadrupled.[52]

In exchange for $100 million in IMF loans, in 1982 the Costa Rican government was forced to lay off 3,300 public employees, increase its charges for water and electricity by 150 percent, raise public transport fees, and eliminate most of its subsidies on basic foods.[53] Only when thousands of poor Costa Ricans took to the streets in protest did the government at least roll back the increase in electricity prices.[54]

The final overt aid channel we will discuss is the World Bank. In 1985, the World Bank lent over $14.3 billion, over 40 percent more than all forms of economic assistance.[55] Although technically multilateral—with 148 member countries—the United States is unmistakably the bank's most powerful member, wielding 20 percent of the votes and appointing the bank's president.[56]

The Mahaweli Dam project in Sri Lanka has received substantial funding from the World Bank. At $2 billion, this venture is the world's largest aid-financed project involving four new megadams along the Mahaweli River. Their purpose is to provide electric power and irrigation, but by nearly every account the results have been disastrous. Rain forests have suffered irreparable damage, and 1.5 million people are being forcibly removed from their homes.[57]

Even the bank is dissatisfied, though not because of the disruption of people's lives or the destruction of the rain forest. Rather, the bank claims that the Sri Lankan government doesn't charge enough for water and access to the newly irrigated land.[58] If, as is likely, the Sri Lankan government caves in to the bank's demands for higher water charges, the smaller farmers will have even less chance of farming the irrigated land.

Less Hunger, More Security

After years of studying our foreign aid program, we have learned that *foreign aid is only as good as the recipient government*. A foreign policy that fears change ends up bankrolling a Ferdinand Marcos who not only robbed the Filipino people but the U.S. treasury as well. Or it ends up pumping more than $1 billion into an El Salvador while that country's own upper class drains as much out of the country and into its private savings accounts and investments abroad.[59]

Foreign aid only reinforces what is there. It cannot transform an antidemocratic process working against the majority into a participatory government shaped in its interests. Where the recipient government answers only to a narrow economic elite, our aid not only fails to reach the hungry, it girds the very forces working against them.

As we began this chapter, we pointed out that whether U.S. foreign aid can benefit the hungry depends on how our government defines the national interest. Thus a first step in putting ourselves on the side of the hungry is *to work to change our government's definition of our national interest*. As we detail in the next chapter, less control—less striving to make the world conform exactly to our model and to our fears—will actually mean more security. An immediate step we as citizens can take is to tell our representatives that stopping both military and economic assistance to third world governments that block demands for fundamental change is a concrete move in the direction of both less hunger in the third world and more security for us.

Understanding the nature of U.S. government assistance does not lead to a there's-nothing-I-can-do dead end. It is actually the first step in perceiving the many and varied actions open to all who are determined to end world hunger. In our concluding essay, and in the other publications of our institute, we offer suggestions as to how to seize the opportunities all around us.

CHAPTER ELEVEN

MYTH · 11

We Benefit from Their Hunger

MYTH: No matter how much Americans may think we would like to help end hunger in the third world, deep down we know that hunger benefits us. Because hungry people are willing to work for low wages, we can buy everything from coffee to computers, bananas to batteries, at lower prices. Americans would have to sacrifice too much of their standard of living for there to be a world without hunger.

OUR RESPONSE: This myth presumes that our interests are opposed to those of the hungry, that acting to alleviate hunger will mean sacrificing our own well-being. In fact, we are coming to see that the opposite may be true—that the biggest threat to our own well-being is not the advancement but the continued deprivation of the hungry.

Beginning in the 1960s, a revolutionary change in consciousness began to take shape. A first glimmer came in the new concept of ecology, eroding a mechanistic world view in which separate parts could be isolated. Many began to see all life, indeed all the natural processes of our unique planet, as organically connected. Ecology opened our eyes to the intricate ways in which life actually shapes life. From crickets to whales, from ragweed to human beings, we take the form we do through interplay with one another.

Low wages reflect the powerlessness of workers everywhere.

What would it mean to push this understanding one step further—to understand that we have created a world system so intricately tied together that it closely mimics the natural world's ecology? Doesn't it suggest that humanity's fate is just as intimately interwoven?

We think the answer is yes.

With this understanding, everything changes. We no longer think of doing for the poor for their good. We realize that genuine, and very legitimate, self-interest cannot be separated from compassion for others. Such an understanding is the opposite of that implied in the myth. The myth leads us to believe that we would have to do the impossible—forego our own interests—in order to respond to the needs of those who go hungry. It therefore deepens despair; everyone knows that people don't wittingly act against their own interest.

Self-interest, however, is legitimate. The problem is that most of us are currently supporting economic and political arrangements that are neither in the interests of the hungry *nor in our own interests.* Changing these arrangements so that hunger can be ended would not undercut the majority in the so-called rich countries, but benefit them.

This perspective is hard to hold on to. We know, because we have doubts ourselves when eyebrows are raised even among some of our

World Hunger: Twelve Myths

colleagues each time we make this case. Why are Americans so willing to see ourselves as competitors rather than natural allies with the world's hungry majority?

First, our Puritan heritage tells us we can only care about others after we overcome our own interests. Second, we get confused by appearances. The third world leaders we see on television often wear our kind of clothes, live in houses like ours, and may even speak our language. Naturally, we come to identify with them. It is hard to keep in mind that they represent a tiny fraction of their countries' people, and to imagine that our real allies may be the Indian peasant in a white dhoti or the illiterate Brazilian coffee picker. Finally, our government's rhetoric of dominance, telling us that the United States must be number one, encourages us to identify our well-being with winning out over others.

The idea that most Americans have common interests with the hungry in the third world is not widely shared. Nevertheless, in this chapter we are asking you to consider such an alternative framework.

Hunger and Violence

We too are victims of the violence necessary to sustain hunger.

Because people do not go on watching their loved ones die needlessly, it takes violence to keep people hungry. Describing the government of El Salvador that in 1980 killed his sister, nun Ita Ford, Bill Ford told us that a government bent on protecting the privileged comes to see the poor as its enemy.[1] Such governments increasingly arm themselves against the hungry, as the preceding chapter stressed.

What are the consequences for us at home? Because our government identifies U.S. interests with protecting the status quo, even the status quo of hunger, we Americans pay a heavy price—directly in tax dollars, and indirectly in the undermining of our economy's health.

Our foreign policy becomes increasingly militarized. So far in this century, the United States has already intervened abroad 65 times—an average of once every 16 months, not counting the two world wars.[2] Today about 245,000 active-duty troops are part of forces especially trained in quick-response, counterinsurgency, and covert operations.[3]

In the last chapter, we described how American taxpayers foot the bill for military aid to third world governments, but to round out any account of the U.S. military role in the third world, we must add at least part of the far greater cost of maintaining a U.S. military presence around the globe—now including 333 major bases on foreign soil.[4] That cost came to nearly *one-half* the Pentagon budget in 1985—about $138 billion.[5] For every American household, that amounts to roughly $1,400 in tax dollars every year,[6] compared to $115 tax dollars going to housing and $126 to education.[7]

But the heaviest economic costs of increased militarization may be less visible—a bigger national deficit, for example. Just in the first four years of the 1980s, increases in military spending contributed $35 billion or 16.5 percent to the 1985 deficit.[8] And militarization undermines a sound economy in other ways. Economists tell us that it is no coincidence that the United States ranks first among 17 major industrial countries in percentage of gross national product going to military spending, but *last* in capital growth in manufacturing and manufacturing productivity.[9] Militarization also means jobs foregone, because investments in military buildup generate many fewer jobs than the same dollars invested elsewhere in the economy.[10]

Just as distressing, U.S. policies end up generating what many Americans fear most—increased Soviet credibility and influence in the third world. Consider Central America. Throughout this century, the United States has consistently backed governments representing the oligarchy against the peasant majorities and has overthrown those attempting genuine reform, as in Guatemala in 1954.[11]

Given that record, can we honestly be shocked or even surprised that those fighting for change in Central America turn elsewhere for help? Have we given them any choice? Ironically, many Central Americans working to overthrow antidemocratic governments have been more inspired by the example of our own American Revolution than the Soviet model. "The constitution of the new United States and the new ideas that inspired it traveled by muleback through Central America like contraband," Nicaragua's Vice President Sergio Ramirez wrote recently.[12]

Americans are angry and bewildered that we face mounting hostility from third world people. But maintaining repressive governments whose policies impoverish so many of their own citizens invariably ends up creating what *Wall Street Journal* writer Jonathan Kwitny calls "endless enemies."[13]

Sales of arms from U.S. corporations to governments that use them against their people can have the same effect. Is it any surprise that people react with anger when their rights are denied with the help of made-in-the-U.S.A. weapons? As we pointed out in chapter 10, the United States ranks second only to the Soviet Union as the leading vendor of military equipment and services to the third world.[14] Arms sales under U.S. government auspices during the 1970s were almost $100 billion—eight times greater than the previous two decades combined. And in 1983, for the first time, the U.S. government began licensing instruments of torture for international sale.[15]

And to what use are U.S.–made weapons put? Robert Fisk of the *London Times* filed this report on Egypt's 1977 food riots in which 75 persons were killed:

> One after another, young policemen wearing gas masks ran forward, knelt on one knee and fired cannisters into the crowd. . . . One group of demonstrators chanted anti-American

slogans, charging that all the tear gas came from the United States. Indeed, this appeared to be true. Every empty gas canister which I picked up bore the words "CS 518—Federal Laboratories, Inc., Saltsburg, PA."[16]

How did we as a people wind up helping to quell a riot over—of all things—food?

Once the poor become the enemy, war no longer means only military against military. Americans rightfully view international terrorism with horror and outrage, but when civilians become targets, the line between war and terrorism disappears. When our government supports regimes killing thousands of noncombatants, as in El Salvador,[17] or arms rebels notorious for barbaric treatment of civilians, as in Nicaragua,[18] is not our government's credibility and effectiveness as an opponent of terrorism destroyed?

Surely both the hungry and we are hurt as long as our governments pretend that stability is possible where people are made to go hungry. As long as there is hunger, *working for stability means working to make room for change.*

Hunger and Our Job Security

Enforced hunger threatens our jobs, our wages, and our work environment.

In societies with widespread hunger, the majority are simply too poor to buy what we produce. As it is, one out of six jobs in the United States depends on exports.[19] We will never know the potential of such trade with the third world as long as the majority are kept too poor to buy our goods.

Societies in which people go hungry are also societies in which workers are denied the right to organize and where many workers compete for a few jobs, because neither government nor business makes job creation a priority. Low wages reflect this powerlessness of workers. In 1984, manufacturing workers in Brazil, South Korea, and Taiwan earned 10, 11, and 13 percent respectively of what their American counterparts were paid.[20]

The lure of such cheap labor is almost irresistible. Over the last 30 years, advances in telecommunications and transportation have allowed many leading national corporations in the United States to become multinational, able to shift production and service operations (such as data processing) to sites where low wages keep their costs down. Between 1978 and 1982, one out of every three jobs in manufacturing—almost 7 million—were lost to plant closures,[21] in part because of capital flight by companies relocating overseas.[22]

Such globally operating corporations are quick to claim that shifting production from a high-wage facility in the United States to a low-wage one in the third world means American consumers now get cheaper imported goods. But Americans are producers as well as consumers, and unless we can find jobs and earn a decent income, lower-priced video recorders and foreign cars will not be of much benefit to us.

A global corporation that isn't accountable to a work force or to a national economy has workers and governments at its mercy. U.S. workers take pay cuts just to keep their jobs, while the government walks away from the minimum wage and health, safety, and environmental protection standards. And it fails to support strong collective bargaining rights for workers—all with the excuse of keeping America competitive.[23]

Even many old-line corporations that once operated major manufacturing facilities in this country have switched to buying goods manufactured abroad and simply sticking their label on them. This trend is leading to what *Business Week* has dubbed with alarm "America's hollow corporations." Detroit's Big Three auto makers are gearing up to buy massive numbers of foreign-made cars, the magazine reports, with the expected loss of 90,000 jobs here by 1988.[24] Not only blue-collar jobs but jobs requiring design, engineering, and management skills are being shifted out of the United States.

Some economists will say that the decline of U.S. manufacturing isn't that significant; after all, they point out, we are becoming a service economy. Approximately 90 percent of all new jobs in the next 10 years will be in services, says the Labor Department.[25] But even in the services, "managers are scanning the globe for cheaper labor," reports *Business Week*.[26] In 1983, for example, American Airlines shifted the keypunching of all used passenger tickets from Tulsa, Oklahoma to Barbados, claiming $3.5 million in wage savings.[27]

In any case, a service job is a poor substitute for one in manufacturing. Few service jobs pay enough to support a family. "It takes two department store jobs or three restaurant jobs to equal the earnings of just one average manufacturing job," says Barry Bluestone, director of the Social Welfare Research Institute at Boston College.[28]

In an economy dominated by footloose corporations and a government ideologically opposed to curbing their power in the national interest, U.S. workers are becoming ever more like their third world counterparts. In 1986, after three years of "economic recovery," the average hourly wage, adjusted for inflation, is lower than it was 10 years before.[29]

Clearly, a healthy U.S. economy—affording work opportunities at livable wages—cannot be achieved by squeezing workers to make wage and other concessions just to keep their jobs. Is there another course, one recognizing the common interests of the American people with workers in the third world who face even greater obstacles? We believe there is. One example of such international solidarity was recently displayed by 350 black workers at a 3M plant near Johannesburg, South Africa. These courageous workers were willing to risk their jobs, arrest, and harassment by the local South African authorities in order to stage a half-day walkout protesting the layoff of 172 workers at a sister 3M plant in Freehold, New Jersey.[30]

In a global economy, our own jobs, wages, and working conditions will only be protected when working people in *every* country establish their rights to organize and protect their interests. For organized labor in this country, working to wrench U.S. government props out from under repressive regimes abroad may be just as critical to achieving their goals as organizing American workers.

Hunger and the Debt Crisis

The majority of Americans as well as the poor majorities in the third world end up paying the price for lending institutions that are unaccountable and undemocratic.

By now, everyone who reads a newspaper or watches the six o'clock news has heard of the international debt crisis. In the 1970s, many third world governments hit by rising oil import costs found it easy to borrow billions of dollars—especially from U.S. banks—and before long sank deeply in debt. By the early 1980s, when the global recession cut into their export earnings, many third world nations found it hard even to make interest payments.

For their part, bankers—unaccountable to the credit needs of farmers, small business people, home buyers, and others in their home countries—had eagerly swallowed the lure of the much higher rates of return on third world loans.[31] The total exposure of U.S. banks alone in the third world tripled from $34 billion in 1975 to $100 billion in 1985.[32] Any large default would seriously disrupt the U.S. and world banking systems.[33]

Couched in terms of desperately debt-ridden countries versus creditor banks, the true significance of the debt crisis eludes us. Those striking the big lending deals were bankers in the industrial nations and third world elites, *but the real payers are the average citizens of both third world and creditor nations.*

Where did all that borrowed money go?

In the third world, a big chunk has been spirited right out of the debtor countries in the form of legal or illegal capital flight.[34] Economists estimate that Marcos and his cronies—to take one example—may have shipped as much as $20 billion abroad, an amount startlingly close to the Philippines' total foreign debt![35]

Much of the borrowed money went into showcase projects—conference centers, large urban hospitals, and administrative buildings—with little hope of generating enough foreign exchange earnings to pay off the loans.[36] Some went to import consumer goods, invariably for the better off. On average, 15 to 20 percent of the borrowing was sunk into arms purchases and other military expenditures,[37] also unlikely to produce goods that might help in repaying loans.

The impact of so much irresponsible borrowing and lending has been most severe on those who had nothing to say about the loans and how they were spent in the first place: the poor and the middle class here and in the third world.

Especially since the early 1980s, many third world governments—desperate to get new loans to pay off the old ones—have had to turn to the International Monetary Fund for help. The preceding chapter described the measures numerous governments had to enact in order to qualify. For Zaire, an IMF-mandated currency devaluation of 500 percent in the early 1980s meant sharply higher prices of basic goods and increased hunger. Those in Zaire lucky enough to have government jobs now earn roughly the price of two sacks of cassava a month, barely enough to feed a family.[38]

Some used laughter to try to ease the pain. After IMF-related austerity measures in the early 1980s, this joke circulated in Peru: an IMF official says, "You'll just have to tighten your belt." And the citizen responds, "I can't. I ate it yesterday!"

While the media sometimes give us a glimpse of the terrible costs to ordinary third world citizens of the irresponsible lending behind the debt crisis, little is said about the costs to the majority of Americans.

Worried about possible defaults, U.S. banks have been made less able to serve the needs of our people. Bankers are now trying to build up reserves and have reduced flexibility in allocating resources.[39] The deepening impoverishment of the poor majorities in the third world also hurts us because we lose markets for our goods. The United States and the other industrial countries lost $85 billion worth of export earnings just in the first two years of the 1980s as a result of reduced ability of third world nations to import.[40] Contributing to the biggest trade deficit in history, the U.S. deficit with the third world has grown to $53 billion—up 40 percent just since 1980.[41] Of course, lost exports mean lost jobs, as we noted above. Nearly 1.4 million jobs were lost or did not materialize as the result of declining U.S. exports to the third world between 1980 and 1984.[42]

Who will pick up the pieces when this house of cards falls?

While major U.S. banks still expect hefty profits from their third world lending (as long as borrowing governments continue to pay interest), what if something goes wrong? U.S. bankers know they have us, the taxpayers, to bail them out. The precedent is clear from the federal government's $4.5 billion bailout of the Continental Bank of Illinois in 1984: the U.S. government will not let a major bank collapse.[43]

More than $1 trillion in loans to the third world over a dozen years have strengthened the forces that generate poverty and hunger while undermining the capacity to repay the loans. Ordinary citizens in the third world as well as in the United States and other creditor countries pay the costs. We therefore share a common interest in restructuring financial institutions to include responsibility to majority concerns.

Hunger and Our Food Security

Hunger in the third world generates agricultural exports that undercut U.S. farmers and threaten U.S. food safety and security.

How can this be? Aren't third world countries the major food *importers* and a boon to U.S. farmers?

Not really. The United States and other industrial countries are the world's major food importers, importing approximately 70 percent of all agricultural commodities in world trade.[44] Even the United States, the world's leading agricultural exporter, imports over 60 percent as much in farm commodities as it exports,[45] much of it from countries where the majority lack a healthy diet.

Throughout our book we have suggested the logic behind this flow of food from the hungry to the well-fed. As elites tighten their hold on the land and other productive resources, more and more of their compatriots are dispossessed, becoming too poor to make their need for food felt in the marketplace. Landowners therefore shift production toward those who can pay—better-off foreign consumers. At the same time, in the United States and other industrial countries, agribusiness corporations—wholesale food brokers, food processors, commodity firms, and supermarket chains—seek the cheapest sources of supply. They find third world landowners make ready partners.

In the process, U.S. producers of certain crops are undercut by producers based in the third world.

Overall, imports of tomato products have increased almost four-fold just since the early 1980s, for example.[46] U.S. producers—primarily in California and Florida—are feeling the squeeze. For the first time, Mexico's market share of fresh winter vegetables may surpass Florida's.[47] Moreover, sizable and rising quantities of cucumbers, bell peppers, and onions are entering the U.S. market from Mexico.[48]

In a joint venture with the wealthy Canelo brothers, a division of Castle and Cooke operates a 5,000-acre tomato operation in the state of Sinaloa, Mexico. At the height of the summer season this one farm puts half a million pounds of tomatoes on California home and restaurant tables every day. Their workers are paid under $3.00 for a 14-hour day.

U.S. citrus growers are also being hard hit. The share of the U.S. frozen juice market supplied by Florida orange growers has fallen from 92 percent between 1979 and 1980 to less than 50 percent between 1984 and 1985, while Brazil's share has increased proportionately.[49] Cargill, the largest privately owned company in the United States, now accounts for 15 percent of Brazil's total exports of frozen orange juice.[50]

Today agribusiness is scanning the Caribbean and Central America for new, even cheaper "offshore" production sites from which to undercut U.S. producers. Coca-Cola, the biggest grower in Florida (through its giant Minute Maid subsidiary),[51] announced in 1985 that it was investing in 50,000 acres of Belize's virgin forest land as a new test cite for its orange groves.[52]

But don't U.S. consumers gain in cheaper produce? After adding in profits to the big growers and multinational marketers, plus transportation costs and tariffs, there is no evidence that we do.[53] The winners are big growers and marketers, not consumers.

The cost to U.S. producers from third world production sites is not just in imports undercutting the domestic market, but the loss of foreign markets as well. Corporations headquartered in the United States have been at the forefront in developing the capacity of third world countries to export feed crops. Cargill has been investing for years in soybean plantations in South America.[54] In 1985, only strong U.S. farmer protest stopped Cargill from importing wheat from Argentina into the United States.[55] Predictably, U.S. grain farmers are losing their world market share, and total farm exports have been shrinking.[56]

Imports of produce from the third world also pose an invisible threat to Americans. U.S. chemical corporations routinely export pesticides to the third world that have been banned or severely restricted in the United States. Since most are used on export crops, they wind up as residues on the food we import. Over half of the shipments of many of our major food imports contain pesticide residues, according to the Food and Drug Administration (FDA).[57] Here at the Institute for Food and Development Policy we call this insidious threat the circle of poison.[58]

No one can say with authority what the long-term effects of these chemical residues are or what levels are "safe," but many of the pesticides are strongly suspected to cause cancer, birth defects, and other serious harm to human health.[59]

Most disturbing, the FDA inspects only a small fraction of imported food for pesticide contamination. Of the 2 billion pounds of oranges imported in 1982, for example, the equivalent of only one crate for every 200 million pounds was inspected![60] Even when the FDA does check food imports for chemical residues, its standard tests detect fewer than half of the pesticides that may have been applied.[61] And when pesticide contamination is found to violate the law, there's no guarantee the food won't wind up on our tables anyway—because laboratory tests are quite slow, fresh produce leaves the docks before lab results are available.[62]

So far, only imports of fresh vegetables, fruits, and a few other crops have come to supply a significant share of U.S. consumption. But as we have seen, the trend in this direction is driven by the dynamic of hunger in the third world. The impoverishment of so many means low wages and lower production costs in the third world, it also forces producers in the third world to look for paying customers abroad.

Hunger and Immigration

Neither we nor the third world's poor benefit if they are made economic and political refugees, forced to flee their homelands to find safety and opportunity.

Refugees fleeing communist oppression are not the only immigrants to our shores. The majority may well be fleeing poverty and hunger. Many more people have fled under Pinochet's authoritarian government whose policies have increased hunger in Chile, for example, than under the previous elected socialist government. And Central American refugees are mostly from El Salvador and Guatemala, where protesting against hunger jeopardizes one's life even more than the hunger itself. Those who can, leave, even at great risk.

People should have the right to pursue a decent life in their homeland; and Americans understandably want immigrants to our country to come for positive, not negative reasons. Thus, on the question of immigration we also share common interests with the hungry.

The Third World Comes Home

In our response to this myth, we suggest just a few of the many ways in which present international economic institutions—and increased militarization protecting them—fail to serve the interests of both the majority in the third world and the majority of U.S. citizens.

But don't some Americans gain from third world poverty? What about all the corporations and banks with lucrative investments? Our answer is yes, of course, some do gain. But they are not the majority. Two-thirds of us live in households earning less than $35,000 a year—not enough money for most people to buy a home, much less invest in the stock market.[63]

Once we looked at world development from the perspective of common interests, we also came to realize that economies governed by world-spanning economic institutions inevitably *begin to look alike*. Within an overriding, antidemocratic financial system, we can't expect individual societies to remain democratic. In our opening chapter, we defined democracy as a principle of accountability—decision makers kept accountable to those whose lives are affected by their decisions. Such a principle applies equally well to economic as to political life.

If our economic life is governed by fewer and fewer anti-democratic corporate structures with a global reach,[64] we are inevitably thrown into competition with societies in which the majority have virtually no voice. It's no coincidence, then, that in our economic life the voice of the majority is becoming weaker.

The signs of that change are all around us.

The gap between rich and poor in the United States is widening and beginning to resemble the third world. In 1984, for example, the poorest two-fifths of the population received only 15.7 percent of our national income—less than in any year since data began being collected in 1947![65] The wealthiest 20 percent, by contrast, captured almost 43 percent, the highest proportion on record.[66] According to the World Bank, the distribution of household income in the United States is as unequal as in Bangladesh, Sri Lanka, or India.[67]

No longer a predominantly middle-class society,[68] we are becoming more and more divided between those who can live by their wealth—the top 2 percent who own half of all stock[69]— and those unable to live by their work. The minimum wage earned on a full-time, year-round basis provides a family of four an income one-third *below* the poverty line.[70]

Whose voices are heard in an undemocratically structured economy? One further statistic suggests the answer to that question. Average hourly earnings of workers rose a mere 6 percent in the 1970s; salaries of top executives shot up 71 percent.[71]

Here, as in the third world, women stay poor. Despite the substantial increase in women's employment between 1979 and 1984, their average income relative to men did not improve.[72] Currently, more than 1.5 million U.S. families headed by women are living below the poverty line, a number that has been steadily increasing for the last 20 years.[73]

Inequalities are worsening along racial lines. By 1985, the median income of blacks had fallen to 56 percent of that of whites, compared to 62 percent in 1970.[74]

The family farm is giving way to an agricultural system dominated by ownership concentration and absentee landlords.[75] Moreover, American farmers have been made more vulnerable as they have increasingly become dependent on a narrow band of crops, much like the coffee-cocoa-banana trap into which many third world producers are caught.

Most tragically, children are the primary victims of hunger and poverty, just as in the third world. More than one in five American children are growing up in a home struggling against poverty, at risk of hunger.[76] In 1984, a nutritionist testifying before the Texas Senate Interim Committee on Hunger reported treating children with kwashiorkor and marasmus, diseases of malnutrition associated with the third world.[77] Doctors from Chicago corroborated her findings in their local hospital, Cook County.[78] An infant born in our nation's capital has less chance of survival than one born in Jamaica.[79]

Civil liberties are eroding as the government tries to protect itself against views and actions that threaten the status quo. Secrecy and national security are becoming synonymous. In recent years, the government has significantly curtailed citizens' access to information about government activities.[80] In 1981, the CIA was formally authorized to operate domestically.[81] The United States is the only Western democracy to exclude foreign visitors on ideological grounds, denying entry because of their political views to a growing number of foreigners seeking to visit this country.[82] The government also prohibits U.S. citizens to travel to selected countries.

Finally, where the majority have little voice in matters of economic life, they are made to sacrifice in times of crisis. This chapter describes how the poor are paying for the third world's debt, and the pattern holds here, too. The poor and the middle class have borne the brunt of the austerity measures of the 1980s. This point we return to in our next chapter when we explore the meaning of freedom as it relates to economic life.

All of these trends suggest that the very character of our society is changing. With high-tech alarms and guarded streets, the wealthy here create walled enclaves much like the ones seen in Latin American cities. Fear rules rich and poor alike.

Self-Interest and Compassion

Having focused on some of the ways Americans are hurt by a global economy that generates hunger for so many, we can also state our response in the positive. Only as the poor in the third world achieve decent livelihoods and dignity can we achieve economic and national security ourselves.

Because some might misread this chapter as an appeal to materialistic self-interest, we want to reiterate our very different perspective. Legitimate self-interest and compassion for others need not and *cannot* be separated.

What do we mean by legitimate self-interest? We assume that most of us Americans, like most people, want to be free from institutions that violate our deepest values—fairness, protection of innocent lives (especially children), accountability of decision makers, and opportunity for all—just as we desire the basic security and stability needed to pursue our individual goals.

Compassion is just as central. Without compassion we cannot put ourselves in the shoes of others, which is required if we are truly to grasp the many parallels and interconnections suggested in this chapter. But compassion alone too easily slides into pity for the less fortunate. And pity leads us to believe that we have to do for rather than work side by side with those struggling for dignity and security in the third world.

Thus a first step in working toward a more life-serving world is a leap of consciousness. We no longer see the hungry as a threat or a burden to us but understand their liberation as essential to our own. Once shifting to this perspective, virtually every time we pick up the newspaper we uncover new ties linking our fate to that of the hungry. And we are also called upon to seek out alternative sources of information, some of which we suggest at the end of this book.

But this chapter still begs one critical question: why have we acquiesced to the creation of world-linked economic institutions that are neither in our best interests, nor in the interests of the majority in the third world? Why have we let it happen?

To answer that we are victims of the tightening concentration of political and economic power is at best partial. We must go deeper. To understand why so many Americans give in to such usurpation of our own and others' rights, requires that we probe our most deeply held beliefs. In our concluding essay, we suggest that we cannot answer why unless we are willing to challenge the role of received economic dogma of both the world's giant "isms"—capitalism and statism. Taken as dogma, both subvert the most fundamental human values that we profess. Widespread hunger is the most tragic evidence of this subversion.

But first, it is necessary to take a close look at what we mean by one of those values—freedom.

CHAPTER TWELVE

MYTH · 12

Food vs. Freedom

MYTH: Societies that eliminate hunger also end up eliminating the freedoms of their citizens. A tradeoff between freedom and ending hunger is distasteful, but it appears to be a fact of life. People may just have to choose one or the other.

OUR RESPONSE: Taking freedom to mean civil liberties, we can think of no theoretical or practical reason why it should be incompatible with ending hunger. In fact, there are good reasons to expect greater progress toward ending hunger in societies where civil liberties are protected. Freedom of the press and freedom to organize, for example, are critical vehicles through which citizens make a government accountable to their needs or change it for one that is.

Surveying the globe, we find many industrial societies, such as the Scandinavian countries, Switzerland, the Netherlands, Austria, and Japan, that have come very close to eliminating hunger—some closer than the United States—and at the same time enjoy civil liberties similar to our own. Others, such as the USSR and Eastern European nations, do not protect civil liberties.

In the third world, we find very few countries where citizens' rights are protected. But the record does not bear out the view that *greater* infringement on civil liberties is taking

Franklin Delano Roosevelt: "Necessitous men are not free men."

place where hunger is being successfully overcome—China or Cuba, for example. Abuses of citizens' rights are just as common where hunger has been deepening—in Chile, South Africa, Pakistan, Ethiopia, and many Central American countries. In the latter group, citizens have been routinely tortured and killed for exercising what we would consider basic civic prerogatives. In other third world countries, such as Sri Lanka and Costa Rica before the late 1970s, considerable progress toward ending hunger has gone hand in hand with more respect for civil liberties than we typically find in third world countries.

Nevertheless, the myth that food and freedom are incompatible points to fundamental value questions worthy of debate and reflection.

In one sense, the assumption embodied in this myth is absolutely correct. One definition of freedom *is* both theoretically and practically incompatible with ending hunger. It is not the definition of freedom expounded by our nation's founders, but that extolled by the Reagan presidency. It is not the definition embedded in

World Hunger: Twelve Myths

classical and Judeo-Christian traditions, but it is the definition of freedom promoted by a minority of well-heeled, vocal Americans.

Let us explain what we mean.

Freedom as Unlimited Accumulation

President Reagan declared in the early 1980s that the distinctive feature of American society is that here anyone is free to become a millionaire. The right to take all one can is one definition of freedom. The core protector of such freedom is the right to unlimited accumulation of wealth-producing property, and the right to use that property however one sees fit.

We hold that this definition of freedom *is* in fundamental conflict with ending hunger.

Once society starts to operate from this understanding of freedom—the right to unlimited private accumulation—certain consequences follow. Because money makes money and wealth begets wealth, economic power becomes increasingly concentrated. By the 1980s, for example, an almost unbelievable 0.1 percent of U.S. corporations held two-thirds of all corporate assets.[1] Today, with the top fifth of the population receiving 43 percent of all income while the bottom fifth ends up with less than 5 percent,[2] concentration of income is no better in the United States than in some third world countries, as we emphasized in chapter 3.

Why is ending hunger incompatible with such economic concentration?

The answer is easiest to grasp in terms of a finite resource like farmland. Where a few can accumulate vast acreage, many are left with no land from which to provide for themselves, as we have suggested throughout our book.

But perhaps even more important, ending hunger is incompatible with economic concentration because along with economic power comes political power. Those with little or no income have little or no political clout. Protecting citizens' access to life-giving necessities, such as food and shelter, becomes difficult if not impossible. Perhaps never has this fact of economic life been more evident than in the impact of the Reagan administration's austerity measures. According to a Congressional Budget Office study, nearly three-quarters of the budget cuts enacted since President Reagan took office affected families earning less than $20,000 a year; by contrast, only 1 percent of the cutbacks touched households earning over $80,000 a year.[3]

Many Americans believe that the right to unlimited accumulation is the guarantor of liberty. They fail to understand that "income-producing property is the bulwark of liberty only for those who have it!"[4] as Yale University economic philosopher Charles

Lindblom coolly reminds us in his classic *Politics and Markets*. In the third world only a tiny minority have such a bulwark to their liberty. And most Americans don't have it either. Eighty percent of us own no stock directly.[5] And the majority of Americans have no net savings.[6]

Security as the Basis of Freedom

Fortunately, however, this understanding of freedom—the freedom of unlimited accumulation—is not the only one. Nor is it consistent with the vision of our nation's founders. They too perceived a link between property and freedom; but they believed that such a link could be positive only when ownership of socially productive property is widely dispersed.

After a conversation on a country road with a desperately poor single mother trying to support two children with no land of her own, Thomas Jefferson wrote to James Madison in 1785, "legislators cannot invent too many devices for subdividing property." The misery of Europe, he concluded, was caused by the enormous inequality in landholding.[7] Benjamin Franklin endorsed the community's right to redistribute what he called superfluous property,[8] and Jefferson believed that land should be redistributed every generation. "Man did not make the earth," declared Tom Paine, "[and] he had no right to locate as his property, in perpetuity, any part of it."[9]

Many dismiss Jefferson's vision of a small-farm-dominated democracy as naive and irrelevant to modern America. But such presumption misses Jefferson's and Franklin's critical insight that the *economic security of citizens is the guarantor of our liberty*. In their day, as well as for many in the third world today, economic security naturally would entail a plot of land, but their insight applies equally well to the industrial era. Translated into the late twentieth century, economic security would also mean the right to a remunerative job, and, if unable to work, the right to life's necessities.

Many political theorists of Jefferson's day and of the seventeenth century believed that unless people were economically independent—that is, had economic security, including access to food—they could not be full citizens of a democracy because *they could not act independently*. Both Oliver Cromwell and the Levellers in seventeenth century England, for example, agreed that "if there be anything at all that is a foundation of liberty it is this, that those who shall choose the law-makers shall be men freed from dependence upon others."[10] Here we find an echo of Plato's view that the essence of freedom is being self-directed.

Such a notion has been largely lost, but might not this age old insight still be relevant? Think for a moment about limits on the independent behavior of workers in our country today. Because the right to employment is not protected, one might question how free are, say, employees of arms contractors to think independently about the military budget. Unsure of alternative employment, would they not feel compelled to push their representatives to vote for arms spending despite possible reservations about the arms race? In the third world, with jobs even more scarce and workers' rights often unprotected altogether, pressure to keep one's views to oneself is even more intense.

Not only is our freedom of action as citizens constrained by economic insecurity, so is our personal freedom. Franklin Roosevelt summed up this insight when he declared "necessitous men are not free men." In 1944, Roosevelt therefore called for a second bill of rights centering on the right to remunerative employment. More recently, University of Maryland philosopher Henry Shue has offered a helpful exploration of precisely *why* subsistence rights— particularly the right to an adequate diet and health care—are basic to freedom.

Shue likens such subsistence rights to the right to physical security—the right not to be subjected to murder, torture, mayhem, rape, or assault. How do we justify the right to physical security? In part by the fact that no other right can be enjoyed without it. Shue argues that subsistence rights are just as basic:

> No one can fully, if at all, enjoy any right that is supposedly protected by society if he or she lacks the essentials for a reasonably healthy and active life. Deficiencies in the means of subsistence can be just as fatal, incapacitating, or painful as violations of physical security. The resulting damage or death can at least as decisively prevent the enjoyment of any right as can the effects of security violations.[11]

Shue goes so far as to argue that the right to the essentials of survival is even *more* basic than the right to be protected from assault. For it is much easier to fight back against an assailant than to challenge the very structure of the social order that denies one access to food.

Such a view of freedom—rooted in security to permit full functioning as a human being—builds, we believe, on our Judeo-Christian and classical heritage. It contrasts sharply with the much more recent notion of freedom defined as unfettered accumulation of property. The former definition is clearly compatible with, indeed essential to, ending hunger; the latter is not.

Freedom: Finite or Infinite?

But we want to probe this myth still further. Behind it lies the fear that freedom is finite, that ensuring everyone's right to eat will require expanding the freedom of some while shrinking the freedom of others, that freedom is a zero-sum equation.

As long as we focus our definition on the freedom to own or control property this view holds considerable truth. But reducing the concept of freedom to mean unfettered control of property drastically curtails our vision. We can begin to embrace the vast breadth and depth of the concept of freedom only by asking the oft-forgotten question: what is the *purpose* of freedom?

For many people—and in most religious traditions—freedom is not an end in itself. Rather its purpose is the development of the uniquely human and individually unique potential of each person— be it intellectual, physical, artistic, or spiritual.[12] Freedom of expression, religion, and participation, and more basically freedom from physical assault (both direct and through deprivation of life's necessities) are prerequisites to such development.

Freedom so understood is not finite. My artistic development need not detract from yours. Your intellectual advances need not reduce my ability to develop my own intellectual powers. And most pertinent to this chapter, assurances of my protection from physical assault, including my right to subsistence, need not prevent you from enjoying equal protection. This is true because, as we have shown throughout our book, sufficient resources already exist in virtually all countries to guarantee subsistence rights for everyone.

Not only is freedom so defined not a zero-sum equation, we see it as a rare case in which the sum truly is greater than its parts. For not only does your freedom to develop your unique gifts not have to limit my expression, my development in part *depends upon* your freedom. How, for example, can I deepen my appreciation and enjoyment of music unless you, with much greater musical talent, are free to develop your gift? Or how can you develop your full potential physical health unless someone else, with talents in science and medicine, is free to cultivate those gifts?

Having thus expanded our understanding of freedom, we can now return our focus to hunger. Here in America the freedom of the poor is being thwarted by poverty and hunger, *and so is the freedom of those who are well-fed*. The failure of our society to protect subsistence rights means that all of its members are deprived of the intellectual breakthroughs, spiritual insights, musical gifts, or athletic achievements of those whose development has been blocked by poverty and hunger. Denied the potential inspiration, knowledge, example, and leadership of those who are directly deprived, all of us experience a diminution of our freedom to realize our fullest potential.

So in this broader sense we conclude that the protection of the right to food is not in conflict with freedom but essential to its maximum realization throughout society.

Freedom: Our Responsibility

We hope we have said enough in our response to this myth to make clear that freedom carries more than one definition. This alone should make us wary of those attempting to impose their definition on others. When the president of the United States calls on Americans to support "freedom fighters" abroad, we might appropriately ask whose definition of freedom they are fighting for.

Since true freedom can only be achieved by a people for themselves, is not our responsibility to other peoples limited to the challenges addressed in the preceding two chapters? We can make sure that our tax dollars and our government's influence are not used to shore up foreign governments that deny their people's rights. And, through knowledge exchange, financial help, or joint campaigns on matters of common concern, we can work in concert with those in other societies who are themselves striving for greater freedom.

Here at home does not a commitment to freedom require that we bring forth into public debate the profoundly conflicting definitions of freedom now held in our society—and clarify how radically the current property-accumulation definition diverges from our cherished heritage? Obviously we hope that in such a debate our book will contribute to a renewed appreciation of the positive link between economic security and freedom, so that Americans who love liberty will want to expand it by establishing the *right* of every citizen to the resources necessary to live in dignity.

Beyond the Myths of Hunger: What We Can Do

Some approaches to world hunger elicit our guilt (that we have so much) or our fear (that they will take it from us). Others imply impossible tradeoffs. Do we protect the environment *or* grow needed food? Do we seek a just *or* an efficient food system? Do we choose freedom *or* the elimination of hunger?

But our search for the roots of hunger has led us to a number of positive principles that neither place our deeply held values in conflict nor pit our interests against those of the hungry. We offer the following principles as working hypotheses, not to be carved in stone but to be tested through experience:

- Since hunger results from human choices, not inexorable natural forces, the goal of ending hunger is obtainable. It is no more utopian than the goal of abolishing slavery was not all that long ago.
- While slowing population growth in itself cannot end hunger, the very changes necessary to end hunger—the democratization of economic life, especially the empowerment of women—are key to reducing birth rates so that the human population can come into balance with the rest of the natural world.
- Ending hunger does not necessitate destroying our environment. On the contrary, it requires protecting it by using agricultural methods that are both ecologically sustainable and within the reach of the poor.

The goal of ending hunger is no more utopian than was the goal of abolishing slavery.

- Greater fairness does not undercut the production of needed food. The only path to increased production that can end hunger is to devise food systems in which those who do the work have a greater say and reap a greater reward.
- We need not fear the advance of the poor in the third world. Their increased well-being can enhance our own.

World Hunger: Twelve Myths

These and other liberating principles point to possibilities for narrowing the unfortunate rifts we sometimes observe among those concerned about the environment, rapid population growth, and world hunger.

Giving Change a Chance

In chapter 10, we explained why most U.S. foreign aid actually sends our tax dollars to work against the hungry. But the question remained, if not promoting more U.S. aid, what *is* our responsibility to the hungry?

We responded that the most important step Americans can take to end hunger is to remove U.S. support—financial, diplomatic, and military—from regimes determined to resist the changes necessary to end hunger.

Even many Americans who agree with our approach to the problem of hunger may balk at this recommendation. "But, we can't do that! If we don't support those regimes, the Soviet Union will fill the vacuum. Nothing new will be allowed to emerge; things will only be worse." How often we have heard this!

We have thought long and hard about this fear. We understand it. We have tried to think through exactly what choices we have. Aren't there really only two? On the one hand, we can allow our government to continue on its present course—blocking change. Or we can give change a chance.

Where does the first choice lead?

Two quite different countries have come to symbolize for us the logical consequences of this course.

The first is Guatemala. In the early 1950s, the U.S. government abetted the overthrow of an elected government attempting to carry out a modest land reform. Over many years, U.S. military and economic aid strengthened the grip of governments responsible for imprisoning, torturing, and murdering tens of thousands of Indian peasants (and making many more into refugees), virtually all opposition leaders, and hundreds of churchworkers—that is, anyone seeking political and economic reforms.

Guatemala has perhaps the worst human rights record in all Latin America. In 1984, the respected human rights organization Americas Watch called Guatemala a "nation of prisoners."[1] That same year the Guatemalan military permitted the election of a civilian as president, but terror against the poor and other dissidents persists. So well entrenched are the oligarchy and their military that many observers doubt the elected government will be able to enact reforms addressing Guatemala's appalling poverty and hunger. And even if the coming years were to bring reform, several decades would be required to undo the damage wrought with U.S. backing. The Philippines, El Salvador, Zaire, Chile, Haiti, South Africa, Paraguay, Indonesia—we could use these and several other countries to make the same point.

Cuba represents an equally predictable consequence of the same course—a policy based on blocking change. Historically, the United States supported corrupt, authoritarian regimes in Cuba even though they perpetuated misery and hunger for many Cubans. When Fidel Castro's government threatened to nationalize a U.S.–owned oil refinery—as decades earlier Mexico had nationalized its oil fields—the United States retaliated with hostilities that continue to this day. Along with multiple failed attempts to assassinate or overthrow Castro, the United States has used all its power to isolate Cuba internationally: trade embargoes, travel restrictions, and lobbying against aid by international lenders. The United States even imposes its policy of fear on its allies, refusing to import goods containing Cuban-made parts.[2]

If U.S. policymakers fear the emergence of a Soviet satellite near our borders, no policy could have been better designed to turn that fear into reality. And if their concern is for political freedom in Cuba, the U.S. government's unrelenting hostility and repeated attempts at subversion help create in Cuba an environment *least* likely to allow the flowering of civil liberties.[3]

Guatemala and Cuba represent the outcome of one choice. Fortunately, there is another choice. Primarily, it would entail our government's obeying the law—both U.S. laws and U.S.–signed international treaties that forbid supporting governments notorious for their human rights violations. It would mean an end to covert and overt operations to "destabilize" societies where reforms necessary to end hunger are under way.

Americans are told that following such a course would pave the road for Soviet satellites throughout the third world, with Cuba cited as proof. But as we have just pointed out, developments in Cuba are in part the outcome of policies based on U.S. hostility to change, *not* on an alternative course.

Years of study about and experience in numerous third world nations have led us to predict a different outcome if the United States were to change its course. Our prediction is based on the observation that any nation that has for decades, even centuries, been under the control of elites beholden to foreign interests will above all yearn for sovereignty. Such movements for change will want to do it *their* way—if they are given the chance. The last thing they will want to become is a puppet of a foreign power. And domestically, they will likely seek to avoid becoming a carbon copy of either dominant model—U.S.–style capitalism or Soviet-style statism.

Our close-up observation of Nicaragua over the last seven years has strongly confirmed our hunch.[4] Looking at the pattern of Nicaragua's aid and trade ties with other countries, we have been struck by the new government's efforts to avoid dependency on any one power bloc. In 1984, most of the value of Nicaragua's imports came from Latin America, Western Europe, and the United States. About one quarter came from the Eastern bloc. In 1984, only 6 percent of Nicaragua's exports went to socialist countries. In loans to Nicaragua, a similar pattern emerges. Between 1979 and 1984, of the almost $3 billion in loans made to Nicaragua, nearly two-thirds came from other Latin American countries, multilateral lending institutions like the World Bank, and Western European countries, while about a quarter came from the Eastern bloc. Only as Western sources of aid have cut back, in large part in response to U.S. pressure to isolate Nicaragua, has the share of its loans from the Eastern bloc increased, reaching 60 percent in 1984.[5]

Nicaragua's domestic economic policies also confirm our sense that third world movements for change will seek to break loose from *both* dominant economic models. About 60 percent of Nicaragua's economy (and over three-quarters of its farmland) is in private hands, and its experiments in political participation include forms tried in neither East nor West.[6]

Americans have been told that Nicaragua, like Cuba, is a direct threat to our own security. But can anyone seriously believe either of these tiny countries could harm the United States? Since the 1962 Cuban missile crisis, the United States has made clear that it would not tolerate weapons installations near our borders that might threaten our security. Satellite-gathered intelligence allows us to be certain that prohibition is not violated. Rather than a threat, both Nicaragua and Cuba could contribute to the U.S. economy if the United States established trading ties, as we now have with China and in certain fields with the Soviet Union.

But if the U.S. government continues its hostility to change, we may be deprived of knowing the full possibilities of economic and political change in the interests of the majority. Any society attacked by a much more powerful enemy will find it difficult to allow free debate or to invest its scarce resources in an alternative development path.

A Relevant Example

If both common sense and historical experience suggest that third world peoples, if allowed to do so, will want to chart new paths, what do Americans have to offer?

We Americans have always thought of our country as a beacon of hope for the world's oppressed. But as we travel throughout the third world, we sense a change. We fear our example is becoming increasingly irrelevant to the poor majority abroad.

While our government extolls the virtues of democracy and freedom, America's present version of these two values appears unrelated to the concerns of the hungry—food, access to land, and jobs. Our government praises third world elections as creating democracies, but most of the hungry people in the world today live in countries—India, Brazil, El Salvador, Pakistan, Sudan, Egypt, Indonesia—where there have been elections, yet the majority of people find themselves no better able to meet their needs.

Even more directly stated, if amid our nation's fantastic food bounty, poor American children are stunted by malnutrition, what example of hope do we offer to children in the third world? If, with an unparalleled industrial and service economy, millions go without work even during a period of economic growth and millions more work full time yet remain in poverty, what hope do we offer the impoverished and jobless in the third world?

We fear the answer is very little as long as Americans' understanding of democracy and freedom fails to address the most central concerns of the poor.

This realization suggests that we can contribute toward ending world hunger not only by helping to remove obstacles in the way of change in the third world but also by what we do right here at home. In the preceding chapter, we quoted philosopher Henry Shue who argues that subsistence rights—what we call economic rights—are just as central to freedom as is the right to security from physical assault.

We would only add that until we expand our understanding of democracy and freedom to include economic rights—a job for all those able to work and income with dignity for those not able—the United States can't be an example of hope in the eyes of the world's poor. Moreover, unless we so enlarge our understanding of democracy here at home, we doubt our government's capacity to understand or tolerate attempts for such change in the third world.

Beyond Economic Dogma

What would be required to expand our understanding of freedom and democracy, necessary both to end hunger here and to allow our nation to open the way to change in the third world?

First and foremost, a willingness to challenge the grip of economic dogma. In the opening essay of this book, we pinpointed what we see as the root of hunger—the antidemocratic concentration of power over economic resources, especially land and food.

But why have we allowed such concentration of power to continue, even at the price of untold human suffering? We began by answering that myths block our understanding. Here we want to probe deeper. We believe the answer lies in our imposed and self-imposed powerlessness before economic dogma.

Seventeenth century intellectual breakthroughs forced us to relinquish the comforting notion of an interventionist God who would put the human house aright. And what a frightening void we then faced! Running from the weighty implication—that indeed *human beings* are responsible for society-inflicted suffering—we've desperately sought a substitute concept. We've longed for overriding laws we could place above human control, thus relieving us of moral responsibility.

With Newton's discovery of laws governing the physical world and with Darwin's parallel discovery in the realm of nature, we became convinced that there must indeed be laws governing the social world.

And we thought we had found them! Here we'll mention two such "absolutes" that relate most directly to the causes of hunger. Though they be human creations, our society has made them sacred.

The first is the market. Who can deny that the market is a handy device for distributing goods? As we stated in chapter 7, any society that has attempted to do away with the market has run up against serious stumbling blocks. But once transformed into dogma, this useful device can become the cause of great suffering. As such, we are made blind to even the most obvious shortcomings of the market—its ability to respond only to the demands of wealth, not to the needs of people, its inability to register the real resource costs of production, and its inherent tendency to concentrate power in ever fewer hands.

Facing up to these shortcomings does not mean that we throw out the market in favor of another dogma, such as top-down state control. It means that we approach the market as a useful device, asking ourselves, under what circumstances can the market serve our values? In chapter 7, we set forth the very simple proposition that *the more widely purchasing power is distributed, the more the market will respond to actual human needs.*

But within a market system in which everything—land, food, human skills—is bought and sold with no restrictions, how can we work toward a more equal distribution of buying power? The answer is we cannot. Yet if we agree that tossing out the market would be foolish, what do we do?

In answering this question, we face the second major stumbling block posed by the prevailing economic dogma, the notion of unlimited private control over productive property.

Taken as economic dogma, the right to unlimited private control over productive property allows many Americans to accept as fair and inevitable the accelerating consolidation of our own farmland in fewer hands and the displacement of owner-operated farms, just as we have seen in much of the third world. In Iowa, a symbol of family-farm America, more than half the land is now controlled by absentee landlords, not working farmers.[7] Similarly, we accept the accelerating concentration of corporate power.

Although many Americans believe that the right to unlimited private control over productive property is the essence of the American way, this was certainly not the vision of many of our nation's founders, as we pointed out in the preceding chapter. In their view, property could serve liberty only when ownership was widely dispersed, and the right to property was valid only when it served society's interests. This view was widely held well into the nineteenth century. "Until after the Civil War, indeed, the assumption was widespread that a corporate charter was a privilege to be granted . . . for purposes clearly in the public interest," writes historian Alan Trachtenberg.[8]

But by 1986, Ford executive Robert A. Lutz could declare without apology that his "primordial duty" is to his shareholders, while lamenting that his company's investment decisions meant the loss of tens of thousands of jobs.[9] Lutz seemed unaware that the notion that a corporation is responsible to its shareholders, but not to its workers nor to the larger society, is in fact a very *new* idea.

More accurately, Lutz's view is the revival of a once-discarded idea. When our nation's founders rejected monarchy their cry was no taxation without representation. It was a demand for the accountability of governing structures. Applied to the much-altered economic world of the twentieth century, their demand seems especially apppropriate vis-à-vis our major corporations. Corporations now "can have more impact on the lives of more people than the government of many a town, city, province, state," notes Yale political scientist Robert A. Dahl.[30] Thus today's claim by corporations of an unfettered right to allocate wealth we all helped to create may be closer to the concept of the divine right of kings than it is to the principles of democracy.

Ownership with Responsibility

Working against hunger requires a fundamental rethinking of the meaning of ownership, certainly when applied to the productive resources on which all humanity depends. Such effort would be a first step in breaking free of the constraints of dogma.

In this rethinking, we believe Americans would be well served by going back to our roots, to the concept of property-cum-responsibility held by our nation's founders and to that of the original claimants to these soils, the American Indian nations. Because the community endures beyond the lifetime of any one indi-

World Hunger: Twelve Myths

vidual, the Indian concept of community tenure carried within it an obligation to future generations as well.[11]

Indeed, we see a worldwide movement toward the rethinking of ownership already under way. In this rethinking, ownership of productive resources, instead of an absolute to be placed above other values, becomes a cluster of rights and responsibilities at the service of our deepest values. It is neither the rigid capitalist concept of unlimited private ownership nor the rigid statist concept of public ownership.

Where do we see movement toward such rethinking? In 1982, we visited one of the most productive industrial complexes in Europe: Mondragon, in the Basque region of Spain. Here some 100 enterprises—including a banking system, technical training school, and social services—are owned and governed by the people who work there. This noncapitalist, nonstatist form of ownership results in very different priorities and values. During the recession of the early 1980s, for example, when Spain suffered 15 percent unemployment, virtually no one in Mondragon was laid off. Worker-owners were retrained to meet the needs of the changing economy.[12]

We can detect a values-first approach to ownership in the third world too. In Nicaragua's pragmatic agrarian reform the goal is not the elimination of private property; indeed many more landowners are being generated by the reform. The keystone is attaching an obligation to the right to own farmland. Since this resource is essential and finite, every owner is obliged to use it efficiently so as to benefit society. Land left idle or grossly underproducing is taken away and given free of charge to families with no land. The concept of ownership is thus protected, but not above a higher value—life itself, the right of all human beings to eat.

Do these examples sound far away, irrelevant, even alien to our own experience? Then consider the recent decision of Nebraskans on this very question of farmland ownership. A few years ago, they amended their state's constitution so that only working farmers and their families can own farmland. Corporations like Prudential Insurance that had been speculating in Nebraska farmland could buy no more. In their support for this amendment, Nebraskans put the value of dispersed ownership in family farm agriculture above the notion of anyone's absolute right to buy whatever their dollars can pay for.[13]

We introduced our discussion of property rights in response to the question, what would be required to achieve such a dispersion of economic power that the market could actually reflect human needs rather than the demands of wealth? Part of the answer, we have suggested, lies in rethinking property rights as a device to serve higher values, not as ends in themselves. But an additional approach is worthy of consideration.

Just Too Important

Price fluctuations in a market economy can be troublesome for the consumer, but in the special case of food, such variation can be catastrophic. For this reason, and because movement toward fairer distribution of income takes time, some societies have simply decided that what is necessary to life itself should not be left to the vagaries of the market.

As we have mentioned in earlier chapters, a number of both capitalist and noncapitalist societies—as vastly different as Sweden and China—have decided that wholesale food prices are too vital to everyone's well-being to be left to the uncertainties of the market. Health care is equally essential to life. Thus some third world societies and all Western industrialized societies except the United States have also concluded that health care should not be distributed by the market, that is, to those who can afford to pay for it, but should be a citizen's right.

These examples are hardly the final word. We present them as signs of growing courage to confront the rigid "isms," courage to put one's deepest values first and judge economic policies according to how they serve those values—not the other way around.

What Can We Do?
Down to the Most Personal Question

Believing in the possibility of ending hunger means believing in the possibility of real change.

Ironically, the greatest stumbling block of all is the notion held by many Americans that in the United States we have achieved the best that can be—no matter how flawed it may appear. Why is this ironic? Because as Americans we have a very different heritage. Near his death, the father of the Constitution, James Madison, said of our newborn nation, "[America] has been useful in proving things before held impossible."[14] Thus the belief that indeed something new is always possible should be our very birthright.

But how is it possible to believe that those who are poor and downtrodden—those who have so much working against them—can construct better lives? Observing ourselves and others, we've come to appreciate how hard it is to believe that others can change unless we experience change ourselves.

With this realization, the crisis of world hunger becomes the personal question, how can I use my new knowledge to change myself so that I can contribute to ending hunger? The answer lies in dozens of often mundane choices we make *every day*.

These choices determine whether we are helping to end world hunger or to perpetuate it. Only as we make our choices conscious, do we become less and less victims of the world handed to us, and more and more its creators. The more we consciously align our life choices with the vision of the world we are working toward, the more powerful we become. We are more convincing to ourselves and more convincing to others.

How do we begin?

A first step is getting alternative sources of information. As we hope to have demonstrated, as long as we only get world news from television and the mainstream press, our vision will remain clouded by myths. That's why the resource section at the end of the book includes a list of useful periodicals that continually challenge prevailing dogma. Without a variety of independent sources, we can't fulfill our role as citizens to help reshape our government's definition of our national interest and its policies toward the third world.

Then we must put that new knowledge to use. We are all educators—we teach friends, coworkers, and family. With greater confidence born of greater knowledge, we can speak up effectively when others repeat self-defeating myths. Letters to the editor, letters to our representatives, letters to corporate decision makers—they all count too.

Perhaps the most important step, however, in determining whether we will be part of the solution to world hunger, is the choice of a career path. The challenge is to think through just how we apply our skills in jobs that confront, rather than accept, a status quo in which hunger and poverty are inevitable.

To have a real choice of career path or to contemplate involvement in social change, we also have to decide what level of material wealth we need for happiness. Millions of Americans are discovering the emptiness of our society's pervasive myth that material possessions are the key to satisfying lives. They are learning that the *less* they need, the more freedom of choice they have in where to work, where to live, in learning experiences.

In every community in America, people go hungry and lack shelter. Through our churches, community groups, trade unions, and local government, we can help address immediate needs and participate in generating a new understanding of democracy—not as a vote one casts every few years but as active participation in community planning for more and better jobs, affordable housing, and environmental protection. Working to elect officials committed to addressing the roots of hunger is essential to such change.

Where and how we spend our money—or don't spend it—is also a vote for the kind of world we want to create. For example, in most communities we can now choose to shop at food stores that offer less-processed and less-wastefully packaged foods, stores managed by the workers themselves, instead of conglomerate-controlled supermarkets. And we can choose to redirect our consumer dollars in support of specific product boycotts, such as the successful boycott of Nestlé that alerted the world to the crisis of infant deaths caused by the corporate promotion of infant formula in the third world, or the boycott of Campbell Soup that brought the company to the negotiating table with a Midwest farmworkers organization.

We can take responsibility for the invisible role our savings play when we put them in the bank. Instead of allowing our savings to be invested in weapons manufacturing, nuclear power, or South Africa, we can use our savings to support our values. Socially responsible investment funds have been created in recent years that use criteria of fairness and environmental protection, along with monetary return, in deciding where to put our money.[15]

But little is possible by oneself. We need others to push us and to console us when we are overwhelmed by the enormity of the problems we face. The points we make about the myth of the passive poor in chapter 9 apply equally well to "passive" North Americans. We, too, need the example of others. *Community is Possible* by Harry Boyte,[16] and *Helping Ourselves* by Bruce Stokes[17] are just two books offering inspiring glimpses into local initiatives for change in America.

Actually *going* to the third world ourselves can profoundly alter our perceptions. A superficial tourist's view might confirm one's despair; but making the effort to meet those working for change, we can discern tremendous energy and hope. And looking back to the United States from abroad, we gain new insights on the role of our government. Today several nonprofit groups and travel agencies offer study-tours to selected third world countries. Individuals with specialized skills can consider actually living for awhile in the third world, offering their services to locally organized initiatives.

At the end of this book, we have included a selected list of some of the organizations working at a number of levels: all are part of the growth in understanding necessary to end hunger.

The Essential Ingredient

Our capacity to help end world hunger is infinite, for the roots of hunger touch every aspect of our lives—where we work, what we teach our children, how we fulfill our role as citizens, where we shop and save. But whether we seize these possibilities depends in large measure on a single ingredient. You might expect us to suggest that the needed ingredient is compassion—compassion for the millions who go hungry today. As we have pointed out, compassion is indeed a profoundly motivating emotion. It comes, however, relatively easy. Our ability to put ourselves in the shoes of others makes us truly human. Some even say it's in our genes and that we deny our innate compassion only at great peril to our own emotional well-being. There is another ingredient that's harder to come by. It is moral courage.

At a time when the old "isms" are ever more clearly failing, many cling even more tenaciously to them. So it takes courage to cry out, "The emperor wears no clothes! The world is awash in food, and all of this suffering is the result of human decisions!"

To be part of the answer to world hunger means being willing to take risks, risks many of us find more frightening than physical danger. We have to risk being embarrassed or dismissed by friends or teachers as we speak out against deeply ingrained but false understandings of the world. It takes courage to ask people to think critically about ideas so taken for granted as to be like the air they breathe.

And there is another risk—the risk of being wrong. For part of letting go of old frameworks means grappling with new ideas and new approaches. Rather than fearing mistakes, courage requires that we continually test new concepts as we learn more of the world—ever willing to admit error, correct our course, and move forward.

But from where does such courage come?

Surely from the same root as our compassion, from learning to trust that which our society so often discounts—our innate moral sensibilities, our deepest emotional intuitions about our connectedness to others' well-being. Only on this firm ground will we have the courage to challenge all dogma, demanding that the value of human life be paramount. Only with this new confidence will we stop twisting our values so that economic dogma might remain intact while millions of our fellow human beings starve amid ever greater abundance.

Notes

Beyond Guilt and Fear

1. World Bank, *Poverty and Hunger: Issues and Options for Food Security in Developing Countries* (Washington, D.C.: World Bank, 1986), 1. Estimates vary; see the next chapter.
2. George Kent, *The Political Economy of Hunger: The Silent Holocaust* (New York: Praeger, 1984), 26.
3. The Hunger Project, *Ending Hunger: An Idea Whose Time Has Come* (New York: Praeger Special Studies, 1985), 7.
4. Charles Clements, *Witness to War* (New York: Bantam, 1984),104.
5. For a useful discussion of the issue of women and agricultural development, see Gita Sen and Caren Grown, "Development, Crises and Alternative Visions: Third World Women's Perspectives," *Monthly Review Press* (Fall 1986); "Women to Women: A World Report," *The New Internationalist*, no. 149 (July 1985); Series of Papers produced for ORSTOM 1985 Conference on Women and Food Production in the Third World (Paris:

French Institute for Development and Cooperation, forthcoming). See also Ruth Leger Sivard, *Women . . . A World Survey* (Washington, D.C.: World Priorities, 1985).

6. Tom Barry, "Roots of Rebellion" (Central America Resource Center, Albuquerque, unpublished manuscript), 1.

7. Milton J. Esman, *Landlessness and Near Landlessness in Developing Countries* (Ithaca: Cornell University, Center for International Studies, 1978).

8. Data are based on an average of 37 developing countries. See Food and Agriculture Organization, "Fighting World Hunger," World Food Day Feature, Rome, 16 October 1985, 6.

9. William Maynes, former assistant secretary of state, quoted in *World Development Forum* 1, no. 26 (31 December 1983): 3.

10. World Conference on Agrarian Reform and Rural Development, *Examen et analyse de la reforme agraire et du developpement rural dans les pays en voie de developpement depuis le milieu des années soixante* (Rome: FAO, 1979), 113.

11. Peter F. Drucker, "The Changed World Economy," *Foreign Affairs* (Spring 1986): 769.

12. UNICEF estimates that 40,000 children die each day from malnutrition, resulting in over 14 million deaths each year. (UNICEF, *The State of the World's Children 1984* (Oxford: Oxford University Press, 1983), 5.

There's Simply Not Enough Food

M Y T H · 1

1. Calculated from Food and Agriculture Organization, *FAO Production Yearbook 1984*, vol. 38 (Rome: FAO, 1985). Over 40 percent of the world's grain supply is now fed to livestock. Most of the land and other resources now used to produce feed grain could be used to grow grain and other foods for human consumption. Feed grains are grown because better-off consumers prefer livestock products, making feed grains more profitable than food grains. According to the FAO, the recommended energy allowance for a U.S. "reference man" in his 20s weighing 155 lbs. and not very active is 2,700 calories/day and for a U.S. "reference woman" weighing 127 lbs. is 2,000 calories/day. Calories adequate to cover energy needs are generally sufficient to meet protein needs, except for people (especially young children) subsisting on low-protein roots, tubers, and plaintains.

2. According to one estimate, if all foods are considered together, enough is available to provide at least five pounds of food per person a day. See Douglas La Roche, "Feeding the World: The

North and South of It," *Plowshare* 6, no. 2 (1981): 11. Root crops are second in importance after grains in the third world (communication from Uwe Kracht, senior economist, World Food Council, 5 May 1986).

3. Barbara Insel, "A World Awash in Grain," *Foreign Affairs* (Spring 1985): 892–911. See also Peter F. Drucker, "The Changing World Economy," *Foreign Affairs* (Spring 1986).

4. Calculated from *FAO Production Yearbook* 1966, 1974, 1984.

5. This refers to prices adjusted for inflation. World Bank, *Poverty and Hunger: Issues and Options for Food Security in Developing Countries* (Washington, D.C.: World Bank, 1986), 14.

6. *FAO Production Yearbook* 1966, 1974, 1984, table 10.

7. Food and Agriculture Organization, *UN Socio-economic Indicators Relating to the Agricultural Sector and Rural Development* (Rome: FAO, 1984), table 27.

8. World Bank, *Poverty and Hunger.* For these estimates, the World Bank used a nutritional standard adequate for an active working life. Even these low percentages are reduced by three-quarters if a lower nutritional standard—a diet adequate to prevent stunted growth and serious health risks—is used.

9. In *Poverty and Hunger*, the World Bank estimates the number of hungry people to be 730 million using a caloric standard necessary to sustain an active life. The FAO, using a nutritional standard lower than that used by the World Bank, estimated that 201 million people in India are undernourished out of a total 435 million hungry people in the third world. See FAO, *Dimensions of Needs* (Rome: FAO, 1982), Part III. Other studies estimate the number of chronically hungry people in India closer to 300 million; see, for instance, U.S. Department of Agriculture, *Agricultural Outlook* (December 1985).

10. World Bank, *Poverty and Hunger*, 20.

11. FAO, *Dimensions of Needs*, Part III.

12. World Bank, *Poverty and Hunger*, 20.

13. Ibid.

14. Thomas T. Poleman, "Quantifying the Nutrition Situation in Developing Countries," *Food Research Institute Studies* 18, no. 1: 9. This article is a good discussion of the multifaceted problems of most agricultural and nutritional statistics. See also Donald McGranahan et al., *Measurement and Socioeconomic Development* (Geneva: United Nations Research Institute for Social Development, 1985).

15. UN Conference on Trade and Development, *Handbook of International Trade and Development Statistics*, 1985 Supplement (Rome: UNCTAD, 1985), table 3.3.

16. Food and Agriculture Organization, *FAO Trade Yearbook 1984* (Rome: FAO, 1985). Calculated by value for nations designated low income by the World Bank (*World Development Report 1985*).

17. "Huge Grain Surplus Poses Problems," *The Economic Times* (of

India), 25 December 1985; Food and Agriculture Organization, *Food Aid in Figures, 1984* (Rome: FAO, 1985), table 5.

18. James K. Boyce, "Agricultural Growth in Bangladesh, 1949–50 to 1980–81: A Review of the Evidence," *Economic and Political Weekly* 20, no. 13 (30 March 1985): A31–A43.

19. Calculated from *FAO Production Yearbook 1984*. To better understand the roots of hunger in Bangladesh, refer to *Needless Hunger: Voices from a Bangladesh Village* (1979, 1982) and *A Quiet Violence: View from a Bangladesh Village* (1983), both by Betsy Hartmann and James Boyce (San Francisco: Food First Books).

20. World Bank, *Bangladesh: Economic and Social Development Prospects: Volume III*, Report no. 5409 (Washington, D.C.: World Bank, April 1985), 18.

21. Steve Jones, "Agrarian Structure and Agricultural Innovation in Bangladesh: Panimara Village, Dhaka District," in *Understanding Green Revolutions*, ed. Tim Bayliss-Smith and Sudhir Wanmali (New York: Cambridge University Press, 1984), 194.

22. "Brazil May Soon Take Heed of Its Have-Nots," *New York Times*, 4 May 1986; Instituto Brasileiro de Analises Sociais e Economicas (IBASE), *A Fome Na America Latina* (Rio de Janeiro, 1985), 4, cites a 1984 study by Claudio de Moura Castro estimating that 86 million Brazilians are undernourished.

23. Calculated from *FAO Trade Yearbook 1984*. Calculations of imports include food aid, according to James Hill, senior economist, North American UN FAO Liaison Office, Washington, D.C. (interviewed by Joseph Collins, May 1986). Otherwise, Sub-Saharan Africa would appear an even stronger net exporter. For some detailed data and descriptions of agricultural exports from Africa, see Barbara Dinham and Colin Hines, *Agribusiness in Africa* (Trenton, NJ: Africa World Press of the Africa Research and Publications Project, 1984).

24. *FAO Trade Yearbook 1984*, tables 135, 137, 144, 145, 146.

25. Calculated from *FAO Trade Yearbook 1984*. For Chad, Niger, Mauritania, Mali, Burkina Faso, and Senegal, years of net exports were 1980, 1982, and 1983. Years of net imports were 1981 and 1984 due to exceptionally high imports into Senegal and Niger those two years.

26. Calculated from *FAO Trade Yearbook 1975*, tables 5, 35.

27. From interview with chief economist, U.S. Agency for International Development Mission, Ouagadougou, Upper Volta (now Burkina Faso), 17 January 1977.

28. World Health Organization, *Apartheid and Health* (Geneva: WHO, 1983) and Food and Agriculture Organization, *Apartheid, Poverty and Malnutrition* (Rome: FAO, 1982). See also "The Poverty of Apartheid," *The Economist* (June 1984), 73.

29. Calculated from *FAO Trade Yearbook 1984*.

30. *FAO Production Yearbook* 1966, 1974, 1984, table 10.

31. Calculated from U.S. Dept. of Agriculture, Foreign Agricultural Service, "Grains Reference Tables on Wheat, Corn and Total Course Grains Supply-Distribution for Individual Countries," *Foreign Agricultural Circular*, FG19-83 (Washington, D.C., July 1983).

32. Sara S. Berry, "The Food Crisis and Agrarian Change in Africa: A Review Essay," *African Studies Review* 27, no. 2 (June 1984): 59–97. See also Jane Guyer, "Women's Role in Development," in *Strategies for African Development*, ed. Robert J. Berg and Jennifer Seymour Witaker (Berkeley: University of California Press, 1986), esp. 393–396.

33. See Stephen K. Commins et al., eds., *Africa's Agrarian Crisis: The Roots of Famine* (Boulder, CO: Lynne Rienner Publishers, 1985) and Nigel Twose, *Fighting the Famine* (San Francisco: Food First Books, 1985).

34. Paul Richards, "Ecological Change and the Politics of African Land Use," *African Studies Review* 26, no. 2 (June 1983). See also Paul Richards, *Indigenous Agricultural Revolution* (Boulder, CO: Westview, 1985).

35. See Bill Rau, *Feast to Famine* (Washington, D.C.: Africa Faith and Justice Network, 1985), esp. chapter 6; and Bonnie K. Campbell, "Inside the Miracle: Cotton in the Ivory Coast," in *The Politics of Agriculture in Tropical Africa*, ed. Jonathan Barker (Beverly Hills: Sage, 1984), 154–168.

36. International Labour Office, *Rural Development and Women in Africa* (Geneva: ILO, 1984); Martha F. Loutfi, *Rural Women: Unequal Partners in Development* (Geneva: ILO, 1980).

37. Between 1969 and 1983, prices paid to African producers fell on average 17 percent. See Preparatory Committee of the Whole for the Special Session of the General Assembly on the Critical Economic Situation in Africa, "Working Paper on the Critical Economic Situation in Africa," United Nations 86-04793, 1986, 10. See also Robert H. Bates, *States and Markets in Tropical Africa* (Berkeley: University of California Press, 1981).

38. Independent Commission on International Humanitarian Issues, *Famine: A Man-Made Disaster?* (New York: Vintage Books, 1985), 85–89.

39. Budget allocations drawn from World Bank, *World Tables, 1983*, Third edition (Baltimore: Johns Hopkins University Press, 1984), table 2. Includes 24 African nations.

40. Calculated from USDA, *Foreign Agricultural Circular*, FG19-83. See G. Andrae and B. Beckman, *The Wheat Trap* (London: Zed Press, 1985).

41. A typical ad appearing in an African newspaper in the early 1970s, cited in Jean-Yves Carfantan and Charles Condamines, *Vaincre la Faim, C'est Possible* (Paris: L'Harmattan, 1976), 63.

42. Gerald O. Barney, study director, *The Global 2000 Report to the President—Entering the 21st Century*, prepared by the Council on Environmental Quality and the Department of State (New York: Penguin, 1982). Much more optimistic is H. Linneman et al., *Contributions to Economic Analysis No. 124: Model of International Relations in Agriculture* (Amsterdam: North Holland Publishers, 1979).

43. Food and Agriculture Organization, *Land, Food and People*, based on the FAO/UNFPA/IIASA report, "Potential Population-supporting Capacities of Lands in the Developing World" (Rome: FAO, 1984).

44. Ibid., 57.

45. See, for instance, Elizabeth Croll, *The Family Rice Bowl: Food and the Domestic Economy in China* (Geneva: UN Research Institute for Social Development, 1982).

46. Francis Urban and Thomas Vollrath, *Patterns and Trends in World Agricultural Land Use*, U.S. Department of Agriculture, Economic Research Service, Foreign Agricultural Economic Report no. 198 (Washington, D.C., 1984), table 2. The United States has .837 ha/per capita of cropland and China has .102 ha/per capita.

47. The Physician Taskforce on Hunger in America, *Hunger in America: The Growing Epidemic* (Cambridge, MA: Harvard University, School of Public Health, 1985), 4. The report states that up to 20 million Americans go hungry for some period of time each month. Note that because the federal government refuses to sponsor studies on the extent of malnutrition, more precise data are not available.

48. Nick Kotz, *Hunger in America: The Federal Response* (New York: The Field Foundation, 1985), 13, based on Center for Disease Control studies.

49. Editorial, *New York Times*, 11 September 1985.

50. Kenneth Sheets, "A Bountiful Harvest That's Hard to Swallow," *U.S. News and World Report*, 11 November 1985: 82–83.

Nature's to Blame

M Y T H · 2

1. *Church Perspective*, San Francisco Council of Churches, February 1986.

2. Anders Wijkman and Lloyd Timberlake, *Natural Disasters: Acts of God or Acts of Man?* (London and Washington, D.C.: Earthscan, 1984), 23.

3. Interview by Michael Scott of Oxfam America, Boston, 1979.
4. Amartya Sen, *Poverty and Famines* (Oxford: Clarendon Press, 1981).
5. Ibid., 151 and table 10.1.
6. Betsy Hartmann and James Boyce, *A Quiet Violence: View from a Bangladesh Village* (San Francisco: Food First Books, 1983), 189.
7. Talk by Mahmood Mandani, dean of social sciences, Makerere University, Kampala, Uganda, 19 March 1985. Following the speech he was stripped of his citizenship and deported. Abridged version printed in *Dollars and Sense*, no. 109 (September 1985): 6, 7, 15.
8. The exception was mineral-rich Mauritania, which has very little land suitable for cultivation. Information from Marcel Ganzin, director, Food Policy and Nutrition Division, FAO, Rome, 18 December 1975.
9. Calculated from *FAO Trade Yearbook* 1970, 1975. For further background on famine in the Sahel, see Richard Franke and Barbara Chasin, *Seeds of Famine* (Totowa, NJ: Rowman and Allenheld, 1980); Rolando V. Garcia, *Nature Pleads Not Guilty: Drought and Man— The 1972 Case History* (New York: Pergamon Press, 1981), 181–195; and Michael Lofchie, "Political and Economic Origins of African Hunger," *The Journal of Modern African Studies* 13, no. 4 (1975): 551–567.
10. Michael Watts, *Silent Violence: Food, Famine and Peasantry in Northern Nigeria* (Berkeley: University of California Press, 1983), 441–460. See also Michael Glantz, ed., *Drought and Famine in Africa* (Cambridge: Cambridge University Press, forthcoming), esp. chapters by Torry, Watts, Little, and Horowitz; and Nigel Twose, *Drought in the Sahel: Why the Poor Suffer Most* (Oxford: Oxfam, 1984).
11. Telephone interview by Joseph Collins with John Sutter, Rural Poverty Program officer, Ford Foundation, Dakar, Senegal, February 1986.
12. John Scheuring, International Crops Research Institute for the Semi-Arid Tropics (ICRISAT), Bamako, Mali, personal communication to authors dated 8 January 1986. See also Watts, *Silent Violence*, 373–465.
13. Nigel Twose, *Fighting the Famine* (San Francisco: Food First Books, 1985), 18.
14. Michael Watts, personal communication, 21 May 1986.
15. For an introduction to the problems of famine and the environment of the region, see Jeremy Swift, "Disaster and a Sahelian Nomad Economy," in *Drought in Africa*, ed. David Dalby and R. J. Harrison (London: Centre for African Studies, 1973), 71–79; Douglas L. Johnson, "The Response of Pastoral Nomads to Drought in the Absence of Outside Intervention" (Paper commissioned by the United Nations Special Sahelian Office, 19 December 1973); F. Fraser Darling and M. Taghi

Farvar, "Ecological Consequences of Sedentarization of Nomads," in *The Careless Technology,* ed. M. Taghi Farvar and John P. Milton (Garden City, NJ: Natural History Press, 1972); and Wijkman and Timberlake, *Natural Disasters,* 23.

16. Independent Commission on International Humanitarian Issues, *Famine: A Man-Made Disaster?* (New York: Vintage, 1985), 86–87.

17. Lloyd Timberlake, *Africa in Crisis: The Causes, the Cures of Environmental Bankruptcy* (London and Washington, D.C.: Earthscan, 1985), 38. See also Wijkman and Timberlake, *Natural Disasters,* 40.

18. Independent Commission, *Famine: A Man-Made Disaster?*

19. Calculated from *FAO Trade Yearbook 1984.*

20. Because many of our sources for the material on Ethiopia are still working in that country and fear government reaction against them, they have asked to remain anonymous.

21. Interview with Guido Gryseels, vice director, International Livestock Center for Africa, Addis Ababa, 21 January 1985.

22. *Facts on File,* vol. 45, no. 2303, 1–11 January 1985.

23. René Lefort, *Ethiopia: An Heretical Revolution?* (London: Zed Press, 1983), esp. 18–36; and Jason Clay and Bonnie Holcomb, *Politics and the Ethiopian Famine 1984–1985* (Cambridge, MA: Cultural Survival, 1985), 5–23.

24. Eiichi Shindo, "Hunger and Weapons: The Entropy of Militarization," *Review of African Political Economy* 33 (August 1985): 6–22.

25. World Bank, *Ethiopia: Agricultural Sector: An Interim Report,* East Africa Region, Report no. ET 3956a (Washington, D.C., 26 January 1983), 31.

26. Food and Agriculture Organization, *Ethiopia: Report of the High-Level WCAARD Follow-Up Mission, May 3–9, 1982* (Rome: FAO, 1982), 2.

27. World Bank, *Ethiopia: Recent Economic Developments and Future Prospects ,* vol. I (Washington, D.C.: The World Bank, 1983), 23, 29.

28. John M. Cohen, "Agrarian Reform in Ethiopia: The Situation on the Eve of the Revolution's Tenth Anniversary," Development Discussion Paper no. 164, Harvard Institute for International Development, April 1984, 45.

29. "Proclamation to Provide for the Establishment of Cooperative Societies," *Negarit Gazeta* (3 March 1978) cited in Edmond J. Keller, "Ethiopian Socialism and Agricultural Development" (University of California, Santa Barbara, Department of Political Science, unpublished manuscript), 15.

30. Robin Luckham and Dawit Bekele, "Foreign Powers and Militarism in the Horn of Africa," *Review of African Political Economy* 30 (September 1984): 16, citing figures in U.S. Arms Control and Disarmament Agency, *World Military Expenditures and Arms Transfers, 1971–1980.* Some analysts of Ethiopia cite

even higher figures for arms imports. See, for instance, Hailu Lemma, "The Politics of Famine in Ethiopia," *Review of African Political Economy* 33 (August 1985): 51.

31. In 1980 to 1981, the government farms absorbed 80 percent of the agricultural credit, 82 percent of fertilizer imports, 73 percent of the improved seeds, and consumed large amounts of imported oil running their 3,500 tractors. See World Bank, *Ethiopia: Agricultural Sector*, 20–21.

32. Data are from 1984. See Graham Hancock, *Ethiopia* (London: Victor Gollancz, 1985), 52. For comparison with other nations, see tables for third world nations in *South* (September 1985). These figures apparently do not include Ethiopia's sizable air force.

33. Estimate taken from Clay and Holcomb, *Politics and the Ethiopian Famine*, 8.

34. Michael Glantz, Center for Atmospheric Research, Boulder, Colorado, letter, 6 May 1986. In March 1986, the United Nations Office for Emergency Operations in Africa noted that of the five African countries still affected by famine, in four (Ethiopia, Angola, Mozambique, and Sudan) the solution to armed conflicts is the essential condition for ending the famines. See *Status Report on the Emergency Situation in Africa*, Report no. OEOA/3/7 (New York: United Nations, March 1986).

Too Many Mouths to Feed

M Y T H · 3

1. Per capita cropland from Francis Urban and Thomas Vollrath, *Patterns and Trends in World Agricultural Land Use*, U.S. Department of Agriculture, Economic Research Service, Foreign Agricultural Economic Report no. 198 (Washington, D.C., 1984), table 2. Life expectancy from World Bank, *World Development Report 1985* (New York: Oxford University Press, 1985), table 1. According to the *Report of the National Bipartisan Commission on Central America* (also known as the Kissinger Commission), "57 percent of Honduras' families live in extreme poverty, unable to pay the cost of the basic basket of food" (Washington, D.C., 1984), 31.

2. Calculated from *Food Balance Sheets: 1978–81 Average* (Rome: FAO, 1984). Per capita the Netherlands has only about one-fourteenth the cropland of the United States. Yet, if the people of the Netherlands consumed all they produce (i.e., did not export food), almost 5,000 calories of food would be available per person, not even counting imports.

3. Planned Parenthood Federation of America, *Echoes from the Past* (New York: Planned Parenthood, 1979), 181.

4. M. T. Cain, "The Economic Activities of Children in a Village in Bangladesh," *Population and Development Review* 3 (1977): 201–228, cited in William W. Murdoch, *The Poverty of Nations* (Baltimore: Johns Hopkins University Press, 1980), 26.

5. M. Nag, B. White, and R. C. Peet, "An Anthropological Approach to the Study of the Economic Value of Children in Java and Nepal," *Current Anthropology* 19 (1978): 293–306.

6. Murdoch, *Poverty of Nations*, 45.

7. Perdita Huston, *Message From the Village* (New York: Epoch B. Foundation, 1978), 119.

8. World Bank, *The World Development Report 1984* (New York: Oxford University Press, 1984), table 19.

9. Techically Lebanon should be added to this group of six; according to published data, its growth rate fell from 2.9 percent to 0.5 percent between 1960 and 1982. The extreme disruption of the country no doubt is a major contributor and limits the usefulness of including it in any general discussion of population "successes." Also note that the World Bank does not include several island countries like Grenada and Mauritius that also have growth rates below 2 percent.

10. According to the Indian Census, the population growth rate of Kerala averaged 1.8 percent annually between 1971 and 1981 (Census of India, Kerala State, Part 2A, Statements 3 and 8, pp. 28 and 32) (interview by researcher Rachel Schurman with K. C. Zachariah at the World Bank, Population and Human Resources Division, April 1986).

11. Among the 72 low and lower-middle-income countries we're considering here, two small Caribbean nations—Haiti and Jamaica—stand alone with growth rates below 2 percent since the 1960s. But the reasons for their slow growth appear to be in dramatic contrast. Haiti's health and educational levels are horrifyingly low. Its infant mortality is offically 110 per thousand, for example, compared to 10 for Jamaica, although Jamaica's rate is currently rising. Perhaps the explanation of Haiti's slow growth is that so many have been fleeing its deadly poverty. Sociologist Phillips Cutright notes that Caribbean fertility has been falling because of the emigration of men. In Jamaica, in contrast to Haiti, government health services are free and spread throughout the countryside. Literacy is as high as in the United States and two-thirds of Jamaican women work outside the home. In both countries, birth rates were low before the introduction of significant family planning programs.

12. Murdoch, *Poverty of Nations*, 89.

13. Elizabeth Croll, *The Family Rice Bowl: Food and the Domestic Economy in China* (Geneva: UN Research Institute for Social Development, 1982), 82. At the time of this writing, grain rationing is still being practiced in China (Elizabeth Croll, "Food

Supply in China and the Nutritional Status of Children," unpublished manuscript, 1985, 20).

14. Medea Benjamin, Joseph Collins, and Michael Scott, *No Free Lunch: Food and Revolution in Cuba Today* (New York: Grove Press/Food First Books, 1986), 26.

15. Ibid., 92. In 1983, in fact, the Organization of American States reported that Cuba ranked second in per capita food availability in Latin America.

16. U.S. Agency for International Development, *Sri Lanka: The Impact of PL 480 Title I Assistance*, AID Project Impact Evaluation Report no. 39 (Washington, D.C., October 1982), C-8.

17. Ibid., C-13. Since the 1970s, the food consumption of the lowest income groups has fallen both in quantity (less food consumed) and in quality (less dried fish and beans).

18. S. Kumar, *The Impact of Subsidized Rice on Food Consumption in Kerala*, Research Report no. 5 (Washington, D.C.: International Food Policy Research Institute, 1979).

19. World Bank, *World Development Report 1984*, table 28.

20. The study also controlled for per capita GNP differences. The poorest groups here refers to the bottom 40 percent of the population by income. World Bank, *Population Policies and Economic Development*, A World Bank Staff Report, Timothy King, coordinating author (Baltimore: Johns Hopkins University Press, 1974), Appendix A, 147. See also Robert Repetto, *The Interaction of Fertility and the Size Distribution of Income*, Harvard Center for Population Studies, Research Papers Series, no. 8 (Cambridge, MA, October 1974).

21. World Bank, *Population Policies*, 147.

22. Interview by Frances Moore Lappé with T. Paul Schultz, an economist and population specialist at Yale University, May 1986.

23. According to the World Bank, about 96 percent of persons aged 15 to 49 were at some point enrolled in primary school. It's also interesting to note that of the 58 low and lower-middle-income countries for which the World Bank presents data, Colombia ranked eighth in the percentage of females enrolled in secondary schools (World Bank, *World Development Report 1984*, table 5).

24. Interviews by researcher Sarah Stewart with Carmen Diana Deere, Department of Economics, University of Massachusetts, January 1986, and with Sherry Keith, World Bank officer, January 1986.

25. Interview by researcher Rachel Schurman with Nola Reinhart, Department of Economics, Smith College, April 1986.

26. A. V. Jose, "Poverty and Inequality: The Case of Kerala," in *Poverty in Rural Asia*, ed. Azizur Rahman Khan and Eddy Lee (Bangkok: International Labour Organization, Asian

Employment Programme, 1983), 108.

27. John Ratcliffe, "Social Justice and the Demographic Transition: Lessons from India's Kerala State," in *Practicing Health for All*, ed. D. Morley, J. Rohde, and G. Williams (Oxford: Oxford University Press, 1983), 65. See also Ratcliffe's "Toward a Social Justice Theory of Demographic Transition: Lessons from India's Kerala State," *Janasamkhya*, vol. 1, Kerala University (June 1983).

28. Here we have selected those whose crude birth rate has fallen by at least one-third between 1960 and 1982 (World Bank, *World Development Report 1984*, table 20, 256–257).

29. U.S. Agency for International Development, *Women of the World: A Chartbook for Developing Regions* (Washington, D.C.: Bureau of the Census, 1985), 30–33.

30. D. J. Hernandez, *Success or Failure? Family Planning Programs in the Third World* (Westport, CT: Greenwood Press, 1984), 133. See also Interdisciplinary Communications Program, *The Policy Relevance of Recent Social Research on Fertility*, Occasional Monograph Series, no. 2 (Washington, D.C.: Smithsonian Institution, 1974).

31. W. Parker Mauldin, Bernard Berelson, and Zenas Sykes, "Conditions of Fertility Decline in Developing Countries, 1965–1975," *Studies in Family Planning* 9, no. 5 (May 1978): 121. This study includes many different analyses of the data, with estimates of program effort ranging from 14 to 25 percent. Here we used the middle range most commonly attributed to this study. In an update of this work, Mauldin and Robert J. Lapham find a similar net program effort effect ("Contraceptive Prevalence: The Influence of Organized Family Planning Programs," *Studies in Family Planning* 16, no. 3 (May–June 1985)).

32. See discussion in Murdoch, *Poverty of Nations*, 56–57.

33. World Health Organization, *Injectible Hormonal Contraceptives: Technical Aspects and Safety* (Geneva: WHO, 1982), 17–23

34. WHO Collaborative Study of Neoplasia and Steroid Contraceptives, "Invasive Cervical Cancer and Depot-medroxyprogesterone Acetate," *Bulletin of the World Health Organization* 63, no. 3 (1985): 508; L. C. Powell and R. J. Seymour, "Effects of Depot-medroxyprogesterone Acetate as a Contraceptive Agent," *American Journal of Obstetrics and Gynecology* 110 (1971): 36–41. Another preliminary study by the WHO Collaborative Group suggests that Depo-Provera is not linked to increased risk of breast cancer, as originally suspected (WHO Collaborative Study of Neoplasia and Steroid Contraceptives, "Breast Cancer and Depot-medroxyprogesterone Acetate," *Bulletin of the World Health Organization* 63, no. 3 (1985): 513–519).

35. World Bank, *World Development Report 1984*, 135.

36. Judith Jacobsen, *Promoting Population Sterilization: Incentives for Small Families* (Washington, D.C.: Worldwatch, June 1983), 8.

37. Betsy Hartmann, *The Strategic Womb: Women and the War on Population*, forthcoming. Hartmann is the coauthor of *Needless Hunger: Voices from a Bangladesh Village* and *A Quiet Violence: View from a Bangladesh Village* (San Francisco: Food First Books, 1979 and 1983).

38. Betsy Hartmann and Hilary Standing, *Food, Saris and Sterilization: Population Control in Bangladesh* (London: Bangladesh International Action Group, 1985), 17. See also Hartmann, *The Strategic Womb*.

39. John Ratcliffe, "China's One Child Policy: Solving the Wrong Problem?" (unpublished manuscript, 1985), 38.

40. Ibid., citing National Research Council, *Rapid Population Change in China, 1952–1982*, Committee on Population and Demography, Report no. 27 (Washington, D.C.: National Academy Press, 1984), 47; and J. Banister, "Analysis of Recent Data on the Population of China," *Population and Development Review* 10, no. 2 (June 1984): 241–271. If indeed the one-child policy fails, further doubt is cast on the thesis that intrusive government family planning efforts are primarily responsible for the fall in China's birth rates since the 1960s. For a statement of this thesis, see Arthur P. Wolf, "The Preeminent Role of Government Intervention in China's Family Revolution," *Population and Development Review* 12, no. 1 (March 1986): 101–116. Wolf does not even consider the thesis of this chapter—that far-reaching improvements in security and opportunity are key.

Food vs. Our Environment

M Y T H · 4

1. Alan Grainger, *Desertification* (London: Earthscan, 1984), 8.

2. Gerald O. Barney, study director, *The Global 2000 Report to the President—Entering the 21st Century*, vol. 1 (New York: Penguin, 1982), 36. See also Norman Myers, *Conversion of Tropical Moist Forest* (Washington, D.C.: National Academy of Sciences, 1980). Another study projects rates of destruction only one-third as great: UN Environment Programme, *Global Assessment of Tropical Forest Resources*, GEMS Pac Information Series no. 3 (Nairobi: UNEP, April 1982). Even this lower estimate is, of course, alarming.

3. Volume estimate from telephone interview by researcher

Rachel Schurman with David Pimentel, Cornell University, April 1986. Pesticides have become more potent over the years, so the increase in volume used actually underestimates the increased toxicity added to the environment. Information on increased potency obtained in an interview by Rachel Schurman with Gary Ballard, Environmental Protection Agency, Office of Pesticide Programs, April 1986.

4. Estimates of pesticide poisonings span a tremendous range, from a low of 400,000 to a high of 2 million. See Michael J. Dover, *A Better Mousetrap: Improving Pest Management for Agriculture*, Study no. 4 (Washington, D.C.: World Resources Institute, 1985), 2–3. The estimate used for this calculation (1.5 million poisonings) is from the UN Economic and Social Council, as reported in Dover (table 1). Deaths from poisoning come from John E. Davies, ''Health Effects of the Global Use of Pesticides,'' World Resources Institute Report, Washington, D.C., 1985.

5. For background on African agriculture and the impact of colonialism, see Paul Richards, *Indigenous Agricultural Revolution: Ecology and Food Production in West Africa* (Boulder, CO: Westview, 1985), chapters 1–3; Robert Chambers, *Rural Development: Putting the Last First* (London: Longman, 1983), chapters 3–4; Walter Rodney, *How Europe Underdeveloped Africa* (Washington, D.C.: Howard University Press, 1981); and Bill Rau, *From Feast to Famine* (Washington, D.C.: Africa Faith and Justice Network, 1985).

6. Richard Franke and Barbara Chasin, ''Peasants, Peanuts, Profits, and Pastoralists,'' *The Ecologist* 11, no. 4 (1981): 162. For a more complete picture by the same authors see *Seeds of Famine: Ecological Destruction and the Development Dilemma in the West African Sahel* (Totowa, NJ: Rowman and Allanheld, 1980).

7. Randall Baker, ''Protecting the Environment Against the Poor,'' *The Ecologist* 14, no. 2 (1983): 56. The colonial pattern of confining black Africans to the least fertile areas continues today in South Africa and occupied Namibia.

8. Franke and Chasin, *Seeds of Famine*, chapter 3.

9. Preparatory Committee of the Whole for the Special Session of the General Assembly on the Critical Economic Situation in Africa, ''Working Paper on the Critical Economic Situation in Africa,'' United Nations 86-04793, 1986,7; Anders Wijkman and Lloyd Timberlake, *Natural Disasters: Acts of God or Acts of Man?* (London and Washington, D.C.: Earthscan, 1984).

10. Michael Watts, ''Drought, Environment and Food Security,'' in *Drought and Famine in Africa*, ed. Michael Glantz (Cambridge: Cambridge University Press, 1986).

11. Franke and Chasin, ''Peasants, Peanuts, Profits, and Pastoralists,'' 163.

12. Watts, ''Drought, Environment and Food Security.''

13. Frances Moore Lappé and Joseph Collins with Cary Fowler, *Food First: Beyond the Myth of Scarcity* (New York: Ballantine Books, 1979), 44–48, 84–95. See also Jeremy Swift, "Disaster and a Sahelian Nomad Economy," in *Drought in Africa*, ed. David Dalby and R. J. Harrison (London: Centre for African Studies, 1973), 71–79; and F. Fraser Darling and M. T. Farvar, "Ecological Consequences of Sedentarization of Nomads," in *The Careless Technology: Ecology and International Development*, ed. M. T. Farver and John P. Milton (Garden City, NJ: Natural History Press, 1972).

14. The following studies contain a wealth of material on the erosion crisis: U.S. Congress, Office of Technological Assessment, *Impacts of Technology on U.S. Cropland and Rangeland Productivity* (Washington, D.C.: Government Printing Office, 1982); Comptroller General of the United States, *To Protect Tomorrow's Food Supply, Soil Conservation Needs Priority Attention—A Report to Congress* (Washington, D.C.: Government Printing Office, 1977); and National Agricultural Lands Study, *Soil Degradation: Effects on Agricultural Productivity* (Washington, D.C.: Government Printing Office, 1980).

15. Robert Gray, "Farmland Conservation: A Major Breakthrough," *Food Monitor* 35: 6. (No date in issue.)

16. Dennis Cory, "Estimation of Regional Planted Acreage and Soil Erosion Losses for Alternative Export Demand Projections and Conservation Technologies: A Macro-Economic Approach" (Ph.D. dissertation, Iowa State University, 1977), 98ff.

17. Calculated from U.S. Department of Agriculture, Economic Research Service, *Foreign Agricultural Trade of the United States: Calender Year 1984 Supplement* (Washington, D.C.: Government Printing Office, 1985), table 4.

18. Norman Myers, *GAIA: An Atlas of Planet Management* (New York: Anchor Books, Doubleday, 1984), 16f. See also Val Plumwood and Richard Routley, "World Rain Forest Destruction—the Social Factors," *The Ecologist* 12, no. 1 (1982): 16–18.

19. *Tropical Forests: A Call for Action*, Part I: The Plan, Report of an International Task Force of the World Resources Institute, the World Bank, and the United Nations Development Program (Washington, D.C.: World Resources Institute, 1985), 3.

20. Ibid. All figures on rain forest destruction are wide-ranging estimate, but no one questions that the destruction is widespread and rapid. See Alan Grainger, "The Tropical Rain Forest Dilemma," *The Ecologist* 11, no. 1 (January–February 1981): 48ff.

21. Bayard Webster, "Governments Move to Stem Amazon Destruction," *New York Times*, 20 November 1979, C3. At that time, one-fourth of the 2 million square miles of Amazonia rain

forest had been destroyed, the rate of destruction each year averaging 50,000 square miles. See also data from the National Institute for Amazonian Research (INPA) in Philip M. Fearnside, "A Floresta Vai Acabar?" *Ciencia Hoje*, Edicao Especial (1984); and "Deforestation in the Brazilian Amazon: How Fast Is It Occurring?" *Interciencia* 7, no. 2 (March–April 1982): 82–88.

22. Lester R. Brown, *State of the World 1986* (New York: W.W. Norton and Co., 1986), 70. See also Douglas R. Shane, *Hoofprints on the Forest: Cattle Ranching and the Destruction of Latin America's Tropical Forest* (Philadelphia: Institute for the Study of Human Issues, 1986). Shane notes that Latin America as a whole has lost some 37 percent of its original tropical forests—mostly in the last 30 years (Ibid., 4). In Central America in particular, over two-thirds of the tropical rain forests have been destroyed (Ibid., 10).
23. Myers, *GAIA*, 44.
24. Plumwood and Routley, "World Rain Forest Destruction," 5.
25. *Tropical Forests: A Call for Action*, 12.
26. Edward O. Wilson, "The Biological Diversity Crisis," *Bioscience* 35, no. 11 (December 1985): 703.
27. See, for instance, "Multilateral Banks and Indigenous Peoples," *Cultural Survival Quarterly* 10, no. 1 (1986). The entire issue is devoted to the impact of large development projects— many of which involve massive deforestation schemes—on indigenous peoples. See also Statement of Brent H. Millikan before the Subcommittee on Natural Resources, Agricultural Research and Environment of the Committee on Science and Technology, U.S. House of Representatives, Washington, D.C., 19 September 1984, 12–14; Teresa Hayter and Catherine Watson, *Aid: Rhetoric and Reality* (London: Pluto Press, 1985), 192; and Patricia Adams and Lawrence Solomon, *In the Name of Progress* (Toronto: Energy Probe Research Foundation, 1985), 20–21.
28. Myers, *GAIA*, 44, 116–117.
29. *Tropical Forests: A Call for Action*, 15.
30. Francis Urban and Thomas Vollrath, *Patterns and Trends in World Agricultural Land Use*, U.S. Department of Agriculture, Economic Research Service, Foreign Agricultural Economic Report no. 198, (Washington, D.C., 1984), table 2.
31. "The IMF and the Impoverishment of Brazil," Instituto Brasileiro de Analises Sociais e Economicas (IBASE), Rio De Janiero, 8 September 1985, 18. See also Mac Margolis, "Land Disputes Trigger Wave of Violence in Brazil," *Washington Post*, 29 August 1985.
32. Marlise Simons, "Landowners in Brazil Are Viewing 'Land Reform' as Fighting Words," *New York Times*, 1 July 1985.
33. "Politica Agraria o Regime Pos-64," IBASE, Rio de Janeiro, 29 January 1984, 1.

34. *Brazil Information*, edited by IBASE/FASE/CPT, Rio de Janeiro, (October–November 1985), 2.
35. Brent H. Millikan, Congressional Testimony, 19 September 1984, 3–4. See also an interview with a migrant in Rondonia, translated from Atila Calvente, "Formacoes Nao-Capitalistas no Moviemento doe Ocupacao da Amazonia: Colonizacao Agricola em Rondonia, 1970–1980," University of Brasilia, 1980, in Brent H. Millikan, "Rondonia: Migration and Rural Development on an Amazon Frontier" (unpublished manuscript, 1984), 40.
36. "Dossie Amazonia," IBASE, August 1985, 17.
37. See, for example, J. Foweraker, *The Struggle for Land* (Cambridge and New York: Cambridge University Press, 1981). See also Susanna B. Hecht, "Cattle Ranching Development in the Eastern Amazon: Evaluation of a Development Policy" (Dissertation, University of California, Department of Geography, 1982).
38. The Brazilian government has pulled back from actively promoting settlement in Amazonia, and in 1985 the World Bank halted loans to the project in response to worldwide denunciations. See Stephen Schwartzman, "World Bank Holds Funds for Development Projects in Brazil," *Cultural Survival Quarterly* 10, no. 1 (1986): 26.
39. Miguel Varon, "Colombia: Rich Forest Reserves Threatened," *Latinamerica Press* 17, no. 34 (19 September 1985): 3.
40. Plumwood and Routley, "World Rain Forest Destruction," 7. They estimate 60 percent.
41. In offering subsidies the government has been helped by World Bank loans, contributing to Brazil's crushing debt. See Susanna B. Hecht, "Environment, Development and Politics: Capital Accumulation and the Livestock Sector in Eastern Amazonia," *World Development* 13, no. 6 (1985): 663–684. See also Nigel J. H. Smith, "Colonization Lessons from a Tropical Forest," *Science* 214 (13 November 1981); and Lappé and Collins, *Food First*, chapter 7.
42. Data (for 1984) are from the Ministry of External Relations, Banco do Brasil, and were provided by the Brazilian consulate in San Francisco. See Hecht, "Environment, Development and Politics," 669. Brazil has become the world's leading producer of canned corned beef with about 50 to 55 percent of the world market. See also "Bordon Builds an Empire in Brazil's Booming Meat Industry," *Agribusiness Worldwide* 8, no. 2 (March 1986): 20.
43. Hecht, "Environment, Development and Politics," 670–672; and Brent H. Millikan, Congressional Testimony, 19 September 1984.
44. Hecht, "Environment, Development and Politics," 668. See also Plumwood and Routley, "World Rain Forest Destruction."
45. Nigel Smith, "Colonization Lessons from a Tropical Forest," *Science* 214 (13 November 1981): 756.

46. Between 1960 and 70, pasture lands in Panama reportedly increased by 43 percent, in Nicaragua by 48 percent, and in Costa Rica by 62 percent. See Shane, *Hoofprints on the Forest*, 10. Shane also notes that an estimated two-thirds of all arable land in the region is used for the production of livestock.

47. In Costa Rica, for example, nearly half of all agricultural credits through the late 1970s went to cattle ranching. See Bruce Rich, "Environmental Management and Multilateral Development Banks," *Cultural Survival Quarterly* 10, no. 1 (1986): 6. Rich also reports that the total investments channeled into Latin American livestock projects (including government matching funds) by the World Bank and the Inter-American Bank between 1970 and 1977 was $5–7 billion, or about $10–14 billion in 1984 dollars. "No other single commodity in developing countries has ever received such extraordinary outside support," observes Rich (p. 6). See also James D. Nations and Daniel I. Komer, "Rain Forests and the Hamburger Society," *Environment* 25, no. 3 (April 1983): 16.

48. Data on grain productivity (for Honduras) come from Billie DeWalt, "Microcosmic and Macrocosmic Processes of Agrarian Change in Southern Honduras: The Cattle Are Eating the Forest," in *Micro and Macro Levels of Analysis in Anthropology: Issues in Theory and Research*, ed. Billie DeWalt and Pertti J. Pelto (Boulder, CO: Westview, 1985), 176. Data on meat productivity (for Costa Rica) are from Catherine Caufield, *In the Rain Forest* (New York: Knopf, 1985), 117.

49. Billie R. DeWalt, "The Cattle Are Eating the Forest," *Bulletin of the Atomic Scientists* (January 1983): 22.

50. Shane, *Hoofprints on the Forest*, 78.

51. Legal commercial logging is estimated to affect 5 million hectares (12.4 million acres) of undisturbed forests every year. See *Tropical Forests: A Call for Action*. Note: if illegal logging were included, this figure would be far higher. (Trade records from the Philippines and Thailand, for instance, indicate that more trees are logged illegally than legally!)

52. For more on the forces behind rain forest destruction in Indonesia, see K. Kartawinata and A. P. Vayda, "Forest Conversion in East Kalimantan, Indonesia: The Activities and Impact of Timber Companies, Shifting Cultivators, Migrant Pepper-farmers and Others," in *Ecology in Practice*, ed. F. DiCastri, F. W. G. Baker, and M. Hadley (Paris: UNESCO).

53. *Tropical Forests: A Call For Action*, 10.

54. Plumwood and Routley, "World Rain Forest Destruction," 9–11.

55. Ibid., 13.

56. Ibid., 14.

57. Telephone interview by researcher Rachel Schurman with

David Pimentel, Cornell University, April 1986.

58. "Pesticide Industry Sales and Usage: 1984 Market Estimates," Environmental Protection Agency, Economic Analysis Branch, Office of Pesticide Programs (Washington, D.C., September 1985), table 4. See also Philip Shabecoff, "Pesticide Control Finally Tops EPA's List of Most Pressing Problems," *New York Times*, 6 March 1986.

59. Mike Lewis and Allan Woodburn, *Agro-Chemical Service 1984* (London: Wood, Mackensie and Co., 1984), 3, 11.

60. Dover, *A Better Mousetrap*, 2.

61. Robert Wasserstrom and Richard Wiles, *Field Duty: U.S. Farmworkers and Pesticide Safety* (Washington, D.C.: World Resources Institute, 1985), 37–39.

62. Jack Doyle, "Biotechnology's Harvest of Herbicides," *Genewatch* 2, (November–December 1985): 1.

63. David Weir and Mark Schapiro, *Circle of Poison* (San Francisco: Food First Books, 1981), 4.

64. *Suara Sam* 2, no. 5 (October, 1985): 4. Newsletter of Sahabat Alam Malaysia/Friends of the Earth.

65. David Weir, *The Bhopal Syndrome: Pesticide Manufacturing and the Third World* (Penang, Malaysia: International Organization of Consumers Unions, 1986).

66. Shabecoff, "Pesticide Control."

67. Ibid.

68. Ibid.

69. Ibid. A 1984 investigation by the Academy of Sciences found that 64 percent of pesticides have not even been minimally tested for their toxic effects. See National Research Council, "Toxicity Testing: Strategies to Determine Needs and Priorities," March 1984, 11–12, 83–85, cited in Lawrie Mott and Martha Broad, *Pesticides in Food: What the Public Needs to Know* (San Francisco: Natural Resources Defense Council, Inc., 1984), 2.

70. The lower estimate is from the EPA's "Pesticide Industry Sales and Usage," table 3, and the higher estimate, from David Pimentel and Lois Levitan, "Pesticides: Amounts Applied and Amounts Reaching Pests," *Bioscience* 36, no. 2 (February 1986): 86.

71. *New York Times*, 6 March 1986, citing U.S. Department of Agriculture study.

72. Pimentel and Levitan, "Pesticides," 90.

73. Dover, *A Better Mousetrap*, 7. See also U.S. Congress, Office of Technology Assessment, *Pest Management Strategies in Crop Protection* (Washington, D.C.: Government Printing Office, 1979).

74. Interview with Gary Ballard at the Environmental Protection Agency, Economic Analysis Branch, April 1986.

75. David Pimentel et al., "Benefits and Costs of Pesticides in U.S. Food Production," *Bioscience* 28 (1978): 772, 778–783.

76. Correspondence from J. P. Hrabovszky, Food and Agriculture Organization, United Nations, 1976, quoting W. R. Furtick, chief of Plant Protection Service. It is not surprising that pesticides are concentrated on export crops, not staple foods. First, food producers are often the poorest farmers who simply cannot afford their cost. Second, planted uniformly in vast expanses, export-crop operations are much more vulnerable to pests than smaller-scale, mixed-crop farms. Third, since pesticides must be imported in most countries, they are likely to be used on crops that can earn foreign exchange needed to pay for such imports.
77. Communication from John Scheuring, International Crops Research Institute for Semiarid Tropics, Bamako, Mali, 8 January 1986.
78. Robert Repetto, *Paying the Price: Pesticide Subsidies in Developing Countries* (Washington, D.C.: World Resources Institute, 1985), 1.
79. Ibid., 1.
80. Dover, *A Better Mousetrap*, 5–6.
81. L. B. Brattsten et al., "Insecticide Resistance: Challenge to Pest Management and Basic Research," *Science* 231 (14 March 1986): 1255.
82. Georganne Chapin and Robert Wasserstrom, "Agricultural Production and Malaria Resurgence in Central America and India," *Nature* 293, no. 5829 (17 September 1981): 181–185.
83. Ibid., 183.
84. The specific project referred to here is the Polonoreste development scheme discussed earlier in this chapter. It should be noted that, while disbursement of these loans has been halted, the loans have not been cancelled altogether.
85. Jeffrey Leonard, *Divesting Nature's Capital* (New York: Holmes & Meier Publishers, 1985), 109.
86. Environmental Project on Central America, c/o Earth Island Institute, 4089 26th St., San Francisco, CA 94131.
87. Anumpam Mishra, "The Forest Cover 'Chipko Movement' in North India," in *Readings on Poverty and Development* (Rome: FAO, 1980); Pandurang Ummayya and J. Bandyopadhyay, "The Trans-Himalayan Chipko Footmarch," *The Ecologist* 13, no. 5 (1983).
88. Pesticide Education and Action Project, affiliated with the Pesticide Action Network, 1045 Sansome St., San Francisco, CA 94111.
89. Ibid. For the address of this organization and others addressing related problems, please refer to the resource guide at the end of the book.

The Green Revolution Is the Answer

MYTH · 5

1. Christopher J. Baker, "Frogs and Farmers: The Green Revolution in India, and Its Murky Past," in *Understanding Green Revolutions*, ed. Tim Bayliss-Smith and Sudhir Wanmali (New York: Cambridge University Press, 1984), 40. The first major Green Revolution in the Indian Punjab, for example, took place over 100 years ago when Punjabi farmers adopted three new varieties of sugarcane in a single generation, with striking results.

2. See, for example, Frederick H. Buttel, Martin Kenney, and Jack Kloppenburg, Jr., "From Green Revolution to Biorevolution: Some Observations on the Changing Technological Bases of Economic Transformation in the Third World," *Economic Development and Cultural Change* 34, no. 1 (October 1985): 31–55.

3. See Frances Moore Lappé and Joseph Collins with Cary Fowler, *Food First: Beyond the Myth of Scarcity* (New York: Ballantine Books, 1979); Andrew Pearse, *Seeds of Plenty, Seeds of Want: Social and Economic Implications of the Grain Revolution* (New York: Oxford University Press, 1980), a summary of the findings of the UN Research Institute for Social Development on the impact of the Green Revolution in more than a dozen countries; Susan George, *How the Other Half Dies* (London: Penguin, 1976); Keith Griffin, *The Political Economy of Agrarian Change: An Essay on the Green Revolution*, 2nd ed. (London: Macmillan, 1979); Keith Griffin and Jeffrey James, *Transition to Egalitarian Development: Economic Policies for Structural Change in the Third World* (New York: St. Martin's Press, 1981); and George Kent, *The Political Economy of Hunger: The Silent Holocaust* (New York: Praeger, 1984).

4. Husain is chairman of the Consultative Group on International Agricultural Research, quoted in *The Bank's World* 4, no. 12 (1985): 1.

5. World Bank, *Poverty and Hunger: Issues and Options for Food Security in Developing Countries* (Washington, D.C.: World Bank, 1986), 49.

6. Ibid., 1–3. The bank estimates that there are 730 million without enough food for an active working life, among whom are 340 million without enough income to obtain diets to prevent serious health risks and stunted growth. Worldwide this report suggests the proportion of hungry fell slightly, if one assumes

no worsening in income distribution over the decade, an assumption the bank calls "optimistic." We find this assumption to be untenable, given the widely acknowledged deterioration of the position of the poor in Africa, South Asia, Central America, the Caribbean, the Philippines, and Chile. By the 1980s, the position of the poor in Brazil and Mexico had clearly fallen as well.

7. Paul Lewis, "The Green Revolution Bears Fruit," *New York Times*, 2 June 1985.
8. Wheat production per person in South Asia has almost doubled since the mid-1960s, and rice is up significantly in several countries.
9. World Bank, *Poverty and Hunger*, 1.
10. Ibid., 3.
11. "Huge Grains Surplus Poses Problems," *The Economic Times* (of India), 25 December 1985. India also has a $1 billion trade surplus. See U.S. Department of Agriculture, Economic Research Service, *Agricultural Outlook* (December 1985): 14.
12. USDA, *Agricultural Outlook* (December 1985): 18.
13. Food and Agriculture Organization, *Food Balance Sheets 1979–81* (Rome: FAO, 1984) and *Food Balance Sheets 1981–83*. See also U.S. Department of Agriculture, *World Food Aid Needs and Availabilities* (Washington, D.C.: USDA Economic Research Service, July 1984), table 40.
14. R. U. Qureshi, "Nutrition Considerations in Agriculture," FAO Regional Office for Asia and the Pacific, Bangkok, 1982, cited in George Kent, "Aid, Trade, and Hunger," *Food and Nutrition Bulletin* 7 (December 1985): 73–79. Calculated from *FAO Production Yearbook*, vols. 30 and 38 (Rome: FAO, 1976 and 1984).
15. Food and Nutrition Research Institute, *First Nationwide Nutrition Survey of the Philippines*, GP11, October 1979.
16. In 1979, Mexico's National Nutrition Institute reported that 52 percent of the population of Mexico existed on diets that did not meet minimal nutritional standards. On 16 June 1985, it was reported in *La Jornada* that 66 percent of the population was nutritionally deficient.
17. "Report on the Root Causes of Hunger and Food Insufficiency in Africa," Churches Drought Action in Africa (CDAA), Studies Subcommittee, coordinated by Catholic Relief Services, World Council of Churches and other churches, November 1985, 29.
18. "Rural Poverty," prepared by the Food and Agriculture Organization for World Food Day 1985, 2. See also Milton J. Esman, *Landlessness and Near Landlessness in Developing Countries* (Ithaca: Cornell University, Center for International Studies, 1978), 15, 36b; and Ghonemy et al., *Studies on Agrarian Reform and Rural Poverty*, Food and Agriculture Organization, Economic and Social Development Series no. 27 (Rome: FAO, 1984), 46.

19. Michael Lipton, "Inter-Farm, Inter-Regional and Farm Non-Farm Income Distribution: The Impact of the New Cereal Varieties," *World Development* 6, no. 3 (1978): 330. Lipton cites four studies from 1973 to 1974.

20. Azizur Rahman Khan and Eddy Lee, *Poverty in Rural Asia* (Bangkok: International Labour Organization and the Asian Employment Programme, 1984), 13.

21. Ibid., 11. Referring to real wages.

22. Consultative Group on International Agricultural Research, *Summary of International Agricultural Research Centers: A Study of Achievements and Potential* (Washington, D.C.: World Bank, 1985), 10.

23. Between 1973 and 1983 the number of tractors increased 94 percent in the "developing market economies." *FAO Production Yearbook*, vols. 29 and 38 (Rome: FAO, 1975, 1984).

24. Khan and Lee, *Poverty in Rural Asia*, 126–130.

25. Steven Sanderson, *The Transformation of Mexican Agriculture* (Princeton: Princeton University Press, 1986), tables 4.3, 4.7.

26. For a full explanation, see Cynthia Hewitt de Alcantara, "The Social and Economic Implications of the Large-Scale Introduction of New Varieties of Foodgrain," *Country Report—Mexico* (Geneva: UNDP/UNRISD, 1974).

27. T. J. Byres, B. Crow, and Mao Wan Ho, *The Green Revolution in India*, Third World Studies, Case Study 5 (London: Open University Press, 1983), 30.

28. Consultative Group, *Summary of International Agricultural Research Centers*, 6.

29. Yujiro Hayami and Vernon W. Ruttan, "The Green Revolution: Inducement and Distribution," *Pakistan Development Review* 23, no. 1 (Spring 1984): 37. See also Y. Hayami and V. W. Ruttan, *Agricultural Development: An International Perspective* (Baltimore: Johns Hopkins University Press, 1985). Note too that size is not always equivalent to wealth. Much will depend on the quality of the soil and access to irrigation. When these differences are considered, farmers with "higher incomes tend to be the main adopters" of the new seeds, observed an overview study of three Asian countries. See R. W. Herdt and C. Capule, *Adoption, Spread and Production Impact of Modern Rice Varieties in Asia* (Los Banos: International Rice Research Institute, 1983), 25.

30. D. P. Singh, "The Impact of the Green Revolution," *Agricultural Situation in India* 13, no. 8 (August, 1980): 323. See also M. Prahladachar, "Income Distribution Effects of Green Revolution in India: A Review of Empirical Evidences," *World Development* 11 (1983): 927–44; and G. S. Bhalla, *The Impact of the Green Revolution on Rural Structural Change* (Nagoya, Japan: UN Centre for Regional Development, 1982), 24.

31. Michael Lipton with Richard Longhurst, *Modern Varieties, International Agricultural Research, and the Poor*, Consultative

Group on International Agricultural Research, Study Paper no. 1 (Washington, D.C.: World Bank, 1985), 32.

32. Ibid., 31.
33. In 1983 to 1984, Sergy Floro of the Stanford Food Research Institute surveyed agricultural credit sources in the three Philippine provinces where rice growing is most concentrated. Results show that 80 to 85 percent of all loans are informal, with the majority averaging interest rates of 180 percent per year. Commercial rates available to the remaining 15 to 20 percent of the population were approximately 17 percent per year.
34. Dale W. Adams, Douglas H. Graham, and J. D. Von Pischke, "Overview of the Importance of Interest-Rate Policies" in *Undermining Rural Development with Cheap Credit*, ed. Dale Adams et al. (Boulder, CO: Westview Press, 1984), 63.
35. Small means less than one hectare. Yujiro Hayami and Masao Kikuchi, "Directions of Agrarian Change: A View from Villages in the Philippines," in *Agricultural Change and Rural Poverty*, ed. John W. Mellor and Gunvant M. Desai (Baltimore: Johns Hopkins University Press, 1985), 132ff. Both authors are noted Japanese economists formerly associated with the International Rice Research Institute, a center of Green Revolution research.
36. Lipton with Longhurst, *Modern Varieties*, 7.
37. World Bank, *World Development Report 1984* (New York: Oxford University Press, 1984), table 6.
38. For a discussion of pesticide dependency, see chapter 4. In India, an additional ton of fertilizer now produces less than half the yield of two decades ago, according to Steve Percy and Mike Hall, "Cornucopia for the Rich," *Spur*, newspaper of the World Development Movement, London, April 1986.
39. See, for example, Per Pinstrup-Andersen and Mauricio Jaramillo, "The Impact of Technological Change in Rice Production on Food Consumption and Nutrition in North Arcot, India," IFPRI/TANU Workshop on Growth Linkages, International Food Policy Research Institute, 1986, 19. Actually this village study shows a 44 percent increase in income but a threefold increase in expenditures from the early 1970s to the early 1980s, and chooses to use the expenditure figure as a more accurate meaure of income. Room is open for doubt. Moreover, this study shows a significant increase in land cultivated, so drawing any conclusion about the income contribution of the new seeds alone is difficult.
40. See, for example, John Harriss, "What Happened to the Green Revolution in South India? Economic Trends, Household Mobility and the Politics of an 'Awkward Class,'" IFPRI/TNAU Workshop on Growth Linkages, International Food Policy Research Institute, 1986, 29–30.
41. Hiromitsu Umehara, "Green Revolution for Whom?" in *Second*

View from the Paddy, ed. Antonio J. Ledsma et al. (Manila: Institute of Philippine Culture, Ateneo de Manila University), 34. Umehara is a senior research officer at the Institute of Developing Economies, Tokyo.

42. C. Ramasamy et al., "Changes in Village Household Welfare," IFPRI/TNAU Workshop on Growth Linkages, International Food Policy Research Institute, 1986. Small farmers compensated for lower farm income by performing wage labor for others, but larger farmers didn't and their total income fell.

43. John Harriss, "What Happened to the Green Revolution," 31.

44. Sulak Sivaraksa, "Rural Poverty and Development in Thailand, Indonesia, and the Philippines," *The Ecologist* 15, no. 5/6 (1985): 267.

45. U.S. Department of Agriculture, Economic Research Service, *Economic Indicators of the Farm Sector: Income and Balance Sheet Statistics*, 1983 and 1984 (Washington, D.C.: Government Printing Office), tables 2 and 13.

46. U.S. Department of Agriculture, Economic Research Service, "Profile of the Superfarms," *Farmline* (August–September 1983): 4.

47. USDA, Economic Indicators of the Farm Sector, 1984, tables 27 and 28. In 1984, for the bottom 50 percent of all farms, average net farm income was $6,166 and income from off-farm sources was $6,807. Calculated from USDA, *Economic Indicators of the Farm Sector*, 1984, tables 27, 33, and 34.

48. See the following chapter for a discussion of the comparative efficiency of large and small farmers.

49. Not only can the biggest farms take advantage of bulk discounts in purchasing and premium prices for large volume sales, but they also benefit disproportionately from contracts with processors and from tax policies favoring large capital investments.

50. Umehara, "Green Revolution for Whom?" 37.

51. U.S. General Accounting Office, "U.S. Food/Agriculture in a Volatile World Economy: Agriculture Overview," November 1985, 8. See also James Wessel with Mort Hantman, *Trading the Future* (San Francisco: Food First Books, 1983), Chapter 6; and Ingolf Vogeler, *The Myth of the Family Farm: Agribusiness Dominance of U.S. Agriculture* (Boulder, CO: Westview Press, 1981).

52. Jack Doyle, "The Agricultural Fix," *Multinational Monitor* 7, no. 4 (February 1986): 3.

53. Frederick H. Buttel and Randolph Barker, "Emerging Agricultural Technologies, Public Policy, and Implications for Third World Agriculture," *American Journal of Agricultural Economics* 67, no. 5 (December 1985): 1170–1175.

54. Martin Kenney and Frederick Buttel, "Biotechnology: Prospects

and Dilemmas for Third World Development," *Development and Change* 16 (1985): 61–91.

55. Doyle, "The Agricultural Fix," 3. See also Jack Doyle, *Altered Harvest: Agriculture, Genetics and the Fate of the World's Food Supply* (New York: Viking, 1985).
56. Kenney and Buttel, "Biotechnology," 68.
57. Ibid., 68–69.
58. A. de Janvry and K. Subbarao, "Agricultural Price Policy and Income Distribution in India," *Economic and Political Weekly* 19 (December 1984): A-177.
59. Pierre Spitz, *Food Systems and Society in India* (Geneva: UN Research Institute for Social Development, 1985), 346. Others argue that the protein foregone in legumes is made up in the greater intake of wheat with its higher protein content compared to most other grains. It would seem, however, hard to document that the poor have access to enough of the new wheat to make up for such a dramatic cutback in legumes (given that most legumes contain three times the protein of grains). The argument also ignores the fact that legumes and grain consumed together yield more usable protein than either eaten alone. Finally, the argument ignores the question of taste and satisfaction altogether.
60. Some claim that in general it has. See Per Pinstrup-Andersen and Peter B.R. Hazell, "The Impact of the Green Revolution and Prospects for the Future," International Food Policy Research Institute, 13.
61. Lipton with Longhurst, *Modern Varieties*, citing Siamwalla and Haykin, *The World Rice Market: Structure, Conduct and Performance*, Research Report no. 39 (Washington, D.C.: International Food Policy Research Institute, 1983).
62. Prices for food consumed by agricultural workers in India increased by 25 percent relative to agricultural worker's wages in the period 1972 to 1984. See International Labour Office, *Yearbook of Labor Statistics*, 1982 and 1984 (Geneva, ILO), tables 21 and 24. In Mexico, food prices increased by 10.7 percent relative to consumer price index over the period 1972 to 1981 (Ibid.). In India, food prices climbed faster after the Green Revolution began than in the period 1950 to 1966, before it had taken off, according to Spitz, *Food Systems*, 159. In Pakistan, rice and wheat prices rose by 2.7 percent relative to the consumer price index in the period 1971 to 1984, *Pakistan Statistical Yearbook* 1975, 1985, tables 17.6 and 17.20. And in the Philippines, internal rice prices nationwide nearly tripled relative to wages in Manila during the period 1973 to 1980, according to the Republic of the Philippines National Economic and Development Authority, *Philippine Statistical Yearbook* (Manila, 1984), table 2.32, and the International Monetary Fund, *International*

Financial Statistics Yearbook, vol. 38 (Washington, D.C.: IMF, 1985), table 2.

63. de Janvry and Sabbarao, "Agricultural Price Policy," A-177.
64. According to the National Nutrition Institute of Mexico, 66 percent of the population is nutritionally deficient. Reported in *La Jornada*, 16 June 1985.
65. Sanderson, *Transformation of Mexican Agriculture*, tables 4.7 and 4.8.
66. Ibid., table 4.1.
67. Billie R. DeWalt, "Mexico's Second Green Revolution," *Mexican Studies* 1, no. 1 (Winter, 1985): 30.
68. Ibid., 49.
69. David Barkin and Billie R. DeWalt, "Sorghum, the Internationalization of Capital and the Mexican Food Crisis" (Paper presented at the American Anthropological Association Meeting, Denver, 16 November 1984), 14.
70. Ibid., 16.
71. Sanderson, *Transformation of Mexican Agriculture*, table 4.3.
72. DeWalt, "Mexico's Second," 49.
73. Interview by researcher Jeremy Sherman with Pan A. Yotopoulos, agricultural economist, Stanford Research Institute, May 1986. Yotopoulos's calculations are based on FAO, *Food Balance Sheets*, 1983–84.
74. Pan A. Yotopoulos, "Competition for Cereals: The Food-Feed Connection," *Ceres* 17 (September–October 1984): 23.
75. Calculated from *FAO Production Yearbook and FAO Trade Yearbook*, 1974 and 1984. Estimate based on period 1973 to 1983.
76. Many who refuse to acknowledge greater equity as a precondition of ending hunger use the northwest Indian state of Punjab as their showcase. The Punjab produces 80 percent of India's wheat and almost half its rice on less than 2 percent of its farmland. But the Punjab was among India's most prosperous states well before the Green Revolution. It also received a grossly disproportionate share of government help. Food grain production in the Punjab climbed by two-thirds per person in the decade ending in 1973; nevertheless, the share of people in poverty dropped only 5 points, from 39 to 34 percent. If anything, the experience of the Punjab only reinforces the lessons of this chapter. Even under the most favorable circumstances, its narrow production strategy has not eliminated hunger. In any case, how could the Punjab's development, built on resources able to grow over half of India's wheat and rice on a tiny share of its farmland, be a relevant model for the rest of India or for the rest of the third world? For a helpful discussion, see Sudipto Mundle, "Land, Labour and the Level of Living in Rural Punjab," in *Poverty in Rural Asia*, ed. Khan and Lee, 85.

77. Keith Griffin, "World Hunger and the World Economy" (Paper prepared for a conference on Obstacles in the International Economy to Meeting Food Requirements, Logan, Utah, May 1985, revised July 1985), 26. See also Keith Griffin, *Institutional Reform and Economic Development in the Chinese Countryside* (London: Macmillan, 1984), chapter 1.

78. Bharat Dogra, "Hunger: A Report on India," *Social Change*, Paper no. 5 (New Dehli: Bharat Dogra, 1983). See also C. Gopalan, "Development and Deprivation: The Indian Experience," *Economic and Political Weekly* 18, no. 52 (December 1983): 2164.

79. Interview with David Chu, University of California, Berkeley Center of Chinese Studies, May 1986.

80. A. K. Sen, "Food Battles: Conflicts in the Access to Food," *Food and Nutrition* 10, no. 1 (January 1985): 85.

81. Wild varieties refers to what are technically called landraces, which are genetically related to modern cultivated crops and are used as an index of genetic diversity. Their genes are used to improve cultivated varieties.

82. Pat Roy Mooney, "The Law of the Seed: Another Development in Plant Genetic Resources," *Development Dialog* 1, no. 2 (1983): 11, 14. See also Mooney's *Seeds of the Earth: A Private or Public Resource?* (Ottawa: Interpares Press, 1979), distributed by Food First Books, Institute for Food and Development Policy, San Francisco; and Garrison Wilkes, "Current Status of Crop Plant Germplasm," *CRC Critical Reviews in Plant Science* 1, no. 2 (1983): 133–181.

83. Marcia H. Pimentel, "Food for People," in *Food and Energy Resources* (New York: Academic Press Inc., 1984), 83.

84. Tim P. Bayliss-Smith, "Energy Flows and Agrarian Change in Karnataka: The Green Revolution at Micro-scale," in *Understanding Green Revolutions*, ed. Bayliss-Smith and Wanmali, 169–170. While types of energy are not strictly comparable, such comparisons are meaningful in designing agricultural systems appropriate to farmers with varying access to energy sources.

85. Donald Q. Innis, "Grow More on Less Land," *The New Farm* (January 1984), 38.

86. Miguel A. Altieri and M. Kat Anderson, "An Ecological Basis of the Development of Alternative Agricultural Systems for Small Farmers in the Third World," *American Journal of Alternative Agriculture* 1, no. 1 (1986): 33–34. See also Miguel A. Altieri, *Agroecology: The Scientific Basis of Alternative Agriculture* (Berkeley: University of California, Division of Biological Control, 1983), ix; and William C. Beets, *Multiple Cropping and Tropical Farming Systems* (Boulder, CO: Westview Press, 1982).

87. Altieri and Anderson, "An Ecological Basis," 30.

88. From correspondence with Miguel Altieri, May 1986.
89. Doyle, "The Agricultural Fix," 5.
90. Innis, "Grow More on Less Land." See also Donald Q. Innis, "The Future of Traditional Agriculture," *Focus* 30 (January–February 1980): 3. Also look for Innis's forthcoming *Intercropping: The Scientific Basis of Traditional Agriculture*.
91. For a useful discussion, see Paul Richards, "Ecological Change and the Politics of African Land Use," *African Studies Review* 26, no. 2 (June 1983).
92. Peter H. Freeman and Tomas B. Fricke, "Traditional Agriculture in Sahelia: A Successful Way to Live," *The Ecologist* 13, no. 6 (1983): 210–212.

Justice vs. Production

M Y T H · 6

1. In Brazil, 340 landowners possess more land (117 million acres) than 2.5 million small farmers. Leaving 13 percent completely idle, big Brazilian landowners devote 76 percent to largely unimproved pasture. See *Alguns dados sobre o solo agrario no Brasil*, Instituto Brasileiro de Analises Socias e Economicas (IBASE), August 1982.
2. Food and Agriculture Organization, *Agricultural Development and Employment Performance: A Comparative Analysis*, Agricultural Planning Studies no. 18 (FAO, 1974). Large refers to those over 86 acres. Those below 10 acres cultivated 72 percent. Large landholding interests such as banana, cotton, and sugarcane estates also take control of much more land than they need to plant their crops precisely to make the land unavailable to the majority in the countryside. Land-poor families will then have little choice but to seek work on the estates, even at miserable wages. See also a widely cited study done by the Food and Agriculture Organization in 1960, which shows that large farmers in South America plant little of their land. *Report on the 1960 World Census of Agriculture*, cited in Robert A. Berry and William R. Cline, *Agrarian Structure and Productivity in Developing Countries* (Baltimore: Johns Hopkins University Press, 1979), table D1.
3. Small farms defined as having less than five acres. See Giovanni Andrea Cornia, "Farm Size, Land Yields and the Agricultural Production Function: An Analysis for Fifteen Developing Countries," *World Development* (April 1985): 518.
4. Ibid., 531.
5. Keith Griffin, *The Green Revolution: An Economic Analysis*

(Geneva: UN Research Institute for Social Development, 1972).

6. International Labour Office, *Employment, Incomes and Equality* (Geneva: ILO, 1977).

7. Food and Agriculture Organization, *Land, Food and People* (Rome: FAO, 1984), 59.

8. Thomas A. Miller, Gordon E. Rodewald, and Robert G. McElroy, *Economies of Size in U.S. Field Crop Farming*, Agricultural Economic Report no. 472 (Washington, D.C.: U.S. Department of Agriculture, Economics and Statistics Service). See also J. Patrick Madden, *Economies of Size in Farming* (Washington, D.C.: U.S. Department of Agriculture, Economic Research Service, 1967); and Warren Bailey, *The One-Man Farm* (Washington, D.C.: U.S. Department of Agriculture, Economic Research Service, August 1973).

9. U.S. Department of Agriculture, *A Time to Choose: Summary Report on the Structure of Agriculture* (Washington, D.C.: USDA, 1981), 58f.

10. Calculated from USDA, *A Time to Choose*, table 24. For additional explanation and discussion, see James Wessel with Mort Hantman, *Trading the Future* (San Francisco: Food First Books, 1983), chapter 3, 49–51.

11. About 90 percent of all the land is worked in whole or in part by sharecroppers and day laborers. See F. Tomasson Jannuzi and James T. Peach, "Report on the Hierarchy of Interests in Land in Bangladesh," University of Texas, Austin, for U.S. Agency for International Development, Washington, D.C., September 1977.

12. Ibid. In Bangladesh, sharecroppers generally must hand over one-half to two-thirds of their harvest to landlords. Only rarely do landlords contribute to the purchase of seeds and fertilizers.

13. Iowa studies by John F. Timmons and Wade Hauser of Iowa State University, cited in Erik Eckholm, *Dispossessed of the Earth: Land Reform and Sustainable Development*, Worldwatch Paper 30 (Washington, D.C.: Worldwatch Institute, 1979). The Iowa studies found 21 tons per acre per year losses on the tenant-operated farms compared to 16 tons on the owner-operated farms.

14. North Central Farm Management Research Committee, *Conservation Problems and Achievements on Selected Midwestern Farms* (Wooster: Ohio Agricultural Experiment Station, July 1951), cited in R. Burnell Held and Marion Clawson, *Soil Conservation in Perspective* (Baltimore: Johns Hopkins University Press, 1965).

15. U.S. Department of Commerce, Bureau of the Census, and the U.S. Department of Agriculture, Economic Research Service, *Farm Population of the United States: 1981* (Washington, D.C.: U.S. Department of Agriculture, Farm Population Series P-27, no. 55, 1981), 4.

16. To deal with the problem, the direction of agricultural reforms in recent years in Cuba and a number of socialist countries has been to make a group of workers responsible in effect for a small part of a state farm, with their pay reflecting their productivity. See Medea Benjamin, Joseph Collins, and Michael Scott, *No Free Lunch: Food and Revolution in Cuba Today* (New York: Grove Press/Food First Books, 1986), chapter 12. In Nicaragua, the government's response to a similar problem has been to turn state farmland over to the workers and other land-poor campesinos to work as privately owned cooperatives and individual family farms. See Joseph Collins, with Frances Moore Lappé, Nick Allen, and Paul Rice, *Nicaragua: What Difference Could a Revolution Make?* (New York: Grove Press/Food First Books, 1986), chapter 24.

17. Radha Sinha, *Landlessness: A Growing Problem* (Rome: FAO, 1984), 73.

18. For more detail, see two books by Betsy Hartmann and James Boyce, *Needless Hunger: Voices from a Bangladesh Village* and *A Quiet Violence: View from a Bangladesh Village* (San Francisco: Food First Books, 1979, 1982, and 1983).

19. Calculated from *FAO Production Yearbook 1978*, vol. 32. Averaged 1969 to 1978.

20. A. C. Delgado, "Determinación de pesticidas clorinados en leche materna del departamento de Leon," Monografia, Depto. de Biologia, Facultad de Ciencias y Letras, Universidad Nacional Autonoma de Nicaragua, Leon, 1978.

21. Steve O'Neil, "Hancock Is Willing to Meet the LSP," *The Land Stewardship Letter* (St. Paul, MN, 1985), 1.

22. Keith Schneider, "As More Family Farms Fail, Hired Managers Take Charge," *New York Times*, 17 March 1985, 1.

23. Food and Agriculture Organization, High Level Mission on the Follow-up to the World Conference on Agrarian Reform and Rural Development in Sri Lanka, 1984, 21.

24. Walter Goldschmidt, "160-Acre Limitation: It's Good for Farmers—and the Nation," *Los Angeles Times*, 4 December 1977. Goldschmidt's classic study in the 1940s contrasting two California towns has been reprinted in Walter Goldschmidt, *As You Sow* (Totowa, NJ: Rowman and Allanheld, 1978). Studies carried out in California in the 1970s came up with similar findings. See Isao Fujimoto, "The Communities of the San Joaquin Valley: The Relationship Between Scale of Farming, Water Use, and the Quality of Life," Testimony before the House Subcommittee on Family Farms, Rural Development, and Social Studies, Sacramento, CA, 28 October 1977.

25. R. Albert Berry and William R. Cline, *Agrarian Structure and Farm Productivity in Developing Countries* (Baltimore: Johns Hopkins University Press, 1979), 131.

26. Ibid. See also Eckholm, *Dispossessed of the Earth*, for a good

overview of the issues.

27. Berry and Cline, *Agrarian Structure*, 132.
28. Tania Krutscha, "Brazil's Large Landowners Brace to Resist Reform," *Latinamerica Press* (19 September 1985): 1.
29. See Martin Diskin, *Agrarian Reform in El Salvador: An Evaluation*, Food First Research Report (San Francisco: Institute for Food and Development Policy, 1985) for an in-depth analysis of land reform in El Salvador. See also Americas Watch, *With Friends Like These*, ed. Cynthia Brown (New York: Pantheon Books, 1985), chapter 4, for information on death squad activity.
30. World Bank, *Land Reform: Rural Development Series* (Washington, D.C.: World Bank, July 1974), 62.
31. Measured in kilograms per hectare. Calculated from the *FAO Production Yearbook 1984*, vol. 38, table 15.
32. World Bank, *Land Reform*, 62.
33. Ibid., 61. See also Eckholm, *Dispossessed of the Earth*, 22.
34. World Bank, *Land Reform*, 61. The highly authoritarian Chinese government of Taiwan, however, has not permitted farmers to form associations, so they remain without any collective bargaining power over the prices they pay for farm inputs and the prices they get for their produce. Caught in the price-cost squeeze, many farm families by the 1970s needed off-farm income to stay in farming. See Huang Shu-min, "Agricultural Degradation: Changing Community Systems in Rural Taiwan" (Ph.D. dissertation, Michigan State University, 1977).
35. Elizabeth Croll, *The Family Rice Bowl* (Geneva: UN Research Institute for Social Development, 1982). See also Croll's "Food Supply in China and the Nutritional Status of Children" (unpublished manuscript, 1985); and Paul B. Trescott, "Incentives Versus Equality: What Does China's Recent Experience Show?" *World Development* 13, no. 2 (1985): 205–217.
36. From 1978 through 1984. See U.S. Department of Agriculture, Economic Research Service, "China's Agricultural Revolution," *Agricultural Outlook* (December 1985): 19.
37. Collins et al., *Nicaragua: What Difference Could a Revolution Make?*, esp. chapter 24.
38. "Zimbabwe Success Holds Out Hope for Others in Africa," *Africa Emergency* 4 (September–October 1985): 3.
39. Folke Dovring, "Economic Results of Land Reforms," *Spring Review of Land Reform* (Washington, D.C.: U.S. Agency for International Development, June 1970).
40. Schlomo Eckstein et al., *Land Reform in Latin America: Bolivia, Chile, Mexico, Peru and Venezuela*, World Bank Staff Working Paper no. 275 (Washington, D.C.: World Bank, April 1978).
41. See Collins et al., *Nicaragua: What Difference Could a Revolution Make?*, for an in-depth look at the attempts of large landowners in Nicaragua to resist reform.
42. James D. Cockcroft, *Mexico: Class Formation, Capital*

Accumulation, and the State (New York: Monthly Review Press, 1983), 177, 195.
43. Diskin, *Agrarian Reform in El Salvador*.
44. An example of a nonauthoritarian, large-scale operation is the Coalition of Collective Ejidos in Mexico, a group of 50 collective farms and 30,000 people. See Medea Benjamin and Rebecca Buell, *The Coalition of Ejidos of the Valleys of Yaqui and Mayo, Sonora State, Mexico* (San Francisco: Institute for Food and Development Policy, 1985).

The Free Market Can End Hunger

M Y T H · 7

1. World Bank, *World Development Report 1984* (New York: Oxford University Press, 1984), table 5.
2. In both countries, banking, foreign trade, and energy are under direct government control while most goods and services are distributed through the market.
3. Donald J. Puchala and Jane Staveley, "The Political Economy of Taiwanese Agricultural Development," and Young Whan Kahn, "Politics and Agrarian Change in South Korean Rural Modernization by 'Induced' Mobilization," in *Food, Politics and Agricultural Development: Case Studies in the Public Policy of Rural Modernization*, ed. R. Hopkins et al. (Boulder, CO: Westview Press, 1979).
4. Cuba is one example. Although Cuba is the only country in the Western Hemisphere to have eliminated hunger, its experience provides no evidence that eliminating the market mechanism is necessary to end hunger. Moreover, the Cuban experience is replete with headaches for having virtually eliminated for many years a market in food. See Medea Benjamin, Joseph Collins, and Michael Scott, *No Free Lunch: Food and Revolution in Cuba Today* (New York: Grove Press/Food First Books, 1986).
5. *New York Times*, 5 January 1983. See also "Move over Cap'n Crunch: Pac-Man & His Pals Are Taking Over," *Business Week* (18 July 1983): 174.
6. Mort Hantman, *Export Agriculture: An Energy Drain*, Research Report (San Francisco: Institute for Food and Development Policy, 1984).
7. For a full discussion of the impact of the export-promotion strategy, see James Wessel with Mort Hantman, *Trading the Future* (San Francisco: Food First Books, 1983).
8. "Do Mergers Really Work?" *Business Week* (3 June 1985). For a discussion of current concentration in the U.S. economy, see J.

R. Munkirs, *The Transformation of American Capitalism* (Armonk, NY: M. E. Sharpe, 1984).

9. John Ratcliffe, "Social Justice and the Demographic Transition: Lessons from India's Kerala State," in *Practicing Health for All*, ed. D. Morley et al. (Oxford: Oxford University Press, 1983), 70–71.

10. See discussion of Ethiopian government policy in chapter 2.

11. A. V. Jose, "Poverty and Inequality—The Case of Kerala," in *Poverty in Rural Asia*, ed. Azizur Rahman Khan and Eddy Lee (Bangkok: International Labour Organization, Asian Employment Programme, 1983), 107ff.

12. Mark B. Lapping and V. Dale Forster, "Farmland and Agricultural Policy in Sweden: An Integrated Approach," *International Regional Science Review*, 7, no. 3 (1982): 297, 299.

13. Interview by Frances Moore Lappé with Tore Johansson of the Federation of Swedish Farmers, Stockholm, September 1982.

14. Javier Secenas Esquivel, "La Industria del Maís en México: Análisis de Precios y Subsidios" (Ph.D. Thesis, Universidad Autónoma Chapingo, México, 1984), table 25.

15. World Bank, *Poverty and Hunger: Issues and Options for Food Security in Developing Countries* (Washington, D.C.: World Bank, 1986), chapter 3.

Free Trade Is the Answer

M Y T H · 8

1. "Latin American Commodities Report," CR-81-15, 31 July 1981.

2. Survey of Brazilian homes conducted by the Brazilian Institute of Economics with the consultation of the U.S. Department of Agriculture, cited in Instituto Brasileiro de Analises Sociais e Economicas, IBASE, *The IMF and the Impoverishment of Brazil* (Rio de Janeiro: December 1985), 17.

3. Interview by researcher Jeremy Sherman with Thanyarat Tom Kulananan, commercial relations officer, Office of Commercial Counselor, Royal Thai Embassy, Washington, D.C., 5 May 1986.

4. Ho Kwon Ping, "Profits and Poverty in the Plantations," *Far Eastern Economic Review* (11 July 1980): 53.

5. Kraisid Trontisirin and Pattanee Winichagoon, *Malnutrition as a Social Indicator: Nutrition Problems in Thailand* (Thai University Research Association, Mahidol University, 1982), 31.

6. Likhit Dhiravegin, "Reaching Out in Silent Hunger," *Thai Development Newsletter* 3, no. 2 (1985): 9–11.

7. Solon Barraclough, director of the UN Research Institute for Social Development, "Agrarian Reform in Central America: Diversion or Necessity" (Paper delivered Washington, D.C., 15–16 May 1985), 2.

8. Billie R. DeWalt, "The Cattle are Eating the Forest," *Bulletin of Atomic Scientists* 39, no. 1 (January 1983): 22.

9. Policy Alternatives for the Caribbean and Central America (PACCA), *Changing Course: Blueprint for Peace in Central America and the Caribbean* (Washington, D.C.: Institute for Policy Studies, 1984).

10. Calculated from World Bank, *World Tables 1983*, 3rd ed. (Baltimore: Johns Hopkins University Press, 1984), tables 1, 2, and 6.

11. Alan Berg, *Malnourished People: A Policy View* (Washington, D.C.: World Bank, 1981), 66; and *World Development Report, 1985* (Washington, D.C.: World Bank, 1985), 220.

12. Jaime Crespi Soler, "El agro Chileno después de 1973: Expansión capitalista y campesinización pauperiante," Grupo de Investigaciones Agrarias, Academia de Humanismo Cristiano, Santiago, June 1981. See also Alain de Janvry, "Perspectives for Inter-American Foundation Programs in Chilean Agriculture," September 1983, 20.

13. Robert Carty, *Miracle or Mirage: A Review of Chile's Economic Model, 1973–1980* (Toronto: Latin American Working Group, 1982), 27.

14. George Kent, *The Political Economy of Hunger* (New York: Praeger, 1984), chapter 4.

15. The ad was reprinted in "Comparative (Dis)Advantage," *Dollars and Sense* 114 (March 1986): 15.

16. International Labor Office, *Yearbook of Labor Statistics* (Geneva: ILO, 1985), table 21. This 1983 wage rate is for agricultural workers in general.

17. G. A. Zepp and R. L. Simmons, *Producing Fresh Tomatoes in California and Baja California: Costs and Competition* (U.S. Department of Agriculture, ESCS Report, February 1980) 32, 37, cited in Steven E. Sanderson, *The Transformation of Mexican Agriculture, International Stucture and the Politics of Rural Change* (Princeton: Princeton University Press, 1986), 79.

18. Information provided by Robert Stauffer, Department of Political Science, University of Hawaii, May 1986.

19. Bernard Wideman, "Dominating the Pineapple Trade," *Far Eastern Economic Review* (8 July 1974).

20. "Latin America Commodities Report," CR-81-15.

21. Sanderson, *Transformation of Mexican Agriculture*, 47–49. See also Cynthia Hewitt de Alcantara, *Modernizing Mexican Agriculture: Socioeconomic Implications of Technological Change 1940–1970* (Geneva: UN Research Institute for Social Development, 1976).

22. According to Wideman, "Dominating the Pineapple Trade," Del Monte officials will not say what payment is made to the government's National Development Corporation for the use of the lands, but it is believed to be $44.78/ha/year. See also Eduardo Tadem, Johnny Reyes, and Linda Susan Magno, *Showcase of Underdevelopment: Fishes, Forest, and Fruits* (Davao City, Philippines: Alternative Resource Center, 1984), 178.

23. "Sugar Projects Threaten Peasant Agriculture," *Sugar World* 8,

no. 1 (March 1985): 6, published by the International Commission for the Co-ordination of Solidarity Among Sugar Workers, Toronto.

24. Ping, "Profits and Poverty," 53.
25. From interviews by Frances Moore Lappé with banana plantation workers, July 1977. See also Tadem et al., *Showcase of Underdevelopment*; and Rigorberto Tiglao, "The Political Economy of the Philippine Coconut Industry" in *Political Economy of the Philippine Commodities* (Quezon City: Third World Studies Program, 1983), 199.
26. World Bank, *World Tables 1983*, tables 2 and 6.
27. Food and Agriculture Organization, *FAO Trade Yearbook 1983*, vol. 37 (Rome: FAO, 1984); and Food and Agriculture Organization, *FAO Trade Yearbook 1975*, vol. 29 (Rome: FAO, 1976). Luxuries defined as meats, feed grains, and alcohol.
28. World Bank, *World Tables 1983*, tables 2 and 6.
29. *FAO Trade Yearbook 1983*, vol. 37 ; *FAO Trade Yearbook 1975*, vol. 29.
30. Exact years referred to are 1971 to 1978, when the urban population grew from 55 million to just under 74 million, the kidney bean harvest fell by 18 percent, corn by 4 percent, plantains by 18 percent, and cassava by 14 percent. See "Latin America Commodities Report," CR-81-15.
31. IBASE, *The IMF and the Impoverishment of Brazil*, 16f. During the period 1979 and early 1985, the minimum wage was increased only half as much as the increase in the prices of staple foods, and in 1982 over 40 percent of all Brazilians in the work force did not even earn the minimum wage. See *Latin America Weekly Report*, 22 March 1985, 12 and *Debt Bondage or Self-Reliance: A Popular Perspective on the Global Debt Crisis* (Toronto: GATT-Fly, 1985), 30.
32. Alan Garcia Perez, "Peru Wants an Historic Re-encounter with Its Land," speech by the president of Peru, *IFDA Dossier* 52 (March/April 1986): 23.
33. Ibid., 20.
34. Lloyd Timberlake, *Crisis in Africa* (London: Earthscan, 1985), 146.
35. See introductory chapter, n. 5.
36. World Conference on Agrarian Reform and Rural Development (WCARRD), *Examen et analyse de la reforme agraire et du développement rural dans les pays en voie de développement depuis le milieu des années soixante* (Rome: FAO, 1979), 113.
37. World Bank, *Price Prospects of Major Commodities* (Washington, D. C.: World Bank, 1984).
38. "Poor Outlook for Poor Nations," *The Economist* (9 November 1985): 81.
39. Peter F. Drucker, "The Changed World Economy," *Foreign Affairs* (Spring 1986): 771.
40. *FAO Trade Yearbook 1983*, vol. 37, 254.

41. Interview by Joseph Collins with Eric Witt, economist, USAID Mission, Khartoum, Sudan, March 1985.

42. Ibid.

43. *FAO Production Yearbook 1983*, vol. 37, table 61.

44. Willy Brandt, Commission on International Development Issues, *North-South Program for Survival* (Cambridge, MA: MIT Press, 1980), 86. This estimate refers to early 1970s.

45. Timberlake, *Crisis in Africa*, 70.

46. A. T. Bull, G. Holt, and M. D. Lilly, *International Trends and Perspectives in Biotechnology* (Paris: Organization for Economic Cooperation and Development, 1982), cited in Jack Doyle, "Biotechnology Research and Agricultural Stability," *Issues in Science and Technology* 2, no. 1 (Fall 1985): 111–124.

47. Barbara Dinham and Colin Hines, *Agribusiness in Africa* (Trenton, NJ: African World Press, 1984), 164.

48. Drucker, "The Changed World Economy," 774–775.

49. Bruce Cumings, "The Origins and Development of the Northeast Asian Political Economy: Industrial Sectors, Products Cycles, and Political Consequences," *International Organization* 38 (Winter 1984): 1–40. See also Larry E. Westphal, "The Republic of Korea's Experience with Export-Led Industrial Development," *World Development* 6, no. 3 (1978): 347–382; and Robert Wade, "South Korea's Agricultural Development: The Myth of the Passive State," *Pacific Viewpoint* 24, no. 6 (June 1983): 22–25.

50. Kumar Rupesinghe, "The Effects of Export-Oriented Industrialization in Sri Lanka," *The Ecologist* 15, no. 4/5 (1985): 246–256.

Too Hungry to Revolt

MYTH · 9

1. Medea Benjamin and Rebecca Buell, *Coalition of Ejidos of the Valleys of Yaqui and Mayo, Sonora State, Mexico* (San Francisco: Institute for Food and Development Policy, 1985).

2. Frances Moore Lappé and Joseph Collins, *Now We Can Speak: A Journey Through the New Nicaragua* (San Francisco: Food First Books, 1982), 106–111.

3. Joseph Collins with Frances Moore Lappé, Nick Allen, and Paul Rice, *Nicaragua: What Difference Could a Revolution Make?* (New York: Grove Press/Food First Books, 1986), chapter 24.

4. Medea Benjamin and Kevin Danaher, "Interview with Marcial Caballero," *Honduras Update* 3, no. 6 (March 1985): 4.

5. Medea Benjamin and Kevin Danaher, "Claiming What Was Ours to Begin With," *Food Monitor* (May 1986).

6. *World Food Assembly Bulletin* (July–December 1985), 7.

7. Wahidul Haque et al., *An Approach to Micro-Level Development:*

Designing and Evaluation of Rural Development Projects (UN Asian Development Institute, February 1977), 15.

8. Lasse Berg and Lisa Berg, *Face to Face* (Berkeley: Ramparts Press, 1971), 154.

9. Willy Randia, *Signes d'Espérance* (Lausanne, 1981), 65–76.

10. Daniel T. Spencer, "Eye Witness: A Week that Shook Port-au-Prince," *Christianity in Crisis* (17 March 1986), 81–83; and George S. Johnson, "Haiti and Lazarus: The Bible Comes Alive in Port-au-Prince," *Seeds* 9 , no. 4 (April 1986): 18–19.

11. "Emigrés: Un retour a la terre," *Famille et Développement*, no. 23 (October 1980): 48–59; "Devenir paysan," *Famille et Développement*, no. 6 (April 1976); and Pierre Pradervand, "Savoir se servir de la saison seche en Savane et au Sahel," *Construire* (27 March 1985) .

12. For a more complete account, see "Kuala Juru: A People's Cooperative," Institute Masyarakat Berhad and Consumer's Association of Penang, Penang, Malaysia.

More U.S. Aid Will Help the Hungry

M Y T H · 1 0

1. World Bank, *World Development Report 1985* (New York: Oxford University Press, 1985), table 18.

2. George Shultz, "Foreign Assistance Request for FY 1986," *Current Policy* no. 656, U.S. Department of State, Bureau of Public Affairs, Washington, D.C., 19 February 1985.

3. Economic assistance refers to development assistance, the Economic Support Fund, and PL 480 (food aid) combined. See U.S. Agency for International Development, *Congressional Presentation Fiscal Year 1987*, Main Volume, Parts I and II.

4. "U.S. Foreign Aid in the 1980s," *Policy Focus*, no. 4. (Washington, D.C.: Overseas Development Council, 1985), table 2. The ODC classifies aid recipients into four groups: low income, lower middle income, upper middle income, and high income. Per capita aid figures for the two middle groups (lower middle income and upper middle income) were $5.82 and $7.95, respectively.

5. United States Agency for International Development, *Congressional Presentation Fiscal Year 1987*, Main Volume, 664–668. Note: emergency Title II food aid funds were excluded from this calculation because they couldn't be associated with any particular country.

6. Ibid., 185–187, 664–668. These estimates were made by adding up the numerators (aid dollars) and denominators (population) across countries first, then dividing. Population data from Food

and Agriculture Organization, *FAO Production Yearbook 1984*, vol. 38 (Rome: FAO, 1984), table 3. Title II food aid includes emergency aid to Africa and supplementals.

7. United States Agency for International Development, *Congressional Presentation Fiscal Year 1987*, Main Volume, 185–187, 664–668. Data refer to 1985 and include supplemental and emergency appropriations for Africa. Population data come from the *FAO Production Yearbook 1984*, vol. 38, table 3. (Note that the Central America figure includes the population of countries that received no U.S. food aid, to be consistent with the Africa figures.)

8. U.S. policy governing the disbursement of Title I food aid is that it must be sold at prices at least as high as those set by the U.S. Commodity Credit Corporation.

9. During the 1984 to 1985 famine, the United States provided almost half of all emergency cereal shipments to Sub-Saharan Africa. See UN World Food Program, "Africa Task Force Secretariat Food Aid: Deliveries to African Countries Affected by Food Emergencies," Status Report no. 21, 1 April 1986, xi.

10. Calculated for period 1980 to 1985 from USAID *Congressional Presentations*, Main Volumes, 1982–1987. In addition, the United States also pays to transport emergency food aid.

11. See, for instance, "A Comparative Analysis of Five PL 480 Title I Impact Evaluation Studies," USAID Program Evaluation Discussion Paper no. 19, December 1983; and U.S. General Accounting Office, *Disincentives to Agricultural Production in Developing Countries*, Report to Congress, 26 November 1975.

12. North-South Institute, "Rural Poverty in Bangladesh: Report to a Like-Minded Group," Canada, April 1985, 70. See chapter 6 for a discussion of the potential of land reform to increase production.

13. Cited by Donald F. McHenry and Kai Bird, "Food Bungle in Bangladesh," *Foreign Policy* (Summer 1977): 74.

14. U.S. Department of Agriculture, Foreign Agricultural Service, *Food for Peace: 1984 Annual Report on Public Law 480* (Washington, D.C., USDA), table 6. Since the mid-1950s, $951 million in wheat and wheat products have been shipped to Africa under the Titles I and III programs of PL 480. This is equivalent to 52 percent of all Title I and III aid to Africa, valued at $1.8 billion.

15. Ernest Feder, *Perverse Development* (Manila: Foundation for Nationalist Study in the Philippines, 1983), 12–22. See also Walden Bello, David Kinley, and Elaine Elinson, *Development Debacle: The World Bank in the Philippines* (San Francisco: Food First Books, 1982).

16. Calculated from the first and second Nationwide Nutrition Surveys of the Philippines dated October 1979 and October 1984, cited in *IBON Facts and Figures* 57 (28 February 1985). See

also Gretta Goldenman, Joel Rocamora, and Kevin Danaher, "Philippines: Fed Up with Hunger," *Food First Action Alert* (San Francisco: Institute for Food and Development Policy, Spring 1986).

17. Based on supply of calories as a percent of requirements as reported in Ruth Leger Sivard, *World Military and Social Expenditures 1985* (Washington, D.C.: World Priorities, 1985), 39.

18. Martin Diskin, *Agrarian Reform in El Salvador: An Evaluation*, Food First Research Report (San Francisco: Institute for Food and Development Policy, 1985).

19. The first vote involved a U.S.–backed resolution condemning the Soviet downing of a Korean airliner, on which Zimbabwe abstained, while the second involved a resolution cosponsored by Zimbabwe condemning the U.S. invasion of Grenada. See Carol Lancaster, "U.S. Aid, Diplomacy and African Development," *Africa Report* (July–August 1984), and "Reagan's Zimbabwe Policy," *Washington Notes on Africa* (Winter 1984).

20. Public Law 98-151, 97th Statute no. 967, passed on 14 November 1983.

21. From a letter to former Chilean President Eduardo Frei, September 1970. Quoted in the U.S. Senate Interim Report of the Select Committee to Study Governmental Operations, "Alleged Assassination Plots Involving Foreign Leaders."

22. Joseph Collins, *Agrarian Reform and Counter-Reform in Chile*, Food First Research Report (San Francisco: Institute for Food and Development Policy, 1979).

23. James Petras and Philip Morley, *The United States and Chile: Imperialism and the Overthrow of the Allende Government* (New York: Monthly Review Press, 1975), 166–167.

24. Joseph Collins with Frances Moore Lappé, Nick Allen, and Paul Rice, *Nicaragua: What Difference Could a Revolution Make?* (New York: Grove Press/Food First Books, 1986).

25. U.S. Agency for International Development, *U.S. Overseas Loans and Grants, Obligations and Loan Authorizations, July 1, 1945–September 30, 1982* (Washington, D.C., 1983), 4; and USAID, *Congressional Presentation Fiscal Year 1987*, Main Volume, 664.

26. Ibid. (Deflator published in the "Security Assistance Volume" of the 1986 *Congressional Presentation*.)

27. Ibid. From $21.1 million in 1980 to $274.2 million in 1985. Adjusting for inflation, military aid to Latin America increased eightfold.

28. Ibid. From $119 million in 1980 to $168 million in 1985.

29. Rigoberta Menchú, *I . . . Rigoberta Menchú, An Indian Woman In Guatemala* (London: Verso, 1984), 133.

30. Charles William Maynes, former assistant secretary of state,

quoted in *World Development Forum* 1, no. 2 (31 December 1983): 3.

31. Sivard, *World Military and Social Expenditures 1985*, 14.
32. *World Military Expenditures and Arms Transfers 1985* (Washington, D.C.: U.S. Arms Control and Disarmament Agency, 1985), 42. Ruth Sivard states that it is not possible to accurately estimate Soviet military aid. She believes it is probably less than U.S. military aid, because the Soviet Union isn't as prone to give it away (interview by researcher Rachel Schurman with Ruth Sivard, April 1986).
33. Report from the Philippine women's group GABRIELA, at the Forum, Nairobi, Kenya, August 1985. Reprinted in *Connexions* 17–18 (Summer/Fall 1985): 53.
34. Based on data provided in Ruth Leger Sivard, *World Military and Social Expenditures 1983* (Washington, D.C.: World Priorities, 1983), 11.
35. See, for example, Guy Gran, ed., *Zaire: The Political Economy of Underdevelopment* (New York: Praeger, 1979); and Jonathan Kwitny, *Endless Enemies: The Making of an Unfriendly World* (New York: Congdon and Weed, 1984), chapter 6.
36. Sivard, *World Military and Social Expenditures 1983*, 19.
37. "Please Forget the Past," *The Economist* (12 October 1985): 48. The amount of aid to Zia comes from USAID *Congressional Presentation Fiscal Year 1987*, Main Volume, 667.
38. Grants and loans from the Economic Support Fund together with military assistance constitute approximately two-thirds of U.S. bilateral aid. Here we are not figuring in the budgetary support generated by recipient governments' resale of much of U.S. food aid.
39. Joint Ministerial Committee of the Boards of Governors of the World Bank and the International Monetary Fund on the Transfer of Real Resources to Developing Countries (also known as the Development Committee), *Aid for Development: The Key Issues* (Washington, D.C.: World Bank, 1985), 41. In the section of this report entitled, "Aid and the Poor," the Development Committee concedes that "rural development programs have usually been unable to benefit 'the poorest of the poor,' i.e., the lowest 20 percent or so of the rural income distribution."
40. "A Synthesis of AID Experience: Small-Farmer Credit, 1973–1985," AID Evaluation Special Study no. 41, October 1985, 11.
41. U.S. Senate, *Foreign Assistance and Related Programs Appropriations for Fiscal Year 1986, Hearings Before a Subcommittee of the Committee on Appropriations*, Ninety-Ninth Congress, Part 2, Appendices, 1985, 43–48.

42. USAID, *Congressional Presentation Fiscal Year 1986*, Main Volume, 659.

43. Frances Moore Lappé, Joseph Collins, and David Kinley, *Aid as Obstacle* (San Francisco: Food First Books, 1980 and 1981).

44. Brigette Erler, *Toedliche Hilfe*. (Frieburg: Dreisam Verlag, 1985), 10–13. Erler writes about the impact of aid programs in Bangladesh, where she was an official of the West German government's aid agency.

45. In fiscal year 1984, for instance, EXIM authorizations (which include loans, insurance, and guarantees) to the third world totaled about $2.6 billion, while CCC credits totaled $4.1 billion. See U.S. Treasury Department, National Advisory Council on International Monetary and Fiscal Policies, *International Finance*, Annual Report FY 1984 (Washington, D.C., 1985), 347–349, and 352–354. That same year, the total value of U.S. development assistance and the Economic Suppport Fund was $4.6 billion. See USAID, *Congressional Presentation Fiscal Year 1986*, Main Volume, 658.

46. Center for International Policy, *Human Rights and the U.S. Foreign Assistance Program: FY 1978*, Part I—Latin America (Washington, D.C., 1977).

47. Kevin Danaher, *The Political Economy of U.S. Policy Toward South Africa* (Boulder, CO: Westview Press, 1985), 68.

48. Export-Import Bank of the United States, *Five Decades of Progress: 1984 Annual Report* (Washington, D.C., 1985).

49. Loans from the multilateral agencies such as the World Bank and Inter-American Development Bank—where the U.S. holds the largest share of votes—have also increased dramatically over the last five or so years. See W. Frick Curry, "Subsidizing Pinochet: Aid and Comfort for the Chilean Dictatorship," *International Policy Report* (Washington, D.C.: Center for International Policy, 1985), 5.

50. International Monetary Fund, *Role and Function of the International Monetary Fund* (Washington, D.C.: IMF, 1985), 94.

51. *Debt Crisis or Self-Reliance: A Popular Perspective on the Global Debt Crisis* (Toronto: GATT-Fly, 1985), 29.

52. Tony Bogues, "Jamaica: IMF Measures Bring Rising Prices, Falling Wages," *Latinamerica Press* (24 October 1985), 5.

53. Marc Edelman, "Back from the Brink," *NACLA Report on the Americas* (November/December 1985), 42–43; Cameron Duncan, "IMF Conditionality, Fiscal Policy, and the Pauperization of Labor in Costa Rica," Department of Economics, American University (Paper prepared for the American Economic Association's Annual Meeting, December 1985).

54. Edelman, "Back from the Brink," 43.

55. World Bank, *Annual Report 1985* (Washington, D.C.: World Bank, 1985), 18; USAID, *Congressional Presentation Fiscal Year*

1987, Main Volume, 664. (Economic assistance includes development assistance, the ESF, and PL 480.)

56. For a critical examination of the World Bank, see Cheryl Payer, *The World Bank: A Critical Analysis* (New York: Monthly Review Press, 1982); Teresa Hayter and Catherine Watson, *Aid: Rhetoric and Reality* (London: Pluto Press, 1985); Bello et al., *Development Debacle*; and Jill Torrie, ed., *Banking on Poverty: the Global Impact of the IMF and World Bank* (Toronto: Between the Lines, 1983).

57. Patricia Adams and Lawrence Solomon, *In the Name of Progress: The Underside of Foreign Aid* (Toronto: Energy Probe Research Foundation, 1985), 89; and John Madeley, "Leaks and Landslides Loom in Sri Lanka," *The New Scientist* (7 April 1983). For a general discussion of the impact of large dams, many of which are funded by the World Bank, see Edward Goldsmith and Nicholas Hildyard, *The Social and Environmental Effects of Large Dams* (San Francisco: Sierra Club, 1984).

58. Madeley, "Leaks and Landslides"; and World Bank, *The IDA in Retrospect* (New York: Oxford University Press, 1982), 70.

59. Between 1979 and 1981, capital flight from El Salvador was estimated to be $1.1 billion dollars. See William Goodfellow, "U.S. Economic Aid to El Salvador: Where Is the Money Going?" *International Policy Report* (Washington, D.C.: Center for International Policy, May 1984).

We Benefit from Their Hunger

M Y T H · 1 1

1. *Faces of War*, video documentary produced and distributed by the Neighbor to Neighbor project of the Institute for Food and Development Policy, San Francisco, 1985.

2. Jonathan King and Steve Rees, *Poor Ronald's Almanac* (San Francisco: Mother Jones, 1982), 54.

3. Center for Defense Information, "America's Secret Soldiers," *The Defense Monitor* 14, no. 2 (1985): 1. This estimate includes 14,900 active Special Operations Forces (SOFs), 32,000 reserve SOFs, and 198,000 Marines. While the Department of Defense does not count the Marine Corps as part of its SOFs, they are specially trained for foreign interventions and amphibious assaults (Ibid., 8), and hence, are included here.

4. Telephone interview by researcher Sarah Stewart with the Department of Defense, March 1986; and Department of Defense, "List of All Military Installations, including FY 1984 Authorized Manpower, Fulltime Permanently Assigned: Territories and Foreign Areas" (unpublished document). To this can be added a total of 888 military installations in the

United States itself and another 19 in U.S. territories, such as Guam, Puerto Rico, and various other islands.

5. Howard Morland, "A Few Billion for Defense, plus $250 Billion More for Overseas Military Intervention," *New Policy Papers* no. 1 (Washington, D.C.: Coalition for a New Foreign and Military Policy, 1986), 2.

6. Estimated using data on federal taxes paid by the average American household in 1985 (published by Jobs for Peace, "How Your Tax Dollars Are Spent," January 1986) and Morland, "A Few Billion."

7. Jobs for Peace, "How Your Tax Dollars Are Spent." Data from the U.S. Office of Management and Budget.

8. Congressional Budget Office, cited in Gordon Adams and Jeff Colman, *The FY 1987 Defense Budget Preliminary Analysis* (Center on Budget and Policy Priorities, Research Report, 5 February 1986), 7. Calculation based on deficit figures given in table B-73, Government Finance, *Economic Report of the President, Transmitted to Congress February 1986*, 339.

9. Council on Economic Priorities, Newsletter, May 1983.

10. According to a recent analysis prepared for the Joint Economic Committee of Congress, government spending on the military creates over 7,400 fewer jobs per $1 billion than would that same amount if spent on infrastructure, education, and health programs. See Barry Bluestone and John Havens, "Reducing the Federal Deficit Fair and Square," prepared for the Joint Economic Committee of the United States Congress, January 1986, 24.

11. Stephen Schlesinger and Stephen Kinzer, *Bitter Fruit: The Untold Story of the American Coup in Guatemala* (New York: Doubleday, 1982). A well-documented account.

12. "An Interview with Sergio Ramirez Mercado, Vice President of Nicaragua," *In These Times* (14–20 November 1984): 12.

13. Jonathan Kwitny, *Endless Enemies: The Making of an Unfriendly World* (New York: Congdon and Weed, 1984).

14. *World Military Expenditures and Arms Transfers 1985* (Washington, D.C.: U.S. Arms Control and Disarmament Agency, 1985), table III, 131 and table A, errata. According to experts at ACDA, these figures may somewhat overstate the value of arms transfers from the Soviet Union due to an overvaluation of the ruble.

15. Interview with Robert Mitchell, an international marketing consultant, June 1984. For more detail, see the U.S. Department of Commerce, *Export Administration Regulations* (1983 and before), Supplement no. 1, Section 5999B.

16. Robert Fisk, *London Times*, 20 January 1977, cited in Michael Klare, *The American Arms Supermarket* (Austin: University of Texas Press, 1984), 196.

17. On the killing of civilians in El Salvador under the government of President Duarte, see testimony before the Subcommittee on Western Hemisphere Affairs, U.S. House of Representatives, 14 May 1986. For a more general discussion of civilian deaths in Central America, see Richard Garfield and Pedro Rodriguez, "Health and Health Services in Central America," *Journal of the American Medical Association* 254, no. 7 (16 August 1985): 936–943. According to Garfield and Rodriguez, national registries put violent death as the most common cause of death in Nicaragua, Guatemala, and El Salvador since 1980 (p. 939). In El Salvador alone, an estimated 40,000 civilians have been killed in the U.S.-funded war since 1979. See Ruth Leger Sivard, *World Military and Social Expenditures 1985* (Washington, D.C.: World Priorities, 1985), 10.

18. Reed Brody, *Contra Terror in Nicaragua: Report on Fact Finding Mission* (Boston: South End Press, 1985). See also "Affidavit of Former Contra Leader Edgar Chamorro to the International Court of Justice: Case Concerning Military and Paramilitary Activies In and Against Nicaragua," *Congressional Record*, 30 January 1986, 1–4; and Joseph Collins, with Frances Moore Lappé, Nick Allen, and Paul Rice, *Nicaragua: What Difference Could a Revolution Make?* (New York: Grove Press/Food First Books, 1986), chapter 14.

19. Brandt Commission, *Common Crisis North-South Co-operation for World Recovery* (Cambridge, MA: MIT Press, 1983), 27.

20. Bill Goold and John Cavanagh, "A Trade Policy for the People," *The Nation* (29 March 1986): 454, citing data from the U.S. Bureau of Labor Statistics.

21. *Business Week* (24 October 1983) cited in Gilda Haas and the Plant Closures Project, *Plant Closure: Myths, Realities and Responses* (Boston: South End Press, 1985), 12. Only part of the loss of manufacturing jobs that have disappeared in America have been lost to low-wage workers overseas. The 1981 to 1982 economic recession was also a factor. Some plants closed because of poor management, and some factories simply relocated within the U.S. away from areas like the Northeast, where generations of organizing had brought workers gains, to the lower-wage South (although studies indicate that from the South, companies often move onwards to the third world).

22. For a probing discussion of such changes in the U.S. economy, see, for instance, Barry Bluestone and Bennett Harrison, *The Deindustrialization of America* (New York: Basic Books, 1982).

23. See, for instance, Samuel Bowles, David M. Gordon and Thomas E. Weisskopf, *Beyond the Wasteland* (Garden City, NY: Anchor Press/Doubleday, 1983); and Center for Popular Economics, *The Economic Report of the People* (Boston: South End Press, 1986).

24. "Even America's Know-how Is Headed Abroad," *Business Week* (3 March 1986): 61.

25. "The Hollow Corporation," *Business Week* (3 March 1986): 59.

26. "The False Paradise of a Service Economy," *Business Week* (3 March 1986): 81.

27. Interview with American Airlines, Barbados, 19 March 1984.

28. Bruce Steinberg, "The Mass Market Is Splitting Apart," *Fortune* (28 November 1983): 78.

29. "The False Paradise," *Business Week*, 79.

30. Donald Warshaw, "South Africa Union Rallies for Freehold Workers," *The Star Ledger* (Newark, NJ), 1 March 1986; "Apartheid Strike, Black 3M Workers in Solidarity," *Associated Press*, 28 February 1986; and "400 South African 3M Workers Protest Peacefully," *Asbury Park Press Monmouth*, 1 March 1986, A1. The apparent reason for the layoff was that 3M wanted to move its cassette manufacturing plant from New Jersey to Minnesota and North Dakota in order to "remain competitive." See Sue Epstein, "Jersey Workers Get South Africa Support," *The Star Ledger*, 28 February 1986; and "400 South African 3M Workers," *Asbury Park Press Monmouth*. Fully one-fifth of the workers facing layoffs in the New Jersey plant were victims of a previous 3M plant closing, which resulted in their relocation to the Freehold setting. See "3M, Don't Abandon Our Hometown: A Message from the 3M Workers in Freehold, New Jersey," Oil, Chemical and Atomic Workers Local 8-760, 1986.

31. The rate of return for U.S. banks' investment in the third world reached a high of 42.8 percent in 1981. The 1984 rate of return of 28.3 percent was still well above the banks' world rate of return of 18.4 percent. See U.S. Dept. of Commerce data cited in Stuart K. Tucker, *Update: Costs to the United States of the Recession in Developing Countries*, Working Paper no. 10 (Washington, D.C.: Overseas Development Council, 1986), table A12.

32. Comptroller of the Currency, Federal Financial Institutions Examination Council, Statistical Release E.16, no. 126, 24 January 1986, 1–3; Richard Feinberg and E. Scott Krigsman, "The Debt Crisis: Can the Costs be Cut?" *Policy Focus* 5 (September 1984): 3.

33. Hang-Sheng Cheng, *FRB San Francisco Weekly Letter*, Federal Reserve Bank of San Francisco, 29 July 1983.

34. Cheryl Payer, "Repudiating the Past," *NACLA Report on the Americas* 19, no. 2 (March/April 1985): 19. Payer cites a *Business Week* report noting that during the three-year period 1980 to 1982, $71 billion flowed out of seven of the world's largest debtor countries (Mexico, Argentina, Venezuela, Indonesia, Egypt, the Philippines, and Nigeria) while the combined debt of these countries rose by $102 billion (referring to *Business Week*, 3 October 1983, 133.) A study by Morgan Guaranty published in

March 1986 estimated that between 1983 and 1985 a total of $30 billion illegally left Brazil, Venezuela, and Mexico; cited in Marlise Simons, "Focus on Latin Flight of Capital," *New York Times*, 27 May 1986.

35. Lawyers Committee for International Human Rights, " 'Salvaging' Democracy: Human Rights in the Phillippines," December 1985.

36. See, for instance, Kathie L. Krumm, *The External Debt of Sub-Saharan Africa* (Washington, D.C.: World Bank, 1985), 11.

37. Rita Tullberg, "Military Related Debt in Non-Oil Developing Countries," in *Stockholm International Peace Research Institute Yearbook 1985* (London/Philadelphia: Taylor and Francis, 1985), 445–455.

38. Glenn Frankel, "Fifteen Months of Harsh Austerity Bring Indications of a Turnaround to Zaire," *Washington Post*, 22 May 1985, A23.

39. Interview by researcher Sarah Stewart with officer in major U.S. bank, March 1986 (not for attribution). See also William Cline, *International Debt and the Stability of the World Economy* (Washington, D.C.: Institute for International Economics, 1983).

40. Brandt Commission, *Common Crisis*, 55.

41. Overseas Development Council, "U.S.–Third World Trade Deficit: Going After the Causes," *Policy Focus* 7 (1985): 1. See also Richard Lawrence, "What's Really Behind the U.S. Trade Deficit?" *Journal of Commerce* (15 November 1985): 17A.

42. *Stuart K. Tucker, Update: Costs to the United States of the Recession in Developing Countries*, Working Paper no. 10 (Washington, D.C.: Overseas Development Council, 1986), v.

43. The experience of Continental Illinois is strong evidence. Robert Lekachman also describes a conversation with financial expert Felix Rohatyn in which Rohatyn confirmed this prediction. See Robert Lekachman, "The Debt Balloon," *Dissent* (Spring 1986): 136.

44. UN Conference on Trade and Development, *Handbook of Trade and Development Statistics 1985*, Supplement (Geneva, 1985).

45. According to the U.S. Department of Agriculture, agricultural imports for fiscal year 1986 are predicted to reach $20 billion while exports will be approximately $32 billion. See U.S. Department of Agriculture, Economic Research Service, *Agricultural Outlook*, Special Reprint (December 1985): 4.

46. Tomato product imports increased from 121,836 MTs of "fresh equivalents" in 1980 to 1981, to 464,678 MTs in 1984 to 1985. See U.S. Department of Agriculture, Foreign Agricultural Service, "Horticultural Products," *Foreign Agricultural Circular*, (Washington, D.C., February 1986), 21. "Imports are displacing American tomato products," says John Welty from the

California Tomato Growers Association. "And we're not talking about the loss of export markets in the case of tomatoes, either. We're talking about inroads into our domestic market (interview by researcher Rachel Schurman, April 1986).

47. U.S. Department of Agriculture, Economic Research Service, *Vegetable Outlook and Situation Report*, TVS-238 (Washington, D.C., February 1986), 5. According to unpublished data from the USDA/ERS, Mexico accounted for a record 90 percent share of the U.S. market of winter vegetables between January and March of 1985 due to our late winter freeze (Ibid., 14.).

48. See Steven E. Sanderson, *The Transformation of Mexican Agriculture* (Princeton: Princeton University Press, 1986), 89. See also Angus Wright, "The Culiacan Valley Farmers," *Catholic Rural Life* (February 1986).

49. Florida Citrus Mutual, Department of Economics, and the U.S. Department of Commerce, Forms IM-1456, for years 1979 to 1980 and 1984 to 1985. Although part of the increase in imports from Brazil in recent years was due to Florida freezes, the state's citrus growers are clearly worried about the threat to their markets posed by Brazil. According to growers at Florida Citrus Mutual, American orange producers simply can't compete with Brazil's low production costs (interview with researcher Rachel Schurman, April 1985).

50. Christine Donahue, "Revenge of the Frostbelt," *Forbes* (5 November 1984).

51. Coca-Cola controls about 20,000 acres of citrus in Florida, most of it through its Minute Maid subsidiary. See David Satterfield, "The Chill Is on the Juice Makers' Margins," *Miami Herald*, 4 February 1985, 21.

52. Robert Graham, "Planting Oranges in a Giant Forest," *Financial Times* (London), 18 November 1985, 14.

53. The state of Florida, for example, imposes a duty on juice imports to bring them up to par in price with locally grown juice oranges. And even though Mexico was able to undercut 1984–1985 costs of Florida producers for five out of six winter vegetables (tomatoes, bell peppers, cucumbers, green beans, and squash—the lone exception was eggplant), export expenses and duties significantly increase the cost of bringing these vegetables to the United States (from 31 percent to 47 percent, depending on vegetable). See Katherine Buckley "Competitive Advantage i n Producing Winter Fresh Vegetables in Florida and West Mexico," in USDA, *Vegetable Outlook and Situation Report*, February 1986, 15.

54. Richard Gilmore, *A Poor Harvest* (New York: Longman, 1982). See also Frances Moore Lappé and Joseph Collins with Cary Fowler, *Food First: Beyond the Myth of Scarcity* (New York: Ballantine Books, 1979), 251.

55. Ward Sinclair, "Cargill's Proposed Import of Grain Reaps Criticism," *Washington Post*, 9 January 1985; and Wendy L. Wall, "Cargill Set to Import Wheat," *Wall Street Journal*, 8 January 1985.

56. Bruce J. Blanton, "U.S. Farmers Greatly Worried by Declining Export Volume," *Journal of Commerce*, 23 April 1984, 6C.

57. Cited in Shelley A. Hearne, "Harvest of Unknowns: Pesticide Contamination in Imported Foods," Research Report by the Natural Resources Defense Council, Inc., New York, 1984, 1.

58. David Weir and Mark Schapiro, *Circle of Poison: Pesticides and People in a Hungry World* (San Francisco: Food First Books, 1981).

59. Ibid. See also Hearne, "Harvest of Unknowns"; and Lawrie Mott and Martha Broad, "Pesticides in Food: What the Public Needs to Know," Research Report by the Natural Resources Defense Council, San Francisco, 1985. Mott and Broad aptly point out that in setting its pesticide tolerance levels and residue limits, the U.S. government fails to consider synergism, or the joint effect of multiple pesticides on human health. In surveying the produce being sold in San Fransisco markets, the Natural Resources Defense Council found that 42 percent of the fruits and vegetables with a detectable pesticide residue contained residues of more than one pesticide (Mott and Broad, "Pesticides in Food," iv.).

60. Hearne, "Harvest of Unknowns," 2.

61. Ibid.

62. Ibid.

63. Data are the latest available and refer to 1984. See U.S. Bureau of the Census, *Current Population Reports*, Series P-60, no. 149, table 3.

64. For a more in-depth look at the role of the multinational corporation, see Richard Barnet and Ronald Müller, *Global Reach* (New York: Simon and Schuster, 1974).

65. Center for Popular Economics, *Economic Report*, 23–24. Data are from the U.S. Bureau of the Census, *Current Population Reports*, P-60 series.

66. Center for Popular Economics, *Economic Report*, 24.

67. World Bank, *World Development Report 1984* (New York: Oxford University Press, 1984), table 28. The comparisons are for 1978 and are not comparable with statistics from the Bureau of Census cited above.

68. Bruce Steinberg, "The Mass Market Is Splitting Apart," *Fortune*, no. 28 (1983).

69. "Study Shows Ownership Concentrated at the Top," *Journal of Commerce* (4 October 1984).

70. Editorial, "Raise the Minimum Wage," *Washington Post*, 3 January 1986.

71. Robert S. McIntyre and Dean C. Tipps, *Inequality and Decline*

(Washington, D.C.: Center on Budget and Policy Priorities, 1983), 15. Actual years covered were 1969 to 1980.

72. Center for Popular Economics, *Economic Report*, 60.

73. Diana Pearce, "Women and Children in Poverty," *Southern Changes* 8, no. 1 (February/March 1986): 1. In the last two decades, women-headed households have increased from 36 percent to 50 percent of all poor families. Three-fourths of America's more than 34 million poor consist of women and their children. This trend has been dubbed by Diana Pearce as the feminization of poverty.

74. Carlyle C. Douglas, "Blacks Losing Ground, Urban League Asserts," *New York Times*, 23 January 1986.

75. See chapter 5.

76. David Moberg, "The Poor Still Getting Poorer," *In These Times*, 22 August–4 September 1984.

77. Physician Task Force on Hunger in America, *Hunger in America: The Growing Epidemic* (Cambridge, MA: Harvard University School of Public Health, 1985), 48.

78. Ibid., 49.

79. Children's Defense Fund, "Poor Mothers and Children Face Nationwide Erosion in Prenatal Care: A Portent of Increasing Infant Mortality and Sickness," 3 January 1984.

80. Eve Pell, *The Big Chill* (Boston: Beacon Press, 1984).

81. Executive Order No. 12333, signed by President Reagan, December 3, 1981.

82. See Mark Schapiro, "The Excludables," *Mother Jones* (January 1986); Stuart Taylor, Jr., "The Unwelcome Mat Is Out for Ideological Undesirables," *New York Times*, 15 July 1984; and Stephen R. Shapiro, "Ideological Visas," *New York Times*, 5 February 1983.

Food vs. Freedom

M Y T H · 1 2

1. Edward Herman, *Corporate Control, Corporate Power: A Twentieth Century Fund Study* (Cambridge and New York: Cambridge University Press, 1981), tables 6.1 and 6.3, 189–192. According to Herman, of more than 2 million firms, fewer than 1,900 control roughly two-thirds of corporate assets.

2. Data are from the U.S. Bureau of the Census, *Current Population Reports*, P-60 Series, cited in Center for Popular Economics, *Economic Report of the People* (Boston: South End Press, 1986), 25.

3. Calculated from table 11 of the Congressional Budget Office, "Major Legislative Changes in Human Resources Programs Since January 1981," Staff Memorandum, Washington, D.C.,

August 1983, 76. Data averaged over the 1982 to 1985 period.

4. Charles Lindblom, *Politics and Markets* (New York: Basic Books, 1977), 49–50.
5. We say directly because some Americans own stock indirectly, through their participation in a pension plan.
6. Calculated by economist David M. Gordon, New School for Social Research, *What's Wrong with the U.S. Economy* (Boston: South End Press, l982), 3, 387 n. 8.
7. Thomas Jefferson, *Democracy*, ed. Saul K. Padover (New York: D. Appleton-Century, 1939), 215.
8. Page Smith, *Dissenting Opinions: The Selected Essays of Page Smith* (San Francisco: North Point Press, 1984), 39.
9. Ibid., 40.
10. C. B. MacPherson, *The Political Theory of Possessive Individualism* (New York: Oxford University Press, 1962), 128. Here MacPherson is quoting Henry Ireton, an ally of Cromwell, expressing a view with which the Levellers "had no quarrel."
11. Henry Shue, *Basic Rights: Subsistence, Affluence, and U.S. Foreign Policy* (Princeton: Princeton University Press, 1980), 24–25.
12. For a provocative discussion of the concept of freedom along similar lines, see C. B. MacPherson, *Democratic Theory: Essays on Retrieval* (Oxford: Clarendon Press, 1973).

Beyond the Myths of Hunger: What We Can Do

1. Americas Watch, *A Nation of Prisoners* (New York: Americas Watch, 1984). For further documentation of human rights abuses perpetrated by the Guatemalan government, see U.S. Department of State, *Country Reports on Human Rights Practices for 1984*, Report submitted to the U.S. Senate Committee on Foreign Relations, February 1985, 541–557.
2. Jonathan Kwitny, *Endless Enemies: The Making of an Unfriendly World* (New York: Cogdon and Weed, 1985), chapter 15; and Warren Hinckle and William Turner, *The Fish Is Red: The Story of the Secret War Against Castro* (New York: Harper and Row, 1981).
3. Most evaluations of Cuban society are so one-sided as to make informed, reasonable discussion impossible. Our institute's study—*No Free Lunch: Food and Revolution in Cuba* by Medea Benjamin, Joseph Collins, and Michael Scott (New York: Grove Press/Food First Books, 1986)—offers a penetrating, critical review of the Cuban food system, discussing both positive and negative lessons.
4. Joseph Collins with Frances Moore Lappé, Nick Allen, and Paul

Rice, *Nicaragua: What Difference Could a Revolution Make?* (New York: Grove Press/Food First Books, 1986); and Frances Moore Lappé and Joseph Collins, *Now We Can Speak: A Journey through the New Nicaragua* (San Francisco: Food First Books, 1982).

5. Central American Historical Institute, Intercultural Center, Georgetown University, Washington, D.C., *Update* 5 (27 February 1986): 6–7.

6. For ongoing information about developments in Nicaragua, see monthly *Envio* and periodic *Updates* from the Central American Historical Institute listed above.

7. *Iowa Land Ownership Survey: Preliminary Report on Land Tenure and Ownership in 47 Counties* (Des Moines: Farmers Unions, 1982), 3, 10.

8. Robert Bellah et al., *Habits of the Heart* (Berkeley: University of California Press, 1985), 289.

9. *Business Week* (3 March 1986): 62.

10. Robert A. Dahl, *Dilemmas of Pluralist Democracy: Autonomy Versus Control* (New Haven: Yale University Press, 1982), 184. For a thoughtful discussion on the issues raised here, see Robert A. Dahl, *A Preface to Economic Democracy* (Berkeley: University of California Press, 1985).

11. For a useful discussion, see William Cronon, *Changes in the Land: Indians, Colonists, and the Ecology of New England* (New York: Hill and Wang, 1983).

12. Based upon interviews by Frances Moore Lappé, September 1982. For a general introduction to the Mondragon experience, see Henk Thomas and Chris Logan, *Mondragon: An Economic Analysis* (London: Allen & Unwin, 1981).

13. For information on Nebraska's constitutional amendment, write to the Center for Rural Affairs, Box 405, Walthill, Nebraska 68067.

14. Robert A. Dahl, *Democracy in the United States*, 3rd edition (Boston: Houghton Mifflin Co., 1981), 32.

15. For more information about one such investment fund, write to Working Assets, 230 California St., San Francisco CA 94111.

16. Harry C. Boyte, *Community Is Possible* (New York: Harper and Row, 1984). See also Boyte's new book, coathored with Sara M. Evans, *Free Spaces: The Sources of Democratic Change in America* (New York: Harper and Row, 1986), for a study of democratic movements in America.

17. Bruce Stokes, *Helping Ourselves: Local Solutions to Global Problems* (New York: W.W. Norton, 1980).

What We Can Do: A Resource Guide

The organizations and publications suggested here represent only a small portion of the many resources that can help to go beyond the myths of hunger and to discover effective action for change. Write for more information to those that sound most interesting to you. For a comprehensive list, refer to the directories at the end of this guide.

Periodicals

Africa News, PO Box 3851, Durham, NC 27702
Catholic Rural Life, 4625 NW Beaver Drive, Des Moines, IA
    50310, 515-270-2634
Central America Update, Box 2207 Station P, Toronto, Ontario
    M5S 2T2, Canada
Community Jobs, 1520 16th Street NW, Washington, DC 20036
Cultural Survival, 11 Divinity Street, Cambridge, MA 02138
Dollars and Sense, 38 Union Square, Room 14, Somerville, MA
    02143, 617-628-8411
The Ecologist, Whitehay, Withiel, Bodmin, Cornwall UK,
    Tel: Bodmin 0208 831231
Food Monitor, World Hunger Year, 350 Broadway, Suite 209,
    New York, NY 10013, 212-226-2714

Foodlines, FRAC, 1319 F Street NW, # 500, Washington, DC 20004
Guatemalan Network News, NISGUA, 930 F Street NW, Suite 720,
    Washington, DC 20004
Honduras Update, Honduras Information Center, 1 Summer Street,
    Somerville, MA 02143, 617-625-7220
In These Times, 1300 W Belmont, Chicago, IL 60657, 312-472-5700
Latinamerica Press, Apartado 5594, Lima 100, Peru
Monthly Review, 155 W 23rd Street, New York, NY 10011,
    212-691-2555
Mother Jones, 1663 Mission Street, 2nd Floor, San Francisco, CA
    94103
Multinational Monitor, PO Box 19405, Washington, DC 20036,
    202-833-3932
NACLA Report on the Americas, 151 W 19th Street, New York,
    NY 10011
The Nation, Box 1953, Marion, OH 43306
National Catholic Reporter, PO Box 281, Kansas City, MO 64141,
    816-531-0538
New Internationalist, 42 Hythe Bridge Street, Oxford OX1 2EP
    England/UK; 113 Atlantic Avenue, Brooklyn, NY 11201
Nicaraguan Perspectives, Nicaraguan Information Center, PO Box
    1004, Berkeley, CA 94701, 415-549-1387
Nutrition Action, Center for Science in the Public Interest, 1501
    16th Street NW, Washington, DC 20036
The Progressive, 409 E Main Street, Madison, WI 53703
Seeds, 222 East Lake Drive, Decatur, GA 30030, 404-378-3566

Organizations

U.S. Focus

American Agricultural Movement, 100 Maryland Avenue NE, Box
    69, Washington, DC 20002, 202-544-5750
Center for Rural Affairs, PO Box 405, Walthill, NE 68067,
    402-846-5428
Center for Science in the Public Interest, 1501 16th Street NW,
    Washington, DC 20036, 202-332-9110
Center for Studies in Food Self-Sufficiency, PO Box 1397,
    Burlington, VT 05402, 802-658-3890
Children's Foundation, 815 15th Street NW, Suite 928, Washington,
    DC 20005, 202-347-3300
Community Nutrition Institute, 2001 S Street NW, Suite 530,
    Washington, DC 20009, 202-462-4700.
Food Research and Action Center (FRAC), 1319 F Street NW, Suite
    500, Washington, DC 20004, 202-393-5060

Institute for Community Economics, Inc., 151 Montague City Road, Greenfield, MA 01301, 413-774-7956
National Catholic Rural Life Conference, 4625 NW Beaver Drive, Des Moines, IA 50322, 515-270-2634
National Center for Economic Alternatives, 1718 Connecticut Avenue NW, Suite 410, Washington, DC 20009, 202-483-6667
National Family Farm Coalition, Box 414, Circle, MT 59215, 406-485-3324
National Farmers Organization, 720 Davis Avenue, Corning, IA 50841, 515-322-3131
National Farmers Union, PO Box 39251, Denver, CO 80239, 303-371-1760
National Land for People, 35751 Oak Springs Drive, Tollhouse, CA 93667, 209-855-3710
Rural America, 1312 18th Street NW, Washington, DC 20036, 202-659-2800
United Farmworkers (AFL-CIO), PO Box 62, Keene, CA 93531, 805-822-5571
Working Group on Domestic Hunger & Poverty, National Council of Churches, 475 Riverside Drive, New York, NY 10115

U.S./International Focus

American Committee on Africa, 198 Broadway, New York, NY 10038, 212-962-1210
American Friends Service Committee, 1501 Cherry Street, Philadelphia, PA 19102, 215-241-7000
Americans for Peace in the Americas, 2001 S Street NW, Suite 300, Washington, DC 20009, 202-667-8848
Americas Watch Committee, 36 West 44th Street, New York, NY 10026, 212-840-9460
Amnesty International, 322 8th Avenue, New York, NY 10001, 212-827-8400
Boston Industrial Mission, 138 Fremont Street, Boston, MA 02111, 617-742-3118
Bread for the World, 802 Rhode Island Avenue NE, Washington, DC 20018, 202-269-0200
Casa Chile, PO Box 3620, Berkeley, CA 94703, 415-845-9398
Center for Community Change, 1000 Wisconsin Avenue NW, Washington, DC 20007, 202-342-0519
Center for International Policy, 120 Maryland Avenue NE, Washington, DC 20002, 202-544-4666
Center of Concern, 3700 13th Street NE, Washington, DC 20017, 202-635-2757
Central America Resource Center (Guide to Central American Groups), PO Box 2327, Austin, TX 78768

Church World Service, Office of Global Education, 2115 North
Charles Street, Baltimore, MD 21218, 301-727-6106
Clergy and Laity Concerned, 198 Broadway, Room 302, New York,
NY 10038, 212-964-6730
Coalition for a New Foreign and Military Policy, 120 Maryland
Avenue NE, Washington, DC 20002, 202-546-8400
Committee in Solidarity with the People of El Salvador (CISPES),
PO Box 50139, Washington, DC 20004, 202-393-3370
Coordinating Committee on Pesticides, 942 Market, #505, San
Francisco, CA 94102, 415-788-0690
Corporate Data Exchange, 198 Broadway, #707, New York, NY
10038, 212-962-2980
Development Group for Alternative Policies, 2200 19th Street NW,
#206, Washington, DC 20009, 202-332-1600
Earthscan, 1717 Massachusetts Avenue NW, Suite 302,
Washington, DC 20036, 202-462-0900
Free South Africa Movement, c/o TransAfrica, 545 8th Street SE,
Washington, DC 20003, 202-547-2550
Friends Committee on National Legislation, 245 2nd Street NW,
Washington, DC 20002, 202-547-6000
Hunger Program, The American Lutheran Church, 422 South Fifth
Street, Minneapolis, MN 55415, 612-330-3221
INFACT, 186 Lincoln Street, Room 203, Boston MA, 02111,
617-338-6101
Institute for Food and Development Policy: Food First, 145 Ninth
Street, San Francisco, CA 94103, 415-864-8555
Institute for Peace and Justice, 4144 Lindell Street, #400, St. Louis,
MO 63108, 314-533-4445
Institute for Policy Studies/Transnational Institute, 1901 Q Street
NW, Washington, DC 20009, 202-234-9382
Interfaith Action for Economic Justice, 110 Maryland Avenue NE,
Washington, DC 20002, 800-424-7292/202-543-2800
Interfaith Center on Corporate Responsibility, 475 Riverside Drive,
Room 566, New York, NY 10115, 212-870-2936
International Alliance for Sustainable Agriculture, in the Newman
Center at the University of Minnesota, 1701 University Avenue
SE, Room 202, Minneapolis, MN 55414, 612-331-1099
International Center for Development Policy, 731 8th Street SE,
Washington, DC 20003, 202-547-3800
Mobilization for Survival, 853 Broadway, Room 418, New York, NY
10003, 212-533-0008
National Committee for World Food Day, 1001 22nd Street N.W.,
Washington, DC 20437, 202-653-2404
National Network in Solidarity with the Nicaraguan People, 2025 I
Street NW, Suite 1117, Washington, DC 20006, 202-223-2328
National Network In Solidarity with the People of Guatemala, 930 F
Street NW, #720, Washington, DC 20004, 202-483-0050

Neighbor to Neighbor, 2940 16th Street, San Francisco, CA 94013, 415-621-3711

NETWORK, 806 Rhode Island Avenue NE, Washington, DC 20018, 202-526-4070

North American Congress on Latin America (NACLA), 151 W 19th Street, 9th Floor, New York, NY 10011, 212-989-8890

Northern California Interfaith Committee on Corporate Responsibility, PO Box 6819, San Francisco, CA 94101, 415-885-5102

Pesticide Education and Action Project, (mailing address) PO Box 610, San Francisco, CA 94101, 415-771-7327

Working Group on Domestic Hunger and Poverty, National Council of Churches, 475 Riverside Drive, Room 572, New York, NY 10115, 212-870-2308

World Hunger Education Service, 1317 G Street NW, Washington, DC, 20005, 202-223-2995

World Hunger Year (WHY), 350 Broadway, Suite 209, New York 10013, 212-226-2714

Overseas Direct Assistance

American Friends Service Committee (National Office), 1501 Cherry Street, Philadelphia, PA 19102, 215-241-7000

American Friends Service Committee, 2160 Lake Street, San Francisco, CA 94121, 415-752-7766

Committee for Health Rights in Central America (CHRICA), 513 Valencia Street, Room 6, San Francisco, CA 94110, 415-431-7760

Eritrean Relief Committee, 475 Riverside Drive, Room 769, New York, NY 10115, 212-870-2727

Grassroots International, PO Box 312, Cambridge, MA 02139, 617-497-9180

Oxfam America, 115 Broadway, Boston, MA 02116, 617-482-1211

Unitarian Universalist Service Committee, 78 Beacon Street, Boston, MA 02108, 617-742-2120

War on Want, Three Castles House, 1 London Bridge Street, London SE1 9SG England/UK, 01-403-2266

Canadian Organizations

Canadian Council for International Cooperation (CCIC), 200 Isabella Street, 3rd floor, Ottowa, Ontario K1S 1V7, 613-236-4547

Development Education Center, 229 College Street, Toronto, Ontario M5T 1R4, 416-597-0328

DEVERIC, PO Box 3460, Halifax, Nova Scotia B3J 3J1, 902-429-1370

Edmonton Learner Center, 10765 98th Street, Edmonton, Alberta T5H 2P2, 403-424-4371

GATT-Fly, 11 Madison Avenue, Toronto, Ontario M5R 2S2, 416-912-4615

IDEA Center, 60 Maryland Street, Winnipeg, Manitoba R3G 1K7,
204-786-2032

IDERA, 2524 Cypress Street, Vancouver, British Columbia V6J 3N2,
604-732-1496

Latin America Working Group, PO Box 2207 Station P, Toronto,
Ontario M5S 2T2, 416-533-4221

Marquis Project, 107 7th Street, Suite 200, Brandon, Manitoba R7A
3S5, 204-727-5675

One Sky Center, 134 Avenue F South, Saskatoon, Saskatchewan
S7M lS8, 306-652-1571

Ontario Public Interest Research Group Provincial Office (OPIRG),
University of Guelph, Guelph, Ontario NlG 2W1, 519-824-2091

Oxfam Canada, 2524 Cypress, Vancouver, British Columbia V6J
3N2, 604-736-7678

Waterloo Public Interest Research Group, University of Waterloo,
Waterloo, Ontario N2L 3Gl, 519-884-9020

Directories

*Third World Resource Directory: A Guide to Organizations and
Publications*. Thomas P. Fenton and Mary Heffron, editors. New
York: Orbis Books, 1984. 284 pp. $12.95.

Who's Involved With Hunger: An Organization Guide. Linda
Worthington, editor, 3rd edition. Sponsored by the Presidential
Commission on World Hunger, Washington, DC: World
Hunger Education Service, 1982. 54 pp. $4.00.

About the Authors

In the early 1970s, when Frances Moore Lappé's *Diet for a Small Planet* was first published, Dr. Joseph Collins, a fellow at the Institute for Policy Studies in Washington, D.C., was working on *Global Reach: The Power of the Multinational Corporation*. Their research had led them to the same troubling question: why hunger in a world of plenty?

In 1975 they decided to join forces and devote their combined knowledge and resources to a full-time effort to answer that question. Together they founded the Institute for Food and Development Policy—also known as FOOD FIRST—and began work on the 1977 ground-breaking book, *Food First: Beyond the Myth of Scarcity*. Since then they have coauthored *World Hunger: 10 Myths; Aid as Obstacle; Now We Can Speak: A Journey Through the New Nicaragua;* and *What Difference Could a Revolution Make? Food and Farming in the New Nicaragua*. They have also produced a wide range of studies, articles, and other books both individually and in collaboration with colleagues at the institute.

As internationally recognized spokespersons on world hunger, the authors maintain busy speaking schedules and appear frequently on television and radio programs.

About FOOD FIRST

FOOD FIRST is a nonprofit research and education center, dedicated to identifying the root causes of hunger in the United States and around the world since its founding in 1975. Financed by thousands of members, with modest support from foundations and churches, FOOD FIRST speaks with a strong, independent voice, free of ideological formulas and vested interests.

In over 60 countries and in 20 languages, FOOD FIRST provides a wide array of educational tools—books, articles, slide shows, films, and curricula for elementary schools and high schools—to lay the groundwork for a more democratically controlled food system that will meet the needs of all.

For more information write to:

FOOD FIRST
Institute for Food and Development Policy
145 Ninth Street
San Francisco, CA 94103
USA

Other *Food First* Books
Available from Grove Press

No Free Lunch: Food and Revolution in Cuba Today

Medea Benjamin, Joseph Collins, and Michael Scott

Has the Cuban Revolution made a difference in the welfare of its people? In this book, experts in agriculture and economics go beyond polemics and investigate firsthand the realities of food in Cuba today. Is hunger really no longer a problem in Cuba? If the hungry are fed, then why is there food rationing? Are private farmers allowed to operate or does the socialist government maintain an iron grip on agriculture? "An x-ray of individual values, social policy and foreign relations, all of which show up on a supermarket shelf in Havana."— Pat Aufderheide, *Village Voice*

An Evergreen Paperback/$9.95 (Canada $14.95)
ISBN: 0-394-62233-2

Nicaragua: What Difference Could a Revolution Make?

Joseph Collins, with Frances Moore Lappé and Nick Allen

What were the dramatic changes brought by the first seven years of the Sandinista revolution in Nicaragua? How have the lives of the rural poor and rural rich changed? Are the hungry eating better? This book presents some surprising answers. In discussing the new government's efforts to build a food and farming system that can meet the needs of the poor and at the same time increase exports, it shatters many of the misconceptions about Nicaragua created in Washington. "An extraordinarily important book."—*Choice*

An Evergreen Paperback/$8.95 (Canada $13.50)
ISBN: 0-394-62295-2

Available at your bookstore or directly from Grove Press Inc., 10 East 53rd St., NY, NY 10022. We accept check, money order, or charge (Visa, MasterCard, or American Express). No COD. Add $1.50 for shipping and handling of one book and $0.50 for each additional book.

Name _____

Address _____
                  City   State   Zip

VISA ____ MC____ AMEX____ Expire Date_____

Number _____

Signature _____